Robert Gradwell

Succat

The story of sixty years of the life of St. Patrick, A.D. 373-433

Robert Gradwell

Succat
The story of sixty years of the life of St. Patrick, A.D. 373-433

ISBN/EAN: 9783744747189

Printed in Europe, USA, Canada, Australia, Japan

Cover: Foto ©Lupo / pixelio.de

More available books at **www.hansebooks.com**

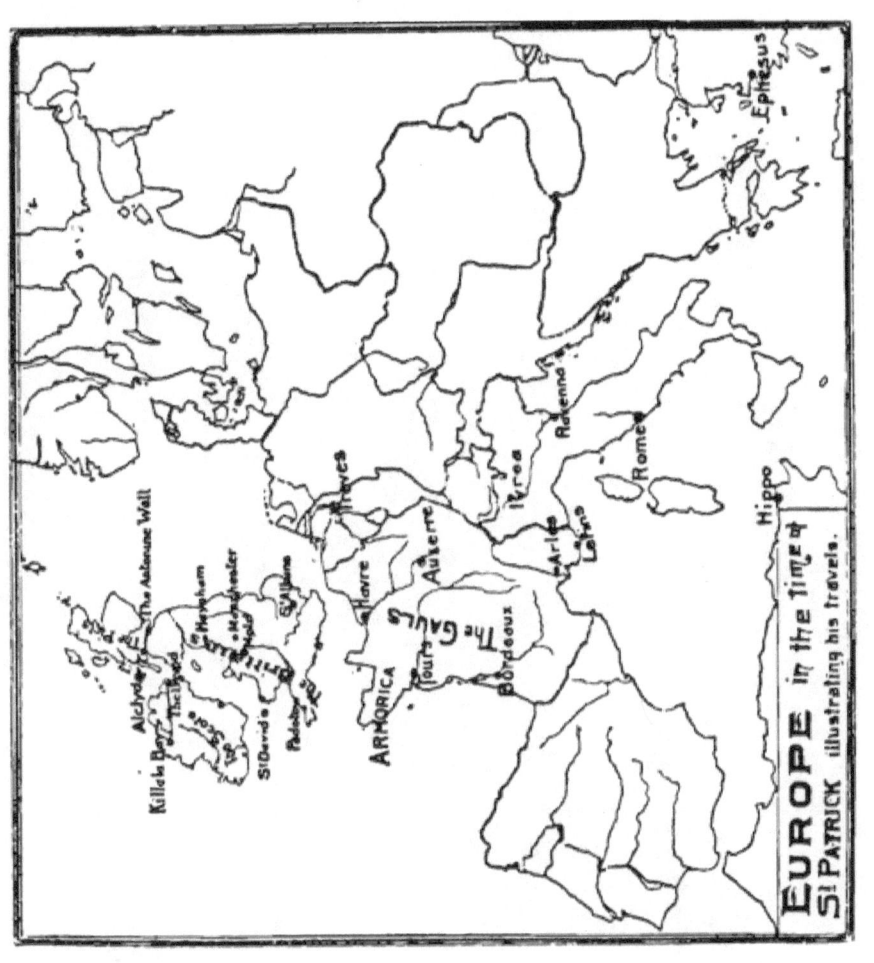

SUCCAT

THE STORY OF SIXTY YEARS OF THE LIFE

OF

ST. PATRICK

A.D. 373-433

BY

MONSIGNOR GRADWELL

"Of the books that are not written, and ought to be written, is . . . a life of St. Patrick." JOHN RUSKIN.

"Indeed I am more and more grateful for every word you write me, and will assuredly examine as far as I am able into all you have so delightfully discovered of St. Patrick." JOHN RUSKIN, *Letter to the Author.*

LONDON: BURNS & OATES, LD.
NEW YORK: CATHOLIC PUBLICATION SOCIETY CO

TO THE

MOST REVEREND CHARLES,

ARCHBISHOP OF GLASGOW,

ARCHBISHOP OF THE DIOCESE IN WHICH ST. PATRICK WAS BORN,

SUCCESSOR OF ST. KENTIGERN,

AND BIOGRAPHER OF ST. CUTHBERT,

A LOVER OF THE CHURCH OF OLD SCOTLAND,

A ZEALOUS BUILDER UP OF THAT OF THE NEW,

AND THE PRINCELY FOUNDER OF AN ECCLESIASTICAL COLLEGE,

THIS WORK, WHICH WAS STIMULATED

BY HIS EXAMPLE

AND ENCOURAGED BY HIS KINDLY AND CONTINUED INTEREST,

𝔍𝔰 𝔇𝔢𝔡𝔦𝔠𝔞𝔱𝔢𝔡

BY HIS HUMBLE AND OBEDIENT SERVANT,

ROBERT GRADWELL.

TABLE OF CONTENTS.

CHAPTER I.

ST. PATRICK'S PARENTAGE AND BIRTH.

                                                                                        PAGE

St. Martin at Amiens. His niece Conchessa—her captivity—her slavery to a Frankish chief—her marriage to her master's son Calpurnius. The Franks conquered by Valentinian. Calpurnius enters the Roman army. Conchessa at Treves. Britain overrun by the Picts and Scots. Calpurnius's legion ordered to Britain. Campaigns of Theodosius. Theodosius at Alclyde. Birth of St. Patrick at Kilpatrick—his baptism...................... 1

CHAPTER II.

BOYHOOD OF ST. PATRICK.

373-388.

Glasgow in the Nineteenth Century. Condition of the country about the Antonine Wall in the Fourth Century. Disposition of the Roman troops in Britain. State of religion at Theodosia. Rebellion of Maximus. St. Martin at Treves. St. Patrick's childhood. Critical state of the Roman Empire on the death of Maximus. Raid of the Scoti on the banks of the Clyde. St. Patrick carried off captive into Ireland.................................... 33

CHAPTER III.

SLAVE IN IRELAND.

388-394.

County Antrim. Ancient notices of Ireland. The Braid Valley. St. Patrick bought by Milcho. God's call to St. Patrick. The religion of Ireland Druidical. St. Patrick makes his escape, he journeys to Fochlut, near Killala Bay, and takes ship for Britain..................................... 54

CHAPTER IV.

RETURN TO DUMBARTON. JOURNEY TO TOURS.

394—ABOUT MARCH TO DECEMBER.

St. Patrick's *Confessio*. His literary style. His voyage from Killala Bay to Morecambe Bay. His landing at Heysham, north of the Lune. Condition of Lancashire at the time. St. Patrick's Well at Slyne. St. Patrick in Patterdale. Arrives in Dumbarton. His vision, in which he hears the voice of the Irish. He sets out for Tours. Lands at Bordeaux. St. Patrick's Thorn Tree on the banks of the Loire. Reaches Marmoutier..................................... 95

CHAPTER V.

AT MARMOUTIER AND LERINS.

394-418.

St. Martin, Bishop of Tours. St. Ninian at Marmoutier. St. Martin's death. Condition of the Roman Empire after the death of Theodosius the Great. St. Patrick at Lerins. Count Montalembert on Lerins 134

CHAPTER VI.

ST. GERMANUS OF AUXERRE.

418-429.

Auxerre. Germanus, Duke of the Province of Lyons, chosen bishop. His austerities and sanctity. St. Patrick becomes one of the clergy of Auxerre..................................... 162

CONTENTS.

CHAPTER VII.

PELAGIUS THE BRITON—CŒLESTIUS THE IRISHMAN.

405-427.

Great increase in the number of Christians. Intellectual activity among the learned. Pelagius high in the esteem of St. Paulinus and St. Augustine. Imbibes the doctrines of Theodorus of Mopsuesta. His repute among the great Christian families of Rome. The Anicii—Demetrias. Taking of Rome by Alaric. Demetrias at Carthage. St. Jerome at Bethlehem. Spread of Pelagianism in Gaul and Britain ... 185

CHAPTER VIII.

SS. GERMANUS AND PATRICK IN BRITAIN.

429-430.

St. Patrick in Armorica. The Emperors Honorius and Valentinian III. St. Celestinus Pope. St. Lupus Bishop of Troyes. St. Germanus sets out for Britain. Meets St. Geneviève at Nanterre. State of Britain. Germanus in Synod—at St. Alban's. At Mold, the Alleluia Victory. St. Patrick at Mancunium and Patricroft ... 211

CHAPTER IX.

ST. PATRICK RECEIVES HIS COMMISSION TO PREACH THE GOSPEL TO THE IRISH FROM ST. CELESTINE AND SAILS FOR IRELAND.

430-433.

St. Patrick returns to Auxerre. St. Germanus goes to Arles. Death of St. Augustine. Mission of St. Palladius to Ireland and his death. St. Patrick goes to Rome and is approved by the Pope. Is consecrated at Ivrea. Seeks the assistance of the British monks and clergy. Lands in Wicklow ... 240

APPENDICES.

I. On St. Patrick's birthplace.................................. 275
II. St. Patrick in Lancashire.................................. 293
III. Travels of St. Patrick.................................... 300
IV. St. Patrick and Old Kilpatrick............................. 301
V. Heysham and Slyne.. 303

CHRONOLOGICAL TABLE.

306-327. Constantine the Great, Emperor.
    313. Constantine defeats Maxentius; gives the Lateran palace to the Popes; adopts the labarum as the Imperial standard.
    317. St. Martin born.
    332. St. Martin at Amiens.
    336. St. Athanasius at Treves.
    360. St. Martin with St. Hilary at Poitiers.—St. Ninian born on the southern shore of Solway Frith.
360-3. Julian the Apostate, Emperor.
364-375. Valentinian I., Emperor.
365 (about). Conchessa in North-Eastern Gaul taken captive by a party of Franks; marries Calpurnius.—Valentinian conquers the Rhineland; fixes his residence at Treves.—Calpurnius enters the Roman army.—Legion of the Batavi.—Calpurnius and Conchessa at Treves.
    365. Picts and Scots overrun Britain to the Thames.
    367. Expedition into Britain of Theodosius the Elder. He advances to Dumbarton; restores the Antonine Wall.—Calpurnius and Conchessa at Dumbarton.
370 (about). Pelagius born.
    371. St. Martin, Bishop of Tours.
    373. St. Patrick, Succat, born.—St. Athanasius died, May 2.
374 (about). St. Martin at Treves at the Court of Valentinian.

CHRONOLOGICAL TABLE.

375. Gratian, Emperor.
378. St. Germanus born.
383. Theodosius the Great, Emperor of the East.—Maximus revolts in Britain; acknowledged Emperor of the West. Death of Gratian.
385 (about). St. Martin at Treves at the Court of Maximus.
388. Maximus put to death.—Calpurnius and Conchessa slain. St. Patrick and his sister carried off as captives to Ireland.—St. Patrick sold to Milcho. Niell of the Nine Hostages, monarch of Ireland.
390. Victricius, Bishop of Rouen.
394. Victricius visits Britain to compose religious troubles.—St. Patrick escapes from slavery; lands at Heysham; traverses Patterdale arrives at Dumbarton.
395. The Emperor Theodosius dies.
404. Honorius fixes the seat of Government at Ravenna.
405. Pelagius broaches his false doctrines on Divine Grace.
406. Gaul overrun by the Goths. Constantine the Briton proclaimed Emperor.
408. Theodosius II., Emperor of the East.—Rome besieged by Alaric the Goth.
409. Armorica declares its independence.—St. Victricius dies.
410. The Roman legions withdraw from Britain.—Rome taken by Alaric.—Demetrias, with her mother, Juliana, and her grandmother, Fultonia Proba, leave Rome for Carthage.—Death of Alaric.—St. Honoratus retires to Lerins.
411. Arles made the seat of Government of Constantine the Briton; he is taken prisoner, and is put to death.—St. Hilary, afterwards Archbishop of Arles; St. Lupus, afterwards Bishop of Troyes; and St. Vincent, author of the "Commonittorium," at Lerins.

CHRONOLOGICAL TABLE.

410-418. Between these two dates St. Patrick at Lerins.

418. St. Germanus, Bishop of Auxerre.—St. Patrick goes to Auxerre.

420. St. Jerome dies in Palestine.

422. St. Celestine, Pope.

(Date uncertain.) St. Patrick sent by Germanus to Armorica.

423. Valentinian III., Emperor of the West.

429. Leogaire, monarch of Ireland.—SS. Germanus and Patrick go to Britain. They meet the little St. Geneviève near Paris.

430. At Easter the Alleluia victory at Mold in Flintshire.—St. Patrick at Mancunium and Patricroft.—The Saints return to Auxerre.—August 28, St. Augustine dies.

431. The Council of Ephesus.—St. Palladius goes to Ireland, and dies among the Picts, July 6.—St. Patrick offers himself for the Irish Mission.

432. St. Patrick crosses the Alps with Segetius; forms an acquaintance with Amatorix at Ivrea; is received by Pope Celestine, and commissioned to preach to the Irish. Received the name of Patrick.

432. Xystus III., Pope.—St. Patrick is consecrated at Ivrea by Amatorex; he sets out for Britain by way of Auxerre; he founds a monastery at Padstow in Cornwall; he seeks the assistance of the British monks and clergy.

433. He sails for Ireland, and lands on the Wicklow coast.

440. St. Leo, Pope.

448. St. Germanus dies at Ravenna.

493. St. Patrick dies.

PREFACE.

Perhaps, throughout the length and breadth of Great Britain and Ireland, there is no spot in which nature exhibits a more rugged and frowning aspect than in Patterdale. The outline of the great mountain ridges which shut in the valley, especially on the eastern side, is so hard and sharp, unbroken for such great distances by projecting bluff or receding brake; the vegetation is so thin and short; the frequent recurrence of fallen earth and stones suggesting tempest and rain—all combine under certain combinations of sky and air to present an unrelieved picture of desolation and barrenness. But there are times when the impression is far different: when, as evening advances and the sun sets behind the western hills, a flood of colour bathes the scarped sides of the opposite range, when gold and purple and red contend with each other to pour out their richest tints and deck those bleak hill-sides with robes which might excite the envy of an empress. The contrast in the physical appearance of the dale is only a type of the moral change which time has wrought in the religious condition of its people. If now the faith is dead and the spiritual destitution is supreme, there was a period when glorious saints trod these rugged wastes, and fervent prayer was marvellously heard, and victory was won by the intercession of heaven's blessed saints over the fiercest assaults of the evil one. The memory of St. Patrick still hangs round this vale; it bears his name, the church is dedicated in his honour, the clear waters spring from St. Patrick's Well. Not merely is his presence here thus commemorated, but his affections too are duly chronicled, and his veneration and love for his great uncle St. Martin are proclaimed in the name of the neighbouring dale, St. Martin's Dale or Matterdale. It is strange, most strange, that two sister dales of Westmoreland, after centuries of oblivion, should still speak to us of our great British saint and of his illustrious relative. I may go further and say that the connection between the two great saints Martin and Patrick, indicated by the names borne by these Cumbrian vales, gives the key to what hitherto has been an unsolved, or only half-solved problem, the parentage and birth-place of St. Patrick.

Others better acquainted with the voluminous literature, which has grown up about the name of Ireland's apostle, may have been familiar with it before, but it is to the pages of the May number of *Merry England*, 1883, that I am indebted for the view which I propose to embody in this narrative. The writer of the paper alluded to is General Butler, C.B., whose time since then had been spent mainly on the banks of the Nile, and whose dashing deeds and power of command have made his name amongst Englishmen familiar as a household word. But he is not merely a brave soldier and a skilful officer, he is a literary man of no mean order, and he has worthily employed his pen in illustrating the dark places in the life of his nation's patron saint. So far from his military instincts and training making him unfit for dealing adequately with his subject, it was that very instinct which caused him to seize on the idea, that the father and grandfather of St. Patrick had been soldiers before they became ecclesiastics, and so, curiously enough, enabled him to unravel the tangled skein of places and nationalities which had been woven about the saint's very cradle. For St. Patrick sprang from a soldier race; his father and grandfather had fought on many a bloody field; his mother was a soldier's daughter, and even she had shared in the dust and clatter, in the excitement and horror of the combat. He himself was all but born in the camp, and the earliest sights and sounds which met his infant eyes and ears were the pomps and clash of arms. No wonder there is something martial even in his sanctity, and that his story reads like that of a hero of the cross, and a bold, skilful commander of an army. But early writers of the saint's life have but dimly perceived this characteristic, and it has been reserved to General Butler to state it in a clear, vivid, and striking form.

It is quite extraordinary the interest which has been concentrated upon the birthplace of St. Patrick; and the learning expended on discussing the point would occupy many bulky volumes. Perhaps it may appear presumptuous for a new writer, one whose thoughts, until recently, had never been seriously fixed on the matter, to suppose that he can add anything worth saying to the already mighty piles of erudition, and yet I hope to add something of value to the mass; or, to adopt a metaphor more consonant with the subject in hand, I fearlessly enter the lists to shiver a maiden lance in maintaining, that St. Patrick is a British saint, born at or near Kilpatrick, near Dumbarton, then a Romano-British fortress, and that along with St. Ninian, of Withern, and St. Kentigern, of Glasgow, he is one of that glorious triad of saints who are the honour and protection —*decus et tutela*—of what was once the British kingdom of Strathclyde. This is the proposition I undertake to illustrate, and very material to this end, as I shall soon show, is the fact that St. Martin and St. Patrick were near blood-relations. For my present purpose it is not necessary to quote any other authority than the Roman Breviary, which, in its fourth lesson for the Feast of St. Patrick, speaks thus: " Patrick, styled the Apostle of Ireland, had for his father Calpurnius, for his mother Conchessa, a reputed blood-relation of St. Martin, Bishop of Tours, and was born in Greater Britain". It is only necessary to bear well in mind these plain elementary facts, and it is surprising how one by one, like scales from the eyes of a blind man restored to sight, the doubts and difficulties surrounding St. Patrick's birthplace fall away and leave the unvarnished simple truth behind.

Thus I wrote in the year 1885. My interest in St. Patrick had been excited by his connection with our north-western coast, and by my becoming acquainted with the traditions about him, which still linger on the shores of Morecambe Bay, and in the dales of Westmoreland. But, as I advanced in my subject, I became strongly impressed with the idea that, in spite of all that has been written on the saint, there was still a gap to be filled, and, after much hesitation, I determined on doing what I could to fill it up. The ancient writers on the Life of St. Patrick had little else in view than to excite in the minds of their readers a love and admiration of their hero. A love of the marvellous, a craving after the supernatural, formed part of the mind of the times; again, the materials for an exact narrative of the facts were scanty in the extreme, and we cannot be surprised, therefore, if the lives of the saints became little else than a record of their virtues and their miracles. There was little criticism then of the laws of evidence, there was little desire in the writer to have trustworthy witnesses, and there was little opportunity for obtaining them, had the desire been ever so great. Besides, their style was, generally speaking, so bald and unadorned, that few moderns, except professed scholars, can take much pleasure in their perusal. That they are invaluable to the scholar is undoubted, for without them he would lack the very foundation on which to build his narrative. They supply the facts, often fragmentary, often out of time, but still facts, which there is no reason for disputing. Though most of the succeeding writers copy, more or less faithfully, their predecessors, reproducing alike their errors and their truths, they often add new incidents, or, at least, fresh details, and these assist a modern compiler in making a more complete and vivid description of the incidents than any single original writer has given. It does not follow that the writer of to-day is a mere workman in patchwork; he knows not his craft unless he can construct a harmonious whole, life-like and breathing, out of the scattered fragments that have come down to him from Fiacc, Tirechan, and Jocelyn. It is the feeling that no such living and human portrait of one of the greatest lights of the fifth century has been drawn that has made me write sketch after sketch of the incidents of St. Patrick's early life. And as a great hero must be viewed in the light of his own times, and of the circumstances and persons amongst which he lived, I have striven with all the power I possess to present the reader with a vivid and graphic description of them.

Of modern writers on the subject it does not become me to say much. Many have done their work admirably; but while some have bewildered their readers with a display of minute learning, others have crowded their pages with controversial matter; consequently the portraiture of the saint has been lost sight of in the heat of the contest with the champions of opposite opinions. I have no theory to maintain, no preconception to advocate. It is St. Patrick that I have constantly kept in view, even when pages pass without his name appearing in them. If I have spoken of Emperors and Popes, of councils and heresies, of rivers and mountains, of the success or defeat of barbarian incursions, it has been with the sole object of illustrating the life of our saint. So, with all humility, I present my little book to the public, as an effort made with goodwill, whatever be its success, to exhibit in detail the long preparation of sixty years, which in faith and in patience St. Patrick made, before he entered on that apostolic career which has given him so high a place among the heroic saints of God, and so firm a hold on the thoughts and love of the people of Ireland.

Perhaps I ought to say a word in excuse for my giving up my task at the moment when St. Patrick landed on the shores of Ireland. My reasons are soon given. I have written at length on a subject that has for the most part been lightly dealt with by historians. I have stopped when the story enters on a field that has been cultivated by a hundred willing and able hands. Besides, I have not the local knowledge, which is essential to one who would do justice to the subject. True it is that I take leave of my work with regret. For more than six years the sayings and doings of St. Patrick have been almost my daily thought. By my solitary hearth, or in my lonely walk, he has been my companion and my friend. If other literary pursuits have called me aside for the nonce, it has been with pleasure that I have resumed the thread of his history. And the one reward I look for is, that his saintly character, his heroic deeds, may be more widely and more clearly known by the millions scattered throughout the world who look up to him as their Father in the faith.

ROBERT GRADWELL.

Claughton-on-Brock,
Feast of SS. Peter and Paul, 1891.

SUCCAT.

CHAPTER I.

ST. PATRICK'S PARENTAGE AND BIRTH.

ST. MARTIN, GREAT-UNCLE OF ST. PATRICK, AT AMIENS—HIS NIECE CONCHESSA—HER CAPTIVITY AND SLAVERY TO A FRANKISH CHIEF—HER MARRIAGE WITH HER MASTER'S SON CALPURNIUS—THE FRANKS CONQUERED BY VALENTINIAN—CALPURNIUS ENTERS THE ROMAN ARMY—CONCHESSA AT TREVES—BRITAIN OVERRUN BY THE PICTS AND SCOTS—CALPURNIUS'S LEGION ORDERED TO BRITAIN—CAMPAIGNS OF THEODOSIUS—THEODOSIUS AT ALCLYDE—BIRTH OF ST. PATRICK AT KILPATRICK.

IN the last decade of the nineteenth century, I am writing the life of a saint who was born in the second half of the fourth century, and whose marvellous length of days reached to the close of the fifth. His times offer as complete a contrast to those of the present day as it is possible to conceive. Then, it was a time of ruin and desolation, and it appeared as if all that had been great and valued for over a thousand years was about to be overwhelmed by a surging flood of barbarism. It was at this epoch that the good providence of God raised up on the extreme borders of the Roman Empire a man who was to found a new civilisation, which abides vigorous and energetic to this day. In the year 373, at what is now the small town of Kilpatrick, a babe was born of Christian parents, who, at his baptism, received the name of Succat. For fifty-nine years he bore this name, and, so far as I know, was called by no other until the day arrived when the Vicar of Christ gave him the name of Patrick.

The mother of Succat was a niece of St. Martin of Tours, and I cannot better commence this history than by giving some account of this very remarkable man. St. Martin was born in 317, some fifty-six years before St. Patrick, and we first meet with him in the important city of Pavia, in northern Italy, where he was living with his father, a veteran soldier, now retired. The father was a Pannonian by birth, had enlisted in the Roman army and risen to the rank of a tribune, corresponding with that of a brigadier in our day. He had never renounced his hereditary paganism, but his son was early attracted to the Christian assemblies, and his great pleasure was to spend whole hours in prayer before the Christian altars. When he was only fifteen years old, his father, in order to remove him from what he considered a serious danger of perversion from the religion of his ancestors and his allegiance to the emperors, took advantage of an imperial decree obliging the sons of veterans to bear arms, and, in spite of his tender age, sent him into Gaul to serve in his former legion of the Heruli. It is probable that an older brother, by name Ochmuis, was already enrolled, and, if the young Martin was placed along with him, the conduct of the father will not appear so harsh. This brother had married, and it was in a city of northern Gaul that his daughter Conchessa was born; so it may well have happened that recollections of her uncle were entwined with the earliest memories of her childhood. We next hear of St. Martin in the severe winter of 336 at the gate of the twins at Amiens. In pity for the destitute condition of a beggar, he, having no other means of relieving his wants, cut his military cloak in two, and clothing the starving wretch with the one half, wrapped himself in the other. The rest of the story is well known. That night St. Martin saw in his sleep the Lord

Jesus dressed in the half of the garment he had given away, was bid to look at it well, and asked if he knew it again. He then heard Jesus say to a troop of angels surrounding him: "Martin, yet a catechumen, has clothed Me with this garment".

We can well imagine how the child Conchessa, growing up in the near neighbourhood of such an uncle, would rapidly ripen into a devout Christian maiden. The bright example of her uncle's charity to God and man would influence her own life, and she would learn that her profession of Christianity was no mere vesture she could put off or on at pleasure, but a real power to mould her heart, to detach it from earth and earthly things, and raise it towards heaven. True, he soon left the army and gave himself up to the more immediate service of God in the Church, but his holy deeds and his inspiring words had done their work, and she grew up a fervent and devout Catholic; and her faith in God, and her courage to serve Him faithfully, took so firm a hold of her life that trials and misfortunes to come might try but could not shake them. And misfortunes came all too soon.

North-eastern Gaul was no secure abode in the fourth century. The Roman power was on the wane, and at no great distance on the east, from the town where Conchessa's childhood was spent, flowed the Rhine, which was but a weak protection against the savage barbarians who seemed to swarm in countless multitudes from north and east. These wild tribes of hardy warriors bore down upon the empire at different points. They were allied in blood, but were called from their arms, now Franks, now Saxons, now Longobards. The Rev. Isaac Taylor tells us that in all probability these were not different races, but merely confederations of the same people taking their names from their distinctive weapons, viz., the Franks from the franca or javelin, the Lombards from the long partisan or halberd, and the Saxons from the seax or sword. From such incursions no part of the immense frontier line of the great Roman Empire was safe. The policy and arms of Valentinian, a skilful and bold warrior, were unequal to the strain put upon them. The watchful barbarians were ever on the alert to make a dash on an unprotected point. Such a sudden attack was made on the city of Mentz about A.D. 365, when the unsuspecting inhabitants were engaged in celebrating a Christian festival, and great numbers of captives, both men and women, were carried off. Some such fate befell Conchessa. She was seized by a band of Frankish spoilers, and, in spite of the efforts of her friends and her own despairing cries and struggles, she was borne off into captivity. She had enjoyed all the advantages of being the child of an officer of high rank; she had been carefully educated as became a Roman maiden of position; and she found herself, without warning, in the midst of a wild horde of savages. Accustomed to the luxuries of a refined Roman household, to be waited on by obsequious slaves eager to do her bidding and even anticipate her slightest wish, the object of the loving care of affectionate parents, this fair flower of northern Gaul now found herself without a friend in the midst of lawless ruffians. She was hurried, without regard to her delicate bringing up, across swamps and through forests, by tracks, suited perhaps to the bold hunter, but little fitted to her tender feet, until the Rhine was reached, and she was assigned as a slave to one of the Frankish chiefs. The new home at best was a miserable hut; her task was to labour in supplying the rude but imperious wants of an exacting master. Many a nature would have given way under these fearful hardships; many a spirit would have been broken under such a crushing disaster; but in that frail girl's bosom beat a heart that rose superior to misfortune, and out of the very depth of misery won for her a deathless name and a place in history.

The Rhine is a grand historical river. The name is familiar to us in stirring story and in glowing verse. To thousands the recollection of the days spent upon its bosom is one they would not willingly let go. They remember the vine-clad slopes, the beetling crags, the picturesque ruins of castle or monastery. These have a far different appearance now-a-days from the scenes which presented themselves to Conchessa's eyes. But to those who read of her sorrows and how she bore them, they will possess a new charm; for here was the school of virtue, where, under the sharp teaching of adversity, she learned those secrets which fitted her to become the mother and trainer of a saint. The Wacht am Rhein has since been sung by thousands of deep voices in exulting triumph. She kept hers in woe and fear, but still with trust in God. She was a niece of St. Martin. She had heard him speak with lofty contempt of death, and with unwavering faith in God; and she feared not. His God was her God, and would watch over His trusting child if she were only faithful on her part.

And so she bent herself bravely to her wearisome task. We can almost see her as she toiled up the hill, bringing water for her master's use from the banks of the Rhine; as she carried the rough faggots from the forest; as she prepared the coarse food for the ravenous appetites of these mighty men. Her hands were becoming rough with work, and her form was bent with toil; her dress was rough and scanty; but above all these sordid appearances shone forth a dignity, a sweetness, and a charm, which insensibly won the hearts of those around her. Her master began to treat her with consideration, and her master's son saw in her what he had never seen in slave before; he loved her, and wished to make her his wife. We know not what was the state of her feelings when she was at home amidst those she loved, but it was a sad change for this fair girl from the elegance and ease of a luxurious home, to be a prisoner and a slave amongst strangers in race, in speech, in religion, and in manners. Many a time must she have from the hill-tops on the eastern banks of the Rhine, in an evening when her day's toil was at an end, looked wistfully to the land of the setting sun, and wonder if any help would come to her in her sore distress. And then her thoughts would turn towards her uncle. Where was he—the brave soldier, the gallant cavalier? Could not he strike one blow in her defence? And she strained her eyes to try if afar off in the distance, where the sun was sinking below the bank of clouds as the night closed in, she could discern the gleaming lances of his cohort as it rode rapidly to the rescue. But no Roman pennon floated on the horizon, no Roman steed pawed the ground eager for the march. She was not to be saved by human hand, nor by the zeal or devotion of friends. Her uncle had long left the army, even before she had reached the age of womanhood. He was now clothed in a cleric's robe, seeking perfection in the religious life under the skilful guidance of an eminent Bishop and Father of the Church, St. Hilary of Poitiers. Perhaps at the time of her capture he was in far-off Pannonia, his own native land, fighting bravely for the cause of the true faith, but not with sword or lance, but courageously submitting his bare shoulders to the executioner's scourge rather than suffer the Arians to blaspheme unrebuked against the divinity of Jesus Christ.

But days, and weeks, and months went wearily by, and no help was forthcoming. Was she forgotten? were her parents and friends helpless as herself, or already numbered with the dead? So time sped slowly on. When she first perceived that the hearts of her captors were softening towards her, it would be with mingled feelings of fear and doubt that she noted the change. And when her master's son made known to her that he loved her, and wished for nothing so much as to make her his wife, promising her the devoted affection of a life, a struggle must have taken place in her heart. Was she, a Roman maiden, to wed with a barbarian? Could she, who might under happier auspices have married into the noblest families of Italy or Gaul, receive as a husband the son of a robber chief? She was a Christian too, and could she become the wife of a worshipper of idols? But she was helpless. She was a slave. She could not fly. And so she became a bride. And a happy day it was for that Frankish family when Conchessa became a member of it. She was like a ministering angel in that rude household; she shrank instinctively from cruelty and rapine and the other vices of the barbarians, and her husband and his father felt that they could not be cruel, or rapacious, or vicious before her. They could not do before her that from which she turned away her eyes: they could not speak words against which she closed her ears: and before her they could not honour gods whom she looked upon as demons, and whose names she could not hear without a shudder. Fierce as they had been, much as they had hated the Roman name, great as had been their disdain for the religion of the Christians, they could not but acknowledge that in that meek woman there was a something before which they must bow down and do reverence. Do not let my readers imagine that I am drawing a fancy portrait, for, in truth, I am only following grave authors. This is what Father W. B. Morris of the Oratory says in page 44 of his *Life of St. Patrick:* "The old chronicler gives a touching picture of the grace and dignity of the high-born slave, and tells us how in the end they won the heart of her master's son Calpurnius". What I have done is merely to amplify this text, and lay before the reader those thoughts and feelings, those hopes and fears, those joys and sorrows, which must have made up her chequered life. Surely there are in Ireland, and in all those countless lands where are scattered the children of Ireland, some who will thank me for picturing to their minds' eyes the romantic story of the mother of St. Patrick; for telling in bright and glowing words what too often has been passed over with the very briefest notice as a dry detail. The children of St. Patrick should love his mother; and I cherish the hope that the name of Conchessa some day may sound as sweet in the ears of an Irish maiden as that of her own St. Bridgid.

One more trial, and this child of strange destiny was to be restored to civilised life; but it was a sharp trial, one to wring her heart with anguish. I have said the Roman power was waning, but it had not set in the second half of the fourth century. The Roman legions might indeed not consist of Italians and Gauls, but they still marched to the sound of a Roman trumpet; they still obeyed the word of command uttered in the sonorous Latin tongue, and the old Roman discipline made them more than a match for any barbarian force, unless taken by surprise, or hopelessly overwhelmed by numbers. So the day came when Valentinian, angry but not disheartened by the reverse his arms had sustained, mustered his forces to revenge past defeats. He was a skilful general, and he prepared a vast army, determined to crush opposition and achieve success. His first assault was on the Germans of the south. In person, accompanied by his son, Gratian, he passed the Rhine at the head of a formidable force. The enemy, unable to prevent the devastation of their villages, fixed their camp on a lofty and almost inaccessible mountain, in what is now the kingdom of Würtemberg, and resolutely awaited the approach of the Romans. The life of Valentinian was exposed to imminent danger by the intrepid curiosity with which he persisted in exploring some secret and apparently unguarded path. A troop of barbarians suddenly rose from their ambuscade, and the emperor, vigorously spurring his horse down a deep and slippery descent, only escaped with difficulty. His armour-bearer, and his helmet, magnificently adorned with gold and precious stones, he was obliged to leave behind. The result was a signal victory for his army. But the Franks lower down the Rhine remained unsubdued, and against them he now directed his arms. It was no part of his plan to effect a permanent conquest of the land, but he resolved on securing his frontier; and to that end the border tribes must be subdued, and precautions taken against a renewal of their attacks. The news spread down the river that the emperor's forces were approaching, and that all the resources of the tribes would be required to make good their defence. Numerous groups of terrified fugitives made their way down the stream, and they had sad tales to tell of the ferocity of the troops and their invincible power. Soon the smoke of the blazing villages and homesteads became visible in the near distance. The chiefs assembled their followers, despatching the women and all their scanty valuables to safe places in the rear, and they prepared for a desperate resistance. To Conchessa it was a terrible time. She truly loved her husband, barbarian though he was, for he was a brave, intelligent man, and he loved her dearly, yet her heart beat fast at the thought that her countrymen were near, and that the dreary period of her captivity was near its end. There was a conflict of hopes and fears in her heart, and she scarcely knew whether victory or defeat would be to her the worse misfortune. But the wise policy of Valentinian saved her from her fearful suspense. He offered peace to the Frankish host on favourable terms. He erected forts and placed garrisons on both banks of the Rhine, from its source to where it all but loses itself in the marshes of Holland, and he completed his conquest by enlisting the young men in his army, placing them in the legion of the Batavi.

Happier days now dawned upon this much-tried sufferer. The emperor chose Treves, on the Moselle, for his capital, for he was anxious to consolidate his conquest, and decided to be himself near the place of danger. His raw levies required laborious drill and training, before they could become soldiers fit to follow a Roman eagle, and he would himself superintend the work. It was not the first time that Treves or Trier had been the residence of an emperor. The great Constantine had spent much time here, and the Empress Helena, his mother, had given up the basilica or great hall of her palace for a church. The Cathedral of St. Peter and St. Helen is still remarkable for the early Byzantine style of its architecture, its altars, and its marble galleries. Another church, that of St. Simeon, also said to have been built in the time of Constantine, is considered the most important Roman monument in Germany. Following her husband —for he had enlisted in the Batavian legion— Conchessa had the unspeakable happiness of hearing again her native language, and of mixing again in cultivated and refined society. Above all, she had the consolations of religion; could kneel at a Christian altar, speak once more with a priest, and receive the holy sacraments. Before long the deepest wish of her heart was granted to her. What she had prayed for even with tears, but had scarcely dared to hope, was given to her, and she had the supreme satisfaction of seeing her husband, now named Calpurnius, and his father, who took the name of Potitus, baptised and fervent Christians. It is difficult to say whether it was at this time she became a mother, but in all she had a numerous family, and it is not improbable that her eldest child was born in Gaul.

It may easily have happened, too, that when at Treves she had the great happiness of seeing once more her uncle, St. Martin. He was at this time with St. Hilary of Poitiers, and it was only some years later that the marvellous sanctity of his life, and the numerous miracles which God wrought by his hands, spread his fame throughout all Gaul. He then became the foremost man amongst the clergy, and his aid was sought by all in distress, in temporal as well as spiritual matters. It was some errand of mercy which took him to the palace of Valentinian, at Treves. The emperor was sincerely attached to the Catholic faith, but he was of a domineering temper, and little disposed to pay any great deference to ecclesiastics, however distinguished. He knew the business which had caused St. Martin to leave his see and his beloved monastery on the banks of the Loire, and undertake the long and fatiguing journey to the Moselle, and he liked it not; so he gave orders that he was not to be admitted to an audience. St. Martin was not disconcerted. His trust was not in princes, but in the King of kings. He had recourse to his usual weapons of fasting and prayer. He put on haircloth and covered his head with ashes. On the seventh day he was ordered by an angel to go boldly to the palace. It is a building of immense extent, imposing ruins of which still remain, the walls in places being ninety feet high and ten feet thick. The saint obeyed the command of the heavenly messenger; he found the doors open, he passed through apartment after apartment, but no one stopped him. Entering the presence chamber, the emperor perceived him, and angrily asked why the officers had let him in, and would not vouchsafe to rise. Suddenly the place where he sat was all in flames, and he was forced to get up. He acknowledged that it was the Divine Hand showing itself; he embraced St. Martin several times, and granted all his requests without even allowing him to mention them. Such was the influence of this holy bishop; and yet Sulpicius Severus, his friend and biographer, tells us that at his election there were some opposed to it, alleging "that he was a contemptible person, unworthy of the episcopate, despicable in countenance, mean in dress, uncouth in his hair".

The event just recorded happened after Calpurnius had left Treves, but it is not unlikely that St. Martin's holy example and teaching had been powerful in the family of his niece, and that he had completed the work her persuasive gentleness had begun, ending in the conversion of both her husband and his father. We have St. Patrick's own words for it that his grandfather Potitus finally became a priest; and the knowledge of this fact has this further significance, it shows us that he was no mere barbarian who had suddenly and perforce submitted to the Roman yoke, but one who heartily embraced its manners and the Christian religion, and, as to become a priest he must have had some acquaintance with reading, we may feel certain that he carefully educated himself, and in his mature age diligently pursued the necessary studies. Here I would guard myself against the charge of having exaggerated the rank and position which St. Patrick's family occupied in Gaul. Again I can quote St. Patrick's own words: " I was of noble birth according to the flesh, my father being a decurio". So he writes in a letter to Corotic, a British chieftain. Like St. Paul himself, he knew how on occasion to appeal to his Roman nationality and his noble parentage.

Were I merely writing a story I might fitly end here with the history of Conchessa. She is once more in congenial society; she is basking in the sunshine of prosperity and court favour. Her strange adventures and her unfailing courage in meeting them have cast a halo of romance about her, and given piquancy to her many engaging qualities. She is breathing that fresh air of Gaul which has ever had an exhilarating effect on the children of the soil, and displays itself to this day in the gaiety and sprightliness of the people. Her husband is honoured and respected in the army and at court. He, too, has shown that he can shine in the council chamber as well as in the field, and that he can acquire the arts of civil life as well as wield the javelin and the spear. We know that he, too, like his father, must have attained considerable proficiency in learning, as otherwise he could never, as his son tells us, have been later on in life admitted to the diaconate. Riches, too, must have been at his command, for service in a Roman legion was liberally paid, and the higher officers had many opportunities of enriching themselves; and we know from St. Patrick himself that he became a landowner on the banks of the Clyde.

But the lives of this pair were intimately bound up with the march of public events. Calpurnius was a soldier, and served an empire which, at the time, was supposed to be world-wide. He was one of an army of men who, to use a modern popular phrase, must be able to do anything and go anywhere. Treves to him was no Capua; he had scarcely become familiar with the Roman discipline and learnt to temper the headlong bravery of the Frank with the foresight and steadiness of the Roman when news reached the court and camp which stirred every heart. Separated by a silver streak of sea from the northern coast of Gaul lies our island of Britain. For centuries it had been at once the pride and care of the Romans. Its fertile soil and the industry of its inhabitants, the readiness of the tribes dwelling in its southerly and central portions to adopt Roman habits and customs, had rendered it a most valuable possession. Only a few years before the period of our story a remarkable exhibition of the great resources of Britain had been furnished, in the reign of the Emperor Julian. The Franks and the Saxons had crossed to the left bank of the Rhine, laid waste an extensive tract of country, and reduced to ashes forty towns. After numerous engagements they were driven back by the emperor, but there remained on his hands the pressing necessity of providing the famishing inhabitants with food. The granaries of Britain offered an immediate and plentiful supply. A fleet of 800 small vessels was collected at the mouth of the Rhine; repeated voyages were made to the British coasts; the cargoes were conveyed in lighters up the river, and the impoverished people received an ample supply of corn, both to sow their lands and support themselves till the following harvest.

But if peace and plenty were the usual condition of the southern part of the island, the northern portion of it was like a thorn in the side of the great empire. If the rich valleys and fertile plains of what is now England made the Roman highly interested in keeping his hold on it, they were equally tempting to the wild and restless inhabitants of the Highland glens. The arms and genius of Agricola had been powerless to tame these children of the heather and the mist; he could conquer them in a pitched battle, but that was all. He could not break them to habits of industry or obedience to the law. They loved their wild liberty, and they hated submission to order or to toil. Yet their bleak hill-sides could not support their teeming numbers; the herds of red deer were no substitutes for the fat cattle of the plains, and the scanty patches of barley or rye only made them long for the rich wheat crops of the lowlands. They were ever ready then for a forage across their borders, and the farms, the villages, and the towns were equally their prey. Under the name of the Caledonians or Gaels of the hills, they are ever appearing in British history during the Roman occupation, and now as Picts they are as self-assertive as ever. Moreover, a tribe of Scoti from the neighbouring isle of Ireland had established itself in what is now Argyleshire, and from this time forward the Scots assume an ever-increasing importance, and in time they give their name to the whole of North Britain. Light-footed and light-armed, they were able to travel immense distances on foot; they had with them no impediments in the way of baggage; their plaid and their kilt, their broadsword and their round target, constituted their whole military equipment. For food and supplies of all kinds they relied on the resources of the country they invaded. Yet, with all their apparent rudeness, there was some political skill directing their assaults. With part of the spoil reserved from past expeditions they maintained spies in the territories ruled by the Romans, and thus had early intelligence of any remissness of the commanders in providing adequate means of defence. They tempted the fidelity of the garrisons, and had little difficulty in seducing many of the foreign auxiliaries to renounce their fealty to Rome and join them in the pursuit of plunder.

This union with disaffected soldiers in the Roman pay gave serious importance to the invasion of 367, and changed what was usually only an inroad of robbers and cut-throats into a menace to the security of the whole island. The general commanding the army of Britain was treacherously murdered, the count of the Saxon shore (including the whole coast from the Humber to Land's End) had fallen in battle, and the flames of devastation spread along the right bank of the Thames. Messenger after messenger reached the court of Valentinian, and at length he became thoroughly aroused to the imminent danger threatening his rule. After some vacillation, the most able of all his generals, Theodosius, was appointed to the command, and a powerful army was placed under him. This celebrated general was the father of a line of emperors; he was brave, skilful, upright, and energetic, and his disinterestedness and sagacity mark him out distinctly from the bulk of the statesmen and captains of his time. To serve under such a leader was the ambition of every brave soldier, and the legions of the Heruli and the Batavi, of the Jovians and the Victors, esteemed it an honour to follow his standard; so it happened that Calpurnius was summoned to take the field with the rest of his legion.

To him the call to arms might perhaps be welcome, but to his wife it was like a clap of thunder in a clear sky. She had once more to break up her home and leave her beloved native land, for she could not think of remaining behind when her husband was serving his emperor in a far-off country. But the thought of her sorrow is lost in the bustle of preparation which is going on all around. The most distinguished of Roman generals is conducting the expedition, the very flower of the Roman youth composes it; the honour of Rome is engaged in its success, and so no pains are spared to provide for and ensure a prosperous issue. The roads between Treves and Boulogne are now crowded with troops of all arms: carts and waggons of all sorts are conveying stores for the numerous requirements of the soldiery. And all along the coast, eastwards and westwards of the port, are collected craft of all sizes and kinds to bear the army over the sea to Britain. A naval expedition was a very different affair then from what it is now-a-days. The science of navigation was ill understood, and the vessels were small in size and of inferior construction. As for the means of making way through the waves, they could rely only on the sail or the oar. Perhaps in the whole flotilla, amounting in mere numbers to over one thousand, there would not be more than one or two vessels which exceeded in bulk a hundred tons; and, at the other end of the scale, the use of skin-covered basket-work or coracles was not despised.

As we read no more of Potitus after this, we may suppose that he stayed behind at Treves. His had been a strange career—wild and lawless in his youth, his pursuits those of a hunter of beasts or a scourge of men, the advent of Conchessa into his house had been the turning-point of his life. Through her he was now a civilised Roman citizen and a devout Christian; and, as he bade her farewell on her setting out with her husband for the sea coast, he must have felt her loss deeply. We know that he found consolation in religion, and that he died a priest of Holy Church.

At Boulogne Conchessa would find a ship assigned for herself and other officers' wives. We know that Theodosius took advantage of favourable weather, and that the passage to Sandwich, on the coast of Kent, was a good one. It must have been a glorious sight on that bright morning in early spring, with a propitious breeze from the south, to watch the vast collection of ships, ranging as far as the eye could reach. The emblem under which the fleet started was no longer the image of Jupiter. Since the time of Constantine the Romans fought under the banner of the Cross, and now from the mast-head of the flag-ship floated the renowned Labarum. A gilded pole bore a cross-bar, surmounted by a crown, having in it the Greek letters X and P, Chi and Rho—the initial letters of the name of Christ; and below was a representation of the emperor and a purple silken banner bespangled with jewels.

In their course they passed the white cliffs of Dover, and anchored in safety in the harbour of Sandwich. It is not necessary for me to describe the two campaigns of this great general. He united in a high degree the qualities of an accomplished military and civil governor. By the skilful disposition of his forces he gradually, but surely, drove back the swarms of the enemy. By his judicious dealing with the people, he established order and good government. The very character of the enemy made it unnecessary for him to fight any great battle; but by dividing his forces, and pursuing vigorously the separated bands of the Gaels and Scots, he forced them to abandon the country and sullenly retire towards their native hills.

I may here mention that Ammianus Marcellinus tells us that he occupied Augusta, formerly called London; and it may be useful for the reader to bear in mind this change of name in so important a city when we come a little later to speak about the vexed question of St. Patrick's birthplace. I may also allude to a curious relic of this expedition, found at Lancaster in 1772, and described by Rev. Father West in his *Guide to the Lakes*. It consists of a tombstone erected to the memory of a Roman cavalry officer, a native of Treves, who died at

Lancaster at the age of thirty years. It reads as follows: "To the Gods, the Shades, Lucius Julius Apollinarius, a citizen of Treves, thirty years of age, a horseman of the Ala Augusta".—(Watkins's *Roman Lancashire*, p. 184.) If this officer died in this campaign, it shows that there were still heathens in the army, as one might reasonably expect that there would be, and that a portion at least of the invading army passed through Lancashire as it crept on cautiously towards the north. Theodosius himself, with the main part of the army, halted not until he had reached the very limit of the Roman dominion. At this time the Wall of Antonine, stretching from the Clyde to the Forth, marked the boundary between civilised and uncivilised life; and at the western end of it rose a great natural fortress, by the Britons called sometimes Nemthor or Empthor, the lone rock, sometimes Alclyde or the rock of the Clyde, and now, in compliment to the great services just rendered by the commandant of the army, it received the name of Theodosia. Later, it was called by the neighbouring Scots Dunbriton, as being the last outpost of the Britons, and this in modern times is familiar to us under the name of Dumbarton. Theodosius carefully repaired the fortifications, strengthened the garrisons in the military stations, and restored the province of Valentia, comprising the country between the Antonine Wall and that of Severus, which runs from the Solway Firth to the mouth of the Tyne. After two years spent in Britain, he left the island, to the great regret of the natives, who accompanied him with their expressions of regard and sorrow till he went on board the vessel which was to carry him back to the continent.

Calpurnius was left behind at the restored city of Theodosia, and his wife, who had shared many of the hardships and some of the perils of the campaign in an enemy's country, found herself a resident in a fortress at the extreme limit of the Roman dominions. Her husband, we may fairly infer from the honourable position in which we afterwards find him, must have served with credit and even distinction. No doubt she felt the change from the imperial city of Treves to this remote outpost at the foot of the bleak hills, where lurked in sullen silence the wild Scots and savage Picts. But she had her family about her, and their care must have fully occupied her time and thoughts. We know from St. Patrick's *Confession* that there were priests in the city; and, besides, the life of St. Ninian (born in Cumberland about 360, a few years before Conchessa's arrival in Britain) informs us that in his youth there were Christian churches in the land. The ancient chronicles tell us that she had five daughters—Lupait, Tigris, Seamain, Darerca, and Cinnenum—and two other sons named Sannan and Ructhi.

The wise precautions taken by Theodosius and the sustained vigilance of the Emperor Valentinian ensured for the time the peace of the northern province of Britain, and, beyond an occasional outbreak of the ever-restless clans, we may presume that security reigned about the strong fortress. It is a very remarkable rock, a mass of basalt, rising sheer up from a flat, marshy plain to a height of 206 feet. It is situated at the junction of the Leven with the Clyde, and the surface at the top is about a mile square. On many sides the face of the rock is all but perpendicular, and it is simply inaccessible. In warlike times it was an important and much-valued place of defence; now it is chiefly renowned for its picturesque and striking appearance, and for its intimate connection with the birth of Ireland's great saint. The surrounding plain was called by the Romans the Campus Tabernaculorum, and by the Britons Magh Tabern, the field of tents, from the encampment there of large bodies of men employed in the defence of the Antonine Wall. A little higher up the river is the village of Old Kilpatrick, where the wall terminated; and we can still trace the sites of four forts connecting this village with the fortress itself.

There, according to Probus and many other writers, our saint was born in the year 373, and there is nothing improbable in the supposition that a distinguished Roman officer should have had a country residence, a little removed from the noise and bustle of the camp. It was for many ages called Hurnia, but this name may easily have been given later, for the word means a house of prayer, and when the fame of St. Patrick's sanctity was spread, from the land he converted to his native place, a church was built on the spot hallowed by his birth, and it became a great resort of pilgrims. There is still a church dedicated to our saint, built on the site of an older one, which had been preceded by a still more ancient building. The parish bears his name, and the range of hills to the north is also styled Kilpatrick. This is not the place to enter into the controversy which has been waged so hotly and so perseveringly about St. Patrick's nationality. I am but telling a plain story, and the groundwork has been substantially laid. I am not aware of any single positive statement of fact for which good warrant cannot be given. In

Cardinal Moran's article in the *Dublin Review* he has exhausted the subject. He has examined every scattered notice of St. Patrick, in Irish or continental writers, ranging from the sixth to the twelfth century. From ancient manuscripts in Irish, beginning with St. Fiac's hymn, in honour of St. Patrick, whom he had known in the flesh, he proves abundantly that it was at Kilpatrick, on the northern bank of the Clyde, in the near neighbourhood of what after the lapse of 1500 years is now Dumbarton, that the great light of the west was born.

We cannot wonder if the coming into the world of so great a servant of God was marked by wondrous signs, and so it was, if we may believe the old writers in this case; and I cannot more fitly end this slight sketch than by quoting Father Morris's account of them, and by adding to his words the striking verses of Mr. Aubrey de Vere: "St. Patrick was one of those upon whom God set His seal, even in infancy, manifesting by miraculous gifts and favours the designs which He had formed concerning him. The priest to whom the child was brought for baptism was blind, and no water could be procured for the sacrament; by a sudden inspiration the priest took the hand of the infant, and with it made the sign of the Cross upon the ground;

forthwith a fountain broke forth, in which the priest baptised the child; then, washing his own eyes in the miraculous waters, his sight was restored."

> How can the babe baptised be
>   When font is none, and water none?
> Thus wept the nurse on bended knee,
>   And swayed the infant in the sun.
>
> The blind priest took that infant's **hand**:
>   With that small hand, above the **ground**,
> He signed **the** Cross. At God's command
>   A fountain rose with brimming bound.
>
> In that pure wave, **from** Adam's sin
>   The blind priest cleansed the **babe with awe**;
> Then, reverently, he washed therein
>   His old, unseeing face, and saw.
>
> He saw the earth; **he saw the skies,**
>   And that all-wondrous **child**, decreed
> A pagan **nation** to baptise
>   And give the Gentiles **light** indeed.
>
>   —(De Vere, *Legends of St. Patrick*.)

CHAPTER II.

BOYHOOD OF ST. PATRICK, 373-388.

GLASGOW IN THE NINETEENTH CENTURY—CONDITION OF THE COUNTRY ABOUT THE ANTONINE WALL IN THE FOURTH CENTURY—DISPOSITION OF THE ROMAN TROOPS IN BRITAIN—STATE OF RELIGION AT THEODOSIA—REBELLION OF MAXIMUS—ST. MARTIN AT TREVES—ST. PATRICK'S CHILDHOOD—CRITICAL STATE OF THE ROMAN EMPIRE AT THE DEATH OF MAXIMUS—RAID OF THE SCOTI ON THE BANKS OF THE CLYDE—ST. PATRICK CARRIED OFF CAPTIVE INTO IRELAND.

It is very difficult for a person living at the end of the nineteenth century, and at all acquainted with the present condition of things on the banks of the Clyde, to imagine what it was when St. Patrick dwelt there at Bannaven Tabernia in the later years of the fourth century. And yet it is obvious that the better we are informed about all the circumstances of that remote time, the more correct will our judgment be on all those things which would materially influence the character of one living at the time and place. In these days the Clyde is one of the most important water-ways in the world; its rising tides bring to the port of Glasgow the merchandise of all parts of the earth, and as those tides ebb they bear away the varied products of the greatest manufacturing district of Scotland. Ships of the largest size are constantly passing up and down the stream, and are visible proofs of the magnitude of the interests they serve. The city of Glasgow now claims the position of being the third city of the empire, even if not of being second only to London. The Clyde itself for twenty miles to its mouth is alive with vessels of all sizes and of all nations of the earth, while its banks are studded in some parts with extensive works for the building of ships and engines, and at others with smiling villas of the city merchants and manufacturers. By incessant care and unwearying industry the bed of the river has been so deepened that ships of thousands of tons burden can now float along the city quays, though at the beginning of the century it was so shallow a few miles below Glasgow that men could wade from shore to shore at low tide. It was not until the May of 1886 that the formidable reef known as the Eldersley Rock, crossing the river at Renfrew, and consisting of a belt of hard whinstone about a hundred yards broad, was entirely removed by dynamite, after an expenditure of £40,000; this operation has greatly increased the depth of water. The great natural features are the same now as ever, and the bold rock of Dumbarton is as conspicuous as Alclyde was in the time of the Roman occupation, but all else has changed. The bed of the river was choked with sand banks and shoals, and no vessel of any size could approach the site of Glasgow within fourteen miles. The city itself did not exist till two centuries after St. Patrick's time, when St. Kentigern settled there and gathered the first commencements of a population around him. The ground was a mere swamp, intersected with streams, in which the natives moored their canoes, and in recent times these have been dug out from a depth of twenty-five feet under the surface, and at a distance of 500 yards from the present margin of the stream.

The district itself was at the uttermost limits of the Roman dominion in Britain; only a few years before St. Patrick's birth, in 373, it had been re-conquered from the invading bands of Picts and Scots by the generalship and skill of Theodosius. On the south of the Antonine Wall the arms of the Romans might ensure some sort of civilisation, but to the north barbarism reigned unchecked. The Picts and Scots were wild and untamed, and one tribe, the Attacotti, occupying the region about Loch Lomond, are described by St. Jerome, a contemporary, as the worst of cannibals. Some of the tribe had enlisted in the Roman army under Valentinian, and St. Jerome met with them in Gaul, and afterwards in Italy and Illyricum, and he assures us they feasted on human flesh. This gives us a lively idea of what it was to live in the near neighbourhood of savage men.

The bold elevation of basaltic rock, on which is now built Dumbarton, rising on the north bank of the Clyde, about twelve miles below Glasgow, had struck the military eye of a Roman general, and it was selected as the citadel of an important station. The great Wall of Antonine, running across the country to the Firth of Forth, had its western extremity close to, and the intervening space was strongly fortified by four towers at short intervals. It is said that at times nearly 10,000 men were employed on the duty of guarding the wall, and keeping up the communication from end to end. Indeed, as was natural, the great bulk of the army in Britain during Roman times was concentrated in the most northern province. In the fourth century there were three great military commands in Britain—those of the Duke of Britain, the Count of Britain, and the Count of the Saxon shore—who all acknowledged as their superior officer the Master of the Horse, stationed on the banks of the Rhine. The Duke of Britain seems to have held command from the northern boundary to the Humber, and his ordinary residence was at York. He had under him 14,000 foot and 900 horse; of these 8000 foot and 600 horse were set apart for the defence of the Northern Wall. The rest were scattered in garrisons throughout the country, being barely sufficient in number to maintain peace and order. The Count of Britain commanded 3000 men and 600 horse, and his authority extended to the rest of England, with the exception of the eastern and south-eastern coasts, which formed the province of the Count of the Saxon shore. He had a force of 2200 foot and 200 horse. In all, Schöll tells us that at the close of the fourth century the Roman army in Britain numbered about 19,000 foot and 1700 horse. Of these nearly half were stationed in the strong line of forts guarding the Antonine Wall. We can then readily imagine how considerable a town would spring up near Dumbarton, or Theodosia, as it was called in late Roman times, for it was the seat of both civil and military government.

The authority on which these figures rest is unimpeachable. It is all but contemporary with the boyhood of our saint, and it has all the weight of an official document. It is called the "Notitia Imperii," drawn up about the year 400, when St. Patrick was about twenty-seven years old, and twelve years after his being sold into slavery. It proves beyond a doubt that Theodosia was the most important military station in all Britain, and, as these stations were also the great centres of Christian influence, we may properly infer that the Christian community was both numerous and influential. If, from time to time, the Roman troops were reduced in numbers, on account of political causes, the great fort and the line of fortifications were too important not to receive careful attention as soon as the pressure on the resources of government was relaxed. It has been a favourite argument with those who question the British birthplace of St. Patrick that Christians and Romans were too few on the banks of the Clyde for the saint's own statement of the great number of prisoners carried away by the pirates to be true about Dumbarton; but the difficulty entirely disappears when we learn for certain that many years after his capture there were nearly ten thousand men in charge of the Antonine

Wall. This great military force would draw to the spot a large civil population, and hence there is ample room for the thousands of St. Patrick's fellow-captives. For centuries the Romans had held an uncertain tenure of the district between the Antonine Wall and that of Hadrian between Carlisle and the mouth of the Tyne; but Theodosius re-conquered the country, and, in compliment to the then Emperor Valentinian, styled it the Province of Valentia.

I cannot supply many details of the state of religion in the province. Certain it is that there was a bishop at York, and it may very well have been that his jurisdiction extended as far as the Roman power reached. In the life of St. Ninian, born about thirteen years before St. Patrick, in 360, on the southern bank of the Solway Firth, we are told that he was the son of a British prince, that he was a Christian from his birth, and that as a boy he was fond of praying in the churches; and from this we may gather that at Carlisle and other great military centres there were many Christian congregations, having their places of worship, and sharing the faith with natives of the island; and St. Patrick himself, in his *Confession*, tells us that there were priests in the districts in which he resided as a boy. At the date of his birth, Pope Damasus occupied the Chair of St. Peter at Rome, having been elected 1st October, 366. Even at this early period the Pope enjoyed a position of great temporal splendour and dignity, so as to excite the sharp comments of pagan writers. A story is told of Pretextatus, the consul elect, who, when exhorted by the Pope to renounce idolatry, answered: "Give me your place and I will be a Christian immediately". The Church counted at the time some of its most distinguished writers and bishops, among others St. Jerome, St. Ambrose, and St. Augustine, while in Gaul St. Martin's influence was wide-spread and powerful. The fortune of war had brought the parents of our saint into Britain in the army of Theodosius in the year 367, and when that general returned to the continent, Calpurnius, his father, remained behind with the garrison guarding the Antonine Wall. The son was born at what is now known as Kilpatrick, close to the western end of the great wall. Of course, from his earliest childhood he would be familiar with the sights and sounds of a great camp. The troops could have had no holiday task in those troubled times, being, as they were, the advanced post of the army, and in sight of the enemy's country. An alarm might be heard at any moment, and orders given to face the Picts and Scots, or to hasten to a portion of the wall where the defenders were sorely pressed.

Patrick was still a mere child when political changes took place in the great Roman world, which had an important influence on his own destiny. In 378, when he was five years old, Theodosius, the son of the brilliant commander under whom his father had served, was associated in the empire by Gratian. He was a Spaniard by birth, and his elevation excited the envy of Maximus, a Spaniard like himself, then serving in the army of Britain. He was declared emperor by the troops, and, though he pretended reluctance to assume the purple, he soon showed that his ambition was not content with rule in the island, but that he aspired to dominion over the West. In 383 he sailed to the mouth of the Rhine with a large army raised in Britain, and thus he nearly drained the country of troops. True, he at times drove back the Picts and Scots who were tempted to renew their incursions by the small number of the soldiers left in the island; but few of the Britons who followed his standard ever revisited their country, and it was left to a great extent defenceless against a restless and insatiable foe. In 388 Maximus experienced on the banks of the Save in Pannonia the first shock to his power, and soon afterwards he was stripped of his imperial ornaments and beheaded. This favourable opportunity was not lost on the Picts and Scots, who poured themselves over the country left with a diminished garrison, and gorged themselves with its spoils. The camp about Dumbarton was kept in a constant state of excitement and alarm by these changes of peace and war.

According to a custom not unusual in those times, the boy Succat, for so St. Patrick was called in his youth, was confided to the care of a nurse residing in the country, and his infancy, at least, was spent amid rustic scenes and pursuits. The ancient authors speak of his taking part in tending sheep, and they further recite many instances of his possessing miraculous powers even at this tender age. His nurse was the wife of a servant of a British chief, who was on friendly terms with the Roman Government, and had a house in Alclyde. This chief was so important a personage that in the Leabhar Breac he is called King of Britain, and his house is styled a palace. Meanwhile the child grew into a boy; as a child he would no doubt learn from his nurse to talk the language of the country, the British or ancient Welsh; but partly from his parents' lips and partly from his school-fellows he would become familiar with the Latin language. One consequence of this was that Latin was never to him the language of thought, and that even to advanced old age he had to translate into Latin the thoughts that came to him in British. As a youth he would be carefully brought up by his pious parents. We know that he was instructed in the Christian religion, in its doctrine and rules, and he seems to have had some knowledge of the history of the Old Testament, for we find him later on, before he had returned from his captivity to civilised life, invoking the aid of Elias. He speaks with great respect of the priests, his instructors, and laments the indifference of himself and his companions to their good advice.

As the father of St. Patrick advanced in years, he seems to have left the army, and to have entered on the duties of civil life. He became a decurio, or provincial senator, and he resided in a villa not far from Bannaven Tabernia. It is not easy to state positively where this was situated. The word Bannaven is a generic name from the Celtic words "ban" or "bun," meaning mouth, and Avon, a river, and signifies "rivermouth". There is a river still bearing the name of Avon which falls into the Clyde about twelve miles above Glasgow, and a range of hills called Bannawk runs along its banks; so that it is sufficiently probable that this was the site of

Calpurnius's villa. Its distance from Theodosia is not an insuperable objection, as a distinguished magistrate may well have had a country as well as a town residence. He long had been a faithful disciple of the Christian law, and he now wished to give himself more immediately to the service of the Church. He received deacon's orders, and so qualified himself to assist at the offices of religion and take part in the instruction of the faithful.

We must not imagine that the family of Calpurnius was cut off from the news of the outer world. There was a constant communication kept up with the headquarters of the army, and a going to and fro of officers and officials between Dumbarton and Treves. In the mess-rooms of the officers the intelligence from the continent was freely talked over, and great news it was for Conchessa when she heard of the high favour which her uncle St. Martin enjoyed at the imperial court of Maximus at Treves. Various calls of charity obliged him to visit that city, to intercede for persons who had incurred the enmity of Maximus by their adhesion to the fallen Emperor Gratian. The greatest consideration was paid to St. Martin, and at a state entertainment given in his honour he was seated next to the emperor. The empress conceived the highest veneration for the saintly old man, and prevailed upon him to be present at a banquet to which she invited the emperor, at which she waited upon him in person. Conchessa would be equally interested when she was told of the earnest pleading of St. Martin for the lives of the unfortunate Priscillianist heretics. For the false teaching of Priscillian he had no sympathy, for he was orthodoxy itself, but he viewed with abhorrence the harshness that was not content with condemning the error, but thirsted for the blood of the heretic. He made use of every influence he possessed to prevent the spilling of blood in the name of religion, and extorted a promise from the Emperor Maximus that the lives of the accused should be spared. His arms were persuasion and gentleness, and persecution and cruelty were abhorrent in his eyes. The firmest champion of true doctrine of his age, he at the same time gave a brilliant example of toleration towards those who had fallen from the faith. We may be sure that Conchessa would often speak to her boy about her venerable uncle, and that he would learn to look up to him with love and respect. St. Martin would become to him a hero, as one to be admired and imitated; and perhaps the idea now began to take shape in his mind that he too would renounce the service of an earthly king to devote himself to that of the King of kings. This at least is certain, that as soon as ever it was in his power he left home and country to place himself under his uncle's care.

It is an interesting study to note the various circumstances made use of by the good providence of God to form the character and direct the life's purpose of one who was in after years to be so great a figure in the Church, and to enjoy after death so undying a renown. Gathered round about the winter's fire of logs in a country villa at Avon-Mouth, on the most remote border of the Roman Empire, might be seen the venerable father showing, under the sombre robe of the ecclesiastic, the erect and stately bearing of the soldier who had fought in many a bloody battle. Beside him was the matron with hair already tinged with grey, for she had endured much in her early maidenhood, but commanding in person, and attracting all by her sweet and winning presence. Then, perhaps, at their feet, conning over a roll of parchment containing passages of Scripture history, or engaged in talking merrily with his many brothers and sisters, was the youthful Succat, a fair boy of not fifteen summers. Of course there is no record in books of such a scene; but surely I am indulging in no very wild flight of fancy when I suggest its probability to the minds of my readers.

And could we have been of that company, we might easily have heard from the boys' lips an earnest request to their fond mother that she would tell them the story of her being carried off a captive from her father's house into a strange and distant land. How they would hang upon her words; how feelings of curiosity would give way to awe, to indignation, and to sorrow as the recital proceeded; and how they would rejoice when she came to the peaceful and happy ending! When the excitement had somewhat subsided, can we not imagine that Calpurnius would very seriously begin to talk about the present situation of affairs in Britain? He would shake his head as he spoke of the absence of Maximus from the island; of the heavy contributions in men and money he had recently drawn in order to make good his claim to rule Italy as well as Gaul. He would become still more in earnest as he spoke of the turbulence of many wild British tribes who had never cheerfully submitted to the Roman yoke, and whose savage instincts were ever ready to assert themselves when a controlling power was wanting to restrain them. He would go on to point out how the frontier garrisons were weak ened to a dangerous extent, and how even at Alclyde or Theodosia there was no force to give protection to the town, much less to the neighbouring country; and he would breathe a prayer that his fears for their security might prove unfounded, and that no such danger as he feared might befall them. He would tell his attentive listeners how he remembered the time when he too was a foeman of Rome, and how at the head of a body of his brave Franks he was ever ready to carry fire and sword into the lands which obeyed the emperor's command. He would proceed to say that he could well recall the day when the news reached his encampment, on the wooded hill-side on the eastern bank of the Rhine, that the Emperor Julian had fallen in battle in the far-off East, vainly fighting against Sapor, the Persian king. How this information was carried he could not tell; but along the vast frontier of nearly three thousand miles, from the shores of the Black Sea to the Antonine Wall in their own neighbourhood, in every village, on every hill-top, the great news was exultingly proclaimed that the emperor was killed, that the Roman power was broken, and that now was the time for Goth and Hun, for Frank and Saxon, for Pict and Scot, to avenge on the helpless Roman the wrongs and defeats of centuries. He would grow more grave still as he mentioned that rumours had just reached Theodosia, though he could not say what truth there might be in them, that the troops of their Emperor Maximus had met with a rebuff from those of Theodosius, the famous and wise Emperor of the East, and even that Maximus himself had by death expiated his crimes and his ambition. If this, indeed, should be true, he could not but feel that evil days were in store for them. Naturally, his thoughts first turned to their near neighbours, the Picts, and he dreaded lest when the news reached them they should pour down from their bleak hills and their rugged valleys and deal out robbery and murder on the unprepared Britons and Romans south of the wall.

Too soon were his misgivings justified, but not from the quarter that he contemplated. While he was thinking about the Picts—a name at once familiar and dreaded—a storm of war was gathering from a very different point. The inhabitants of Ireland had at this time as great a reputation for predatory expeditions by sea as the Danes had a few centuries later. Their object was booty, but an especial part of this consisted of captives, both men and women, of whom they made slaves, offering a portion as due to their princes, and selling the rest at the highest price they could command. It so happened that seven sons of a British prince named Sechmaidhe were in banishment; they took service under an Irish chieftain, and with a numerous fleet of light vessels were ravaging the coast of western Britain. At this time Niell of the nine hostages was the most powerful king in Ireland. History tells us that he devoted much of his time and energies to naval expeditions against the Gauls and Britons; he finally perished in one of them, when he was cruising in the Iccian Sea, the present English Channel: and we can scarcely be wrong in supposing that the sons of Sechmaidhe were serving under him. It must have been an expedition on a more than usually large scale, for we find that the captives they carried off were numbered, not by hundreds, but by thousands. The flotilla entered the Clyde: from the diminished garrison they met with no effectual resistance; and the families of the inhabitants, civil and military, were at their mercy. Whether the soldiers in the strong fort were too weak to protect the town, or whether they held aloof in selfish indifference, the result was the same, and the invaders could work their lawless and savage will. It was a sad sight to behold peaceful homes broken into, the unsuspecting inhabitants seized and carried off, and, whenever opposition was shown, the sword or the fire, slaughtering and burning. The house of Calpurnius was surrounded; on every side surged those fierce warriors, thirsting for their prey. The terrified Conchessa saw renewed those fearful scenes of her youth, when she became the slave of her captors. It is not unlikely that Calpurnius made a valiant resistance, for the old chroniclers record that he and his wife were slain, and that three of his children, Succat and his two sisters Lupiat and Tigris, were carried off captives. They were hurried to the sea coast and placed in different vessels, so that they knew not that they were companions in misfortune. In the Clyde, opposite the Kilpatrick Church, is a rock called St. Patrick's, and tradition has it that the vessel on which he was aboard struck upon it when under full sail but sustained no injury.

Bewildered with the suddenness and rapidity of events, the boy would, when he found himself at length left quiet in the ship, begin to realise the dreadful mischance which had befallen him. His parents murdered, his sisters he knew not where, and he himself perfectly helpless in the hands of cut-throats and savages. Their appearance was wild, their speech was strange, their manners rough and savage. We cannot doubt that he was a boy of high spirit: his after-life assures us of this. His education had been a hardy one, and constant exposure and outdoor exercise had strengthened and invigorated his frame. He had already learnt to brave the fury of the elements, and to contend successfully with wild beasts; but this was a crushing blow. He could not stir a hand to help himself—he could but submit to the imperious will of his new masters. Love of their native land has ever been a characteristic of Britons; they have ever cherished an ardent affection for the land of their birth. This is stronger, as a rule, among those born and brought up amongst hills and moors; and, as this had been the lot of our saint, we cannot wonder that years afterwards he speaks in touching words of his regret at being ruthlessly torn away from the beloved soil of his country. He was but fifteen years of age: and so it was only natural that bitter tears should roll down his cheeks and convulsive sobs shake his breast as he was rudely ordered to keep still, or, perhaps, without waiting for words, smart blows were dealt him to secure obedience.

For a time his eyes could rest on the great rock of Alclyde, the principal feature in the landscape about his home; but as this gradually faded from his view, and the rising waves told him that he was now in the open sea, each hour at an increasing distance from his home, his boy's heart would sink within him. He had been a bold, aspiring youth, and had looked forward when he should reach manhood to do some great work. At one time he had thoughts of being like his father, a brave officer in Rome's mighty army, and later on he conceived the idea of following in the steps of his uncle St. Martin, and being a valiant soldier of the Cross. And was this to be the end of all his dreams of an honourable and distinguished career? Was he now to have no other future before him than that of slavery in a barbarous land? When the exhaustion of weariness followed on the excitement of the few previous hours, when hunger began to tell on his healthy young frame, and the cold arising from being exposed for a lengthened time to the salt sea breeze had chilled his very marrow, he felt, indeed, utterly miserable and forsaken. But the despondency of youth is not of long duration; his hunger was appeased by some coarse food flung to him, and the sight of a strange land soon aroused alike the crew and their helpless prisoners. They seem to have first sighted the coast of Louth, and here they sold into slavery the young sister

Lupiat. Then they pursued their voyage northwards, finally landing on the shore of County Antrim. The ship was run on the sands as the readiest mode of effecting a landing, and the boy was ordered to rise and go on land.

CHAPTER III.

CAPTIVITY OF ST. PATRICK IN IRELAND, 388-394.

PHYSICAL FEATURES OF THE NORTH OF IRELAND—ANCIENT WRITERS ON IRELAND, MELA, PTOLEMY, SOLINUS—THE VALLEY OF THE BRAID—SUCCAT SOLD TO MILCHO—THE WORKINGS OF THE HOLY SPIRIT IN HIS SOUL—THE PAGANISM OF THE IRISH—SUCCAT'S ESCAPE FROM SLAVERY—HIS JOURNEY ACROSS IRELAND—HE TAKES SHIP IN KILLALA BAY.

County Antrim is at the extreme north-east of Ireland. It is distant from the opposite Scottish shore of Wigtonshire about twenty-three miles, and is not more than fifteen miles from the Mull of Cantyre. Between the Irish and Scottish coasts flows the warm gulf stream, which so softens the rigour of the cold that close to the sea are to be found huge hedges of fuchsias and tall hydrangeas, which have for years remained uninjured during the severest winter. But the eastern coast of Antrim is iron-bound. A range of lofty, often precipitous, hills runs close to the sea coast from south to north. Frequently the cliffs rise steep and perpendicular from the water's edge, so that the road which skirts the sea from Larne to Fairhead runs through galleries cut in the living rock. Yet such is the mildness of the air and the fertility of the soil, where there is any, that the vegetation creeps down to the water's edge. Between the projecting headlands are little bays of exquisite beauty, and in these tiny patches of sand have been thrown up by the sea, offering a ready landing-place for boats and small vessels. A curious physical feature of the county is that, for the most part, the rivers do not flow eastwards towards the Irish Sea, but westwards and southwards into Lough Neagh, the largest lake in the British Isles, being twenty miles in length and fifteen in breadth. The district is so little frequented by travellers that a popular authoress, writing an account of her visit to it in the autumn of 1886, calls it "An Unknown Country". The Giants' Causeway, on the northern coast, is, of course, well known to every reader; but the rest of the county is almost neglected by travellers. Yet the authoress just alluded to does not hesitate to say that the coast drive from Larne to Cushendale is little inferior to the best part of the Riviera, and that the "glens of

Antrim" can be compared, not disadvantageously, with the grand, sombre moorlands of the Scottish Highlands. The hills are for the most part of basalt resting on a thick substratum of limestone. Their tops have bold, sharp, rugged, and even fantastic shapes; while in the parts where the sea has beaten for ages on the limestone, vast caves have been hollowed out of the rock, presenting a spectacle, most curious and magnificent, of arch and pinnacle, of tower and buttress, in endless variety and combination.

The earliest geographer who has given us any account of Ireland is the Spaniard, Pomponius Mela, who wrote in the reign of the Emperor Claudius, A.D. 41-54. He travelled in Ireland about the year 40, and he describes in a few pithy sentences the climate, the soil, and the people of that country as he found them at the time. He says that the climate is unfit for ripening grain—" Caeli ad maturanda semina iniqui"—but that the soil is so rich in herbage, not only luxuriant, but sweet, that a very short part of the day suffices for the cattle to take their fill of it, and that, unless driven from the pasture, they burst from eating too much—" Terra autem adeo foecunda herbis non laetis modo sed etiam dulcibus ut se exigua parte diei pecora impleant, et nisi pabulo prohibeantur diutius pasta dissiliant". The people he does not speak favourably of. He says the cultivators are uncivilised and destitute of every virtue —"Cultores ejus inconditi sunt, et omnium virtutum ignari". This was written more than eighteen hundred years ago.

The next writer who gives us any detailed account of Ireland is the Alexandrian author, Ptolemy, who flourished early in the second century. His chapter on Ireland is little more than a transcript, with corrections, of an older work by Marinus of Tyre, who lived a short time before him; and this in turn is supposed to have been drawn from an ancient Tyrian atlas. Ptolemy mentions over fifty names of places in Ireland, but of these nine only can be identified. These names were probably derived from sailors whose ships touched at various points on the Irish coasts: they would catch the sounds very inaccurately, and repeat them in such a manner that they would be still further corrupted. Among the places which can be definitely ascertained, the most notable are: Bououinda—the Boyne; Senos—the Shannon; Nagnatai—Connaught; and Eblana—Dublin. Tacitus, also of the second century, speaks of the ports of Ireland as being better frequented than those of Britain, and he describes the inhabitants as being like to those of Britain.

Indeed, it is recorded by historians that some of the British tribes, unwilling to submit to the Roman yoke, emigrated to Ireland, and settled there in different parts of the country. Among other places, Waterford, Tipperary, and Kilkenny were colonised by bands of Brigantes from Lancashire and Yorkshire.—(Harris's *Ware*.) Solinus, a contemporary of the writers just quoted, gives some curious details of the island, and, among others, mentions that no snake is to be found in it.—(Solinus, xxii. " Illic nullus anguis".) Solinus is so faithful a copyist of the great work of Pliny that he is called Pliny's Ape, and he but reproduces the belief common amongst the learned of his time. Ireland is seldom mentioned by writers of the third or fourth centuries, except as the country from which bold and hardy pirates issued forth to plunder the coasts of Britain and Gaul.

Such was the land into which, in the year 388, the boy Succat, as St. Patrick was then called, was brought by his captors. Their object was to sell him to the highest bidder, and of course until that was done it was no part of their policy to treat him ill and so rob him of any personal advantages he possessed. As they critically surveyed their human prize, they could not but admire the upright, well-knit frame, the easy, elastic, yet firm step, and the bold, fearless bearing of the boy; and as he sprang on shore, still clad in his Roman toga, they flattered themselves that he would bring a good price. The chronicles do not tell us where he landed, but probably enough it would be in the pretty little Bay of Glenarm. The beauty of the spot is such that the Earls of Antrim have chosen it for the site of their castle. Its natural charms might be a matter of little moment to the wild slave-catchers of the fourth century, but even in those remote days it would offer a secure shelter from the raging sea and a safe landing-place for the rude craft then in use. At no great distance dwelt a chieftain named Milcho, a prince of Dalaraida, a district reaching from Newry to the Braid, and to him it was determined that the boy should be offered in sale. To reach his residence, in the valley of the Braid, it was necessary to cross the range of mountains which runs along the coast. For a time the route of the caravan would follow the north bank of the river Glenarm, but soon they would begin to ascend the steep side of the hill, here rising to a height of from 800 to 900 feet. From the summit of the pass on a clear day the British shore can be distinctly seen; and it would be with a sinking heart that Succat would take his last look at his well-loved native land.

The valley of the Braid plays such an important part in the history of our saint that a short space devoted to it will not be thrown away. The readiest approach to it now is by railway from Belfast to Ballymena, and from that town it runs in a north-easterly direction for about fourteen miles, until the mountains above Glenarm on the sea coast shut it in. Except for its connection with St. Patrick, it is not in any way remarkable, and the constructors of railways have shown their appreciation of it by just crossing it at the lower end of the valley. A railway from Larne to Belfast runs on the other side of the hills which form its southern border; and another iron road from Ballymena to Cushendale skirts the northern slope of the hills on the other bank of the Braid. But the traveller who wishes to tread the soil made sacred for evermore by the footsteps of St. Patrick must forsake the beaten track of tourists at Ballymena, and find his solitary way to the source of the Braid, leaving behind him the hum of towns, and finding companions in the rushing waters, the desolate valleys, and the bare mountain-tops.

The name, Braid, is the modern form of Braghad, a gullet or windpipe, and is used to signify a gorge or deeply-cut glen. Joyce, *Irish Names and Places*, i. p. 465, says: "Of this application the river and valley of the Braid near Ballymena in Antrim form a very characteristic example". However, the river soon loses its wild and precipitous character, and, after receiving a confluent at the Forked Bridge, flows in a quiet stream past Broughshane and Ballymena into the Main. Its breadth is rarely over twenty feet, and except in times of flood its waters are shallow. On the north bank, in the parish of Skerry, there is a narrow strip of low, arable land, with a light, gravelly soil; but, this is soon hemmed in by a range of mountains, sometimes rising to a considerable elevation, and in the case of Soarns Hill to 1326 feet. At some little distance from the stream is a basaltic rock of great height, on which are still pointed out what tradition says are the footprints of the Angel Victor, who is said to have here conversed with St. Patrick. But the most remarkable feature in the landscape is the Hill of Slemish. This is on the south bank; it stands somewhat in front of the mountain range separating the valley of the Braid from that of the Glenwherry, and rises suddenly to a height of 1437 feet above the sea-level, from a tract of low-lying moorland. It presents to a spectator looking at it from the west the appearance of half of the orb of the full moon.

The Braid forms the boundary between the parishes of Racavan or Rathcavan on the south, and Skerry on the north of the river. The former, so called from the Rath (or circular mound) of the Cavan (or hollow), contains some curious remains of ancient times. An artificial cave, provided with a species of chimney or air-hole, is surrounded by the foundations of buildings now completely thrown down; the adjoining locality is known in the country as St. Patrick's Chapel. This cluster of ancient buildings was formerly surrounded by a deep ditch and parapet. A small stream called the Cashel Burn runs by it before it falls into the Braid. The word Cashel means a circular mound formed of stone, and no doubt the stream derives its name from the cashel formerly surrounding the buildings.

In a straight line between Slemish and Skerry is the townland of Bally-lig-Patrick, the townland of Patrick's hollow: here, too, is a cave built with remarkable strength and solidity; it had at least three compartments, and one of them is supplied with air by a chimney.—(O'Laverty, *Down and Connor*, p. 438.)

There are some other very ancient stone monuments which may easily have come down from times preceding those of St. Patrick: and the valley is full of places with which traditions of his presence are associated. Stations are still held on the Skerry Rock, where the angel is said to have appeared to the saint; and Colgan, writing in 1647, says: "The place is called Schire Padrine, and is the scene of a great pilgrimage; and crowds of people assemble at it with great devotion".—(O'Laverty, p. 444.)

As the party descended from the summit of the pass, and entered the little valley of the Braid, the youth must have been struck with the extreme desolation of the surrounding country. The hills were either covered with scanty, coarse grass or heather, or presented to view the bare, rugged rock. As they reached the lower ground it was boggy, and scarcely passable. There was no attempt at a road, and there were few signs of human habitation. Succat had been used to the sights and sounds of a busy city: when for a time he went into the country he was always within easy reach of the ceaseless hum of men, and the country about Dumbarton bore the marks of industrious cultivation, and often of taste and luxury. But here nothing caught the eye save the desolate heath, no sound fell on the ear but the screech of a wild bird or the monotonous murmur of falling water. At length they reached the Rath or abode of Milcho.

Milcho was not inclined to purchase a slave

on his own account, and three other persons joined with him, and we may well imagine there would be much bargaining before the matter was settled. While Milcho dwelt upon his youth and the slightness of his frame, alleging that he would be of little value to him, the vendors would enlarge on his handsome appearance and distinguished birth, and declare that he was just the servant for so noble a master. Succat, meanwhile, though he could understand what was said only imperfectly, would know well what was going on, and his proud Roman heart would swell with indignation at the humiliation put upon him. When the bargain was made, and his captors had departed, he found himself in a most embarrassing position, for he was the slave not of one master but of four, and it would be a most difficult matter for one so circumstanced to give satisfaction. While he was doing the behest of one, he was too often wanted by another, and so he had to suffer ill-treatment for what was beyond his power to remedy. After a time, however, Milcho perceived that his new slave was no common person, and that it was well worth his while to secure his undivided service, and so he bought from his partners their share of this human chattel. It must have been a gain to the poor boy, and yet he had a hard lot to endure.

It is evident that Milcho was a close-fisted man, with a keen eye to his own interest, and that he would not spare a slave when anything was to be gained by harshness. Besides his property in the valley of the Braid, he had another estate in Killicarn, a few miles off, where there still remains a considerable Rath, or circular mound of earth, in which he is supposed to have had a residence. But he dwelt principally on the northern slope of Mount Slemish, or, as it was then called, Sliabh Mis. Succat's employment was tending his master's flocks of sheep on the hills, and sometimes a herd of swine which ranged the woods, and subsisted on roots, acorns, and beech nuts. At first it must have been with loathing that he executed his menial and repulsive task. Many a time must his thoughts have turned to the peaceful home from which he had been so ruthlessly torn. Often must he have called to mind his parents' house, and tears must have filled his eyes as he thought of their untiring love and care for him. Then he would think of his companions at school, and of the happy hours he had spent with his brothers and sisters. A sense of utter loneliness and misery would come upon him, and, when he considered the hopelessness of success in attempting an escape, he would be inclined to give way to despair. It was fortunate for him that, in childhood, he had spent much of his time in the country, and that he had even then taken part in the labours of the farm, so that his present task, however irksome, was not altogether new to him.

He would have been more than boy if his soul had not been stirred to anger against his captors, and to a deep desire for their condign punishment. But soon his thoughts took another turn. His occupation forced him into solitude; day after day he was alone on the desolate heath-covered mountain-top, or in the rugged gorges amongst the hills with no other companions than the sheep or the swine under his care: the voice of religion began to make itself heard in his soul. At first it might be in all but inaudible whispers and at occasional moments, but soon he felt that it was God speaking to him, and calling him to His service. Then the remembrance of his past life came to his mind, and filled him with confusion and sorrow. One incident of his life which had occurred only a short time before his being stolen from his home especially caused him anguish and remorse. He speaks of " what he had done in his youth in one day—nay, rather in one hour—because I was not then able to overcome. I know not, God knows, if I was then fifteen years of age; and from my childhood I did not believe in the

Living God, but remained in death and unbelief."—(*Confession*, p. 594.) He does not tell what was his fault, but it was sufficiently serious to be alleged against him years afterwards when it was proposed he should be raised to the episcopate. Indeed, he says of this part of his life: "This I know for certain, that before I was humbled I was like a stone lying in deep mud, until He who is powerful came, and in His mercy raised me up" (p. 585). Yet we cannot have a doubt that he had been well instructed in his religion, and that on the whole he had led a virtuous life, free from any habitual breach of God's commandments: but, now that grace was enlightening his soul, it appeared to him as if he for the first time was beginning to know God. "I knew not the true God," he says, "and I was brought captive to Ireland with many thousand men, as we deserved, for we had forsaken God and had not kept His commandments, and were disobedient to our priests who admonished us for our salvation."—(*Confession*—Cusack's *Life*, p. 581.) Who is there who cannot remember a similar experience in his own life? Who cannot look back to a time when he entered into himself, and seemed to view everything in a new light, so that his past life appeared to him little better than darkness and ignorance of divine things? To many a youth in these times such an awakening to a new life has come with a spiritual retreat, or on hearing a sermon, or meeting some great and sudden sorrow. To our saint it came in the lonely valley amid the desolate hills of Antrim. It pleased his heavenly Guide and Teacher to impress him with a lively and distinct sense of His divine presence, so that he saw God everywhere and in everything, and particularly in the great operations of nature. He beheld God working in the sun by day and the moon and stars by night; and breathing in the winds that swept these wilds, using them as the instruments of His Will. He recognised that it was God's direct action which ruled the course of his own being, tempering mercy with justice, and fitting him for the great work of his life. He now laid that solid foundation of true humility upon which the exalted sanctity to which he attained in later years was built, and he looked upon himself with entire conviction as one who had nought worthy of praise of his own—but owed every good thing to his Maker. He perceived that God was making use of his present lowly state to train him in virtue. "I was severely chastened, and in truth I have been humbled by hunger and nakedness; and I did not come to Ireland of my own will, until I was nearly worn out. But this proved a blessing to me, for I was thus corrected by the Lord, and He made me fit to be what was once far from my thoughts, so that I should care for the salvation of others; for at that time I had no thought even for myself" (p. 594). The most striking characteristic of St. Patrick's piety seems to have been a vivid realisation of God's almighty power and his own utter nothingness before Him, and his entire reliance upon the divine wisdom, goodness, and power. In every circumstance of his after life there appears an entire forgetfulness of himself; it is for his Master he acts, and it is that divine Master who strengthens and upholds him. He thus describes the earnestness and frequency of his prayer to God: "After I had come to Ireland I was daily tending sheep, and I prayed frequently during the day, and the love of God and His faith and fear increased in me more and more, and the spirit was stirred: so that in a single day I have said as many as a hundred prayers, and in the night nearly the same, so that I remained in the woods on the mountain; even before the dawn I was roused to prayer, in snow and ice and rain; and I felt no injury from it, nor was there any slothfulness in me, as I see now, because the spirit was then fervent within me" (p. 587). In a remote valley in Ireland, at the end of the earth, the Holy Spirit was doing in the soul of this lonely youth the same wonderful work of grace which at the time was going on in the hearts of solitaries dwelling in the deserts of Egypt and the wilds of Palestine, and which was directed by the inspired wisdom of St. Anthony's successors.

Probably enough at this time the idea first presented itself to his mind of devoting himself to the conversion of the people among whom he dwelt. Their hands had inflicted upon him the greatest injuries. They had slain his father and mother—they had carried his sister into slavery—they had made of him a bond-slave to a harsh master. Had he listened only to the promptings of nature, he would have indulged in feelings of hatred and a consuming desire for revenge: but he had given himself up to the teachings of that divine Master, who biddeth His sun shine alike upon the good and the wicked, and he had before his eyes the example of Him, true God and true Man, who had given His life for him, and who on the Cross had prayed to His Father for His executioners: "Father, forgive them, for they know not what they do". He forgot the injuries he had suffered—they were as if they had never been; and he longed that the light of the true faith might shine in that land and on that people whom he had learned to love. But what could he do to effect such an end? He was but a youth and a slave. His hard lot had taken from him all means of completing his education. He knew just enough to be fully aware of his disadvantages. At school, and from his father's lips, he had learned the rudiments of knowledge —but his life in the mountains of Antrim, his occupation in tending flocks and herds, his absolute isolation from men of education and refinement, and the utter absence of books, made it impossible for him to pursue his studies. As time went on even the little he had picked up became dim and indistinct, and it seemed as if he had forgotten most of what he had learned. Truly, as far as outward circumstances were concerned, he had little to console or encourage him, but God Himself became his Teacher, and filled his soul with a knowledge surpassing all earthly learning, and with an assurance that success should be given to him.

The boy was living with pagans, for up to this time the light of Christianity had never shone upon Ireland. The Romans had brought it with them into Britain, amongst the troops of various nationalities who composed their legions; but Ireland had escaped invasion and conquest, and no Christian teacher had yet proclaimed on her shores the Gospel of Jesus Christ. The religion of Ireland was a form of Druidism, which prevailed generally among all the peoples of Celtic origin. The objects of worship were chiefly the great works of nature, the sun and the fire, the storm and the whirlwind, the water and the cloud. The lively fancy of the Irish, fostered by the inspiriting songs of the bards, peopled the earth and sky with imaginary beings—some good and kind, some mischievous and cunning, and others downright wicked and malignant. Many of these old superstitions laid such a firm grasp upon the popular mind, that they have survived until even our day. Christianity has changed them into harmless, often salutary practices, but there is many a custom lingering in the rural districts which had its origin in the usages and beliefs of pre-Christian times. The fires on St. John's Eve are the survival of the old fire-sun worship of the Druids, and the reverence paid to holy wells had its precursor in the times when the heathen priests made offerings to them and honoured them as divine. Whether it was from the notions prevalent amongst the people, or, perhaps more probably, from his own deep communings with nature, St. Patrick himself was keenly alive to the changes of the elements; and in the poetry ascribed to him when on his way to Tara he summoned to aid him in his warfare

> The virtue of Heaven,
> In light of Sun,
> In brightness of Snow,
> In splendour of Fire,
> In speed of Lightning,
> In swiftness of Wind,
> In depth of Sea,
> In stability of Earth,
> In compactness of Rock.

It is a common saying now that strangers settling in Ireland become more Irish than the Irish themselves; "Hibernicis hiberniores" was said of the descendants of the Norman warriors who in Henry II.'s reign gained a footing in the land. But it seems to have been true in far more ancient times, and St. Patrick yielded to the charm, and became a true child of the soil. When we try to conjure up a vision of the persons into whose society he was thrown, and of the influences which gradually moulded his character, we have little in written history to help us. But the tenacity with which the Celtic character clings to old usages and treasures up old ideas enables us to form some sort of notion of what was going on round about our youthful saint whilst he was a slave in Milcho's household.

Foremost amongst these was the character of his master. When St. Patrick entered his family Milcho could not have been much over thirty years of age, for he was still living in 433, when his former slave returned to become the Apostle of Ireland forty-six years afterwards. To his rank as hereditary prince of North Dalaraida he united the functions of a Magus or Druidical priest, and he was a fanatical lover of the national worship. He must often have practised heathenish rites in the presence of his household, and thus excited the horror of his Christian slave; and perhaps he may have gone further, and endeavoured to force him to take a part in them.

It is not the place here to enter into the question whether or not the Round Towers of Ireland were pre-Christian: there are weighty authorities on both sides, but there are sufficiently high names who maintain that they were already in existence when the saint was brought to Ireland. If they belong to a later period, when Ireland was Christian, it seems strange that the architects of those times should have displayed such surpassing skill in the construction of these Towers, for which it is difficult to assign any adequate purpose; and, on the other hand, have left us no monuments whatever of a more useful kind. The ruins of the old churches of the sixth and succeeding centuries until the arrival of the Normans are entirely unworthy to be put in comparison with the Round Towers : and we cannot suppose that the ecclesiastics of those times would lavish all the resources of their wealth and the highest talents of their architects in erecting the former, when they have not left to posterity one single church whose dimensions or architectural pretensions are on a level with these famous works. It is likely enough, then, that St. Patrick found on his arrival in Ireland, dotted over the face of the land, these strange, mysterious buildings, which have so wonderfully for more than fifteen hundred years kept their secret. That they were intended for religious purposes scarcely admits of a doubt, and the most probable supposition is that they were in some way connected with the worship of fire or the sun. One of the most perfect specimens still stands in a garden near the town of Antrim. It is over fifty feet in circumference at the base, and is ninety-three feet high. It tapers gradually upwards, and is exquisitely proportioned. Whatever was its original purpose, it was converted to Christian uses, for a cross inclosed in a circle is carved in stone over the doorway, and at the top are the remains of a beam placed across from which a bell has probably been swung. The name of the property on which it stands, tall and upright, is Steeple, and most likely has acquired its name from it.

From his rank as Prince of Dalaraida and his zeal for the national religion, we can well imagine that Milcho would leave his home in the valley of the Braid to take part in the national festivals celebrated near this remarkable Tower. In the neighbourhood there are other memorials still remaining of these ancient superstitions. Near to the foot of the Tower just mentioned is a flat Druidical stone supposed to have been used for sacrifices. Small circular holes made to receive the victim's blood can still be perceived on its upper surface. Near the landing-place at Larne is shown an ancient Cromlech, also belonging to these remote times, and used either for worship or sepulture.

Like every other heathen nation, the Irish did not confine themselves to the worship of nature: they formed to themselves graven images and worshipped them as gods. The great sacred place in the fourth century was Magh-Slecht (the Plain of Adoration) in Cavan on the borders of Leitrim. It was about ninety miles distant from Mount Slemish, but there can be little doubt that Milcho would be careful to be present at the annual festival kept on November the first in honour of the great idol of Crom Cruach. According to a very ancient geographical treatise called "Dinnsenchus," "this was the principal idol of all the colonies who settled in Ireland from time to time, and they were wont to offer to it the firstlings of animals and other gifts".—(Cusack's *Life of St. Patrick*, p. 287.) "It is by no means certain what was the form or exact appearance of the Crom Cruach; the name signifies the bent or sloping monument." (*Ibid.* p. 287.) In the *Tripartite Life of St. Patrick* it is described as "made of gold and silver, and surrounded by twelve other idols formed of bronze". A zealous worshipper of his country's gods, Milcho must certainly have joined in the great throng, who assembled at the close of the year to do honour to this imaginary deity.

The Irish nation was at this time ruled over by a monarch, Niall or Niell, surnamed by historians "the Great". He was the son of Achy Mogmedon, who had reigned over Ireland from A.D. 358-366, and of Carinna, his second wife, a Saxon by birth.—(*Ogygia*, ii. 396.) We are assured by the Roman historian, Ammianus Marcellinus, a contemporary writer, that in the year A.D. 364, the first year of the Emperor Valentinian, a combined army of Picts, Scots, Saxons, and Attacotti invaded Britain and reduced the Britons to the utmost distress.—(*Ogygia*, ii. 297.) And Claudian thus describes the success of the great general Theodosius :—

> Maduerunt Saxone fuso
> Orcades, incaluit Pictonum sanguine Thule
> Scotorum cumulos flevit glacialis Ierne.

The Orkney Isles were dyed with the effusion of Saxon blood;
Thule was warmed with the blood of the Picts;
Icy Ireland wept over the heaps of Scots.

Both writers describe the Saxons and the Scots, as the Irish were then called, acting in concert with the Picts: and O'Flaherty, the author of the *Ogygia*, concludes that there was a common league between the nations, and that intermarriages and commercial intercourse subsisted amongst them (p. 298). This readily accounts for the Irish monarch Achy's friendship with Saxon chiefs, and his marriage with a daughter of that race; but the union must have taken place some years before the great expedition which proved so disastrous to the combined forces of Picts, Scots, and Saxons when Theodosius took the field against them, and drove them before him beyond the Antonine Wall. Niell did not succeed to the throne till the year 379, and he reigned about twenty-six years. Much of his time was spent in hostile expeditions against Britain and Gaul; and in one organised in his reign St. Patrick was brought a captive to Ireland. He was on the whole successful in his enterprises, and received the name "Niell of the Nine Hostages" from the number of peoples whom he had subdued, and from whom he had exacted this token of submission. He inherited from his father his roving tastes, and no doubt the Saxon blood he had from his mother would rather increase than diminish his love of adventure. Another reason why historians have honoured him with the title of "Great" is that many of the chief Irish families are descended from him. During the intervals of his warlike enterprises he made his residence at Tara in County Meath; and here he received the homage of his subject kings and chiefs, for we must remember that, besides the King of Ireland, there were also many others enjoying the royal title, and reigning in Leinster, Munster, Connaught, and Ulster. If we may believe the ancient writers of Ireland, the kings of Ireland lived in great splendour at Tara. O'Hartigan, who died A.D. 973, thus describes their royal state:—

>Three hundred cup-bearers distributed
>Three times fifty choice goblets
>Before each party of great numbers,
>Which were of pure, strong carbuncle,
>Or gold, or of silver all.

Dr. Petrie supports to a certain extent the substantial truth of this statement, when he tells us of the magnificent gold ornaments found at Tara, and now in the possession of the Royal Irish Academy.

O'Curry gives us an extract from the Book of Ballymote, which, in its turn, quotes it from a much older authority, the *Na Chong-bhail*. (Cusack's *Ireland*, p. 103.) No doubt, the writer has freely indulged his fancy in this bardic photograph of Cormac-mac-Airt, but still it is well worth inserting here, as giving us an idea of what an ancient bard of Ireland conceived to be a fitting description of an Irish king of the third century reigning at Tara. "His hair was slightly curled, and of a golden colour; a scarlet shield, with engraved devices and golden hooks, and clasps of silver; a wide-folding purple cloak on him, with a gem-set gold brooch over his breast; a gold torque around his neck; a white collared shirt, embroidered with gold, upon him; a girdle with golden buckles, and studded with precious stones, around him; two golden net-work sandals with golden buckles upon him; two spears with golden sockets, and many red bronze rivets, in his hand: while he stood in the full glow of beauty, without defect or blemish. You would think it was a shower of pearls that were set in his mouth; his lips were rubies; his symmetrical body was as white as snow; his cheek was like the mountain-ash berry; his eyes were like the sloe; his brows and eyelashes were like the sheen of a blue-black lance."

As it was usual for the Irish Ard-righs or chief monarchs to hold Court at Tara, at which the minor kings and the more important chiefs attended in great numbers, sometimes to show their loyalty to the sovereign, sometimes to push forward their own interests or intrigues, and at others to join in annual religious festivities in honour of their national divinities, Milcho would be sure to be present in the throng. He would travel from the banks of the Braid to those of the Boyne with all the state he could muster, and would be attended by a numerous retinue of clansmen and dependants. On their return to their secluded valley, they would bring with them the news of the day; and, unless the Irishmen of those days were very different from those of the present, every point of intelligence, whether of home politics or foreign adventure, would be keenly discussed. The hardy inhabitants of the hills and dales of Antrim did not require the shelter of a building to hold a conference, but whenever there was a meeting, either for business or pleasure, or even a chance rencontre of neigh-

hours, the doings of the Court would be narrated by ready spokesmen, and listened to with greedy ears. In this way Succat, though a slave, would readily pick up the gossip of the day, and would acquire a familiar knowledge of Ireland's affairs. Too often the foreign news would bring to him nothing but sorrow and grief. If he heard anything of Dumbarton or his beloved Strathclyde, it would be but tales of desolation and slaughter, of which he had already only too vivid a recollection. For the rest, the narrative would be little more than an exulting description of the feebleness of the resistance offered by the Britons to the fierce attacks of the troops, led by their warlike king, or a still more rapturous account of the rich spoils the galleys had brought back with them from the sack of Patrician villas or flourishing towns. His own heart would be wrung with anguish at hearing these glowing tales of abundant success on the one side, and abject cowardice on the other; but, as he gazed at the animated faces of the story-teller and his listeners, he longed that the high spirits, the overflowing courage, and the adventurous bravery of this people should have a nobler aim than plunder and carnage, and be employed in the service of his divine Lord and Master. What Apostles of the Cross would these hardy and active men, careless of fatigue or danger, make, if only they could become disciples of the Crucified! When in the solitude on the hill-top, after one of these recitals, he looked up to the broad canopy of heaven, bespangled with its myriads of stars, and reflected upon what he had heard and seen, tears would come into his eyes as he thought of those loved ones whom he had lost: but there was no bitterness now in his soul againt the people among whom he lived, but he poured forth his whole heart in prayer that Ireland might be converted to the faith. Perhaps he began to hope that that humble and most earnest prayer had reached the throne of the Most High, and that he was the vessel of election, the one chosen by God to gather into the fold of Christ the Irish nation.

He had now been nearly six years in Ireland: from a youth he had grown into a man. If his literary education had been abruptly checked, he had accumulated a stock of wisdom from above, a knowledge which raised him above his miserable surroundings, and fitted him for his mighty task. He had but scant intercourse with men, but his conversation was with the angels. There cannot be a doubt that, as time went on, his prayer became supernatural in a high degree. He gazed full into the face of his Maker, and he was given knowledge surpassing what can be learned in schools, or at the feet of the sages of the earth. His master began to perceive there was something uncommon in his slave; but this only aroused in him hatred and distrust. A fanatical worshipper of false gods, he beheld in this once despised youth a something which at once compelled his admiration and excited his fear. The following incident must have greatly increased this feeling:—

"While St. Patrick was with Milcho, this king had a dream or vision, in which he saw his servant come into the house where he was, and flames of fire appeared to issue from his head. Milcho thought that 'the flames broke upon him to burn him,' but he drove it from him, and it did him no harm. His son and daughter were with him, and it seemed as if it consumed them entirely, and their ashes were scattered all over Erin. Milcho called Patrick at once, and told him his vision, which the saint interpreted to him thus: 'The fire which thou sawest on me is the faith of the Trinity which burns within me, and it is this faith which I shall hereafter preach unto thee, but thou wilt not believe. Thy son, however, and thy daughter, they will believe, and the fire of grace shall consume them.'"

From this story we learn that the saint had already an intimation of his high destiny, and that God had revealed to him the knowledge of future events, and we can easily believe that, from this time forward, Milcho regarded his slave with ever-growing ill-will.

It may give some idea of the overbearing and passionate nature of Milcho if I somewhat anticipate the order of time and recount the tragic incidents of his end. He never forgave the escape of his slave; he bore towards him an undying resentment, and when nearly forty years later, in 433, he heard of his landing in Ireland, his long smothered hatred burst into a flame. News was brought to him that his former slave was come to Ireland to destroy the religion of the Druids, and so to annihilate the power and authority which the priests or magi had hitherto enjoyed. He heard that the powerful Prince Dichu, after a fruitless resistance, had acknowledged his mission and ranged himself amongst his disciples, and that Succat himself (for that was the name he had borne when in his service) was coming at the head of a large suite to interview him in his own cashel or stone fort. To add to his indignation, his fellow magi told him prophesy had foretold that their long reign of power and supremacy over the minds of the people was at its end, and that the new faith would henceforth reign in Ireland. St. Patrick had arrived in sight of his master's house, he was gazing intently on the well-remembered scenes when a strange spectacle presented itself to his eyes. The house broke out into flames, and before long there was nothing left of it but smouldering ashes and fitful puffs of smoke. Milcho's passion on hearing of the arrival of the Saint knew no bounds. He would not meet as an equal one who had been his bought slave, and he feared that the meeting might end in his submission or humiliation. His pride refused to bend, and in a paroxysm of rage he set on fire his house and barns, and then leaped himself into the flames. The charity of the Saint was overcome by the obstinacy of the haughty chief.

We will now return to our Saint. A strong desire to be again amongst his own people, to visit Britain, and even Gaul, took possession of Patrick's mind. Everything contributed to strengthen this feeling. His menial task of tending flocks seemed now to him a mere waste of time, when his soul was burning within him with a passion to be a Shepherd of men. His master's growing aversion, shown to him in many ways, contributed to increase his eagerness for a change. But he had learnt by this time to wait for a sign from above before he came to a decision. He was God's servant, and must obey His command, and not follow his own inclination. Probus, who wrote the life of the Saint about the 10th century, tells us that an angel now began to visit him every seventh day, and speak with him as a man is wont to speak to a man. Probably this was the Victor, or Victoricus, of whom St. Patrick himself speaks in his confession, as appearing to him in the night on a memorable occasion, and who became his constant companion and guide. Still, though he awaited patiently for heavenly guidance, we are not to suppose that his mind did not busy itself with devising a mode of escape. He was not ten miles from the sea coast, and that coast was not thirty miles from the nearest shores of Britain, but still, escape was not such an easy matter. There were few points of embarkation on that rock-girt shore, and ships fit to face that stormy sea were few and far between. Besides, the influence of the Chief of North Dalaraida was dominant in all that region. His vengeance on anyone who might aid a fugitive slave would be severe and speedy. In this dilemma help came to him from the quarter from which he had now accustomed himself to look for it. He gives us the following account :— " One night in my sleep I heard a voice saying to me, Thou fastest well, fasting thou shalt soon go to thy country." (*Conf.*,

p. 588.) From this time he ceased to be anxious: his path was clear before him. He knew that God approved of his design, and he waited for Him to point out to him the time and the manner. His patience was not long tried. " After a very short time I heard a voice saying to me, Behold thy ship is ready. Soon after this I fled, and left the man with whom I had been six years." (*Conf.*, p. 588.) The heavenly messenger who directed him ordered him to make a journey of two hundred miles to a place far distant from Antrim, a place which he had never seen, and where he knew no one: but he feared nothing, and set out in the strength of the Lord, who directed his way for good.

At the close of the 4th century the population of Ireland was, as compared with recent times, very small. Probably, in 392, it was not more than 300,000. A writer of some repute has stated that so thoroughly pastoral was the life of the natives there was not a single town, scarcely a good-sized village, in Ireland before the arrival of the Northmen in the 9th century. The chiefs lived in their raths or cashels, surrounded by their septs: there was little cultivation of the ground, enclosures even were rare, and for the most part the occupation of the people was in tending vast herds of cattle. The woods and waste lands occupied great part of the country. A journey of 200 miles through such a district was no light matter, but to St. Patrick it had few terrors. He had been used to the weather in all its moods. Many a night had he passed in the open air. He was accustomed to privation and hardship, and he feared neither fatigue, nor hunger, nor danger. Such a traveller, when he once got a safe distance from Milcho's territory, could find little difficulty in making his way from farm-house to farm-house, and he would be sure of an hospitable welcome. Little can be said of the route he followed. We know of two circumstances only which can in any way help us to fix it. The one is the distance of 200 miles he had to traverse; the other is the mention which the Saint himself makes, in his account of a memorable vision, of the Wood of Fochlut, near the Western Sea. In the narrative he gives us of his early life in his *Confession*, this is the one name of an Irish place which he gives us, and we may be sure that something remarkable must have there happened to impress it thus strongly on his imagination. Whether it was a danger escaped, or a kindness received, he never forgot it. Likely enough it was both; an extensive forest in that remote part of Ireland, for Fochlut is in the County of Mayo, not far from the town and bay of Killala, would be most difficult to traverse, and probably would be infested with wolves or other wild beasts: and had the Saint found a shelter, and warmth and food after escaping from these adventures, he may well have remembered it for a life-time. But whatever it was, his heart was touched, and tears would come into his eyes in after years when Fochlut was named, and even in the presence of King Leoghaire, at Tara, he could not conceal the emotion the recollections of the place excited in his breast.

Though the Saint's narrative of his early life is brief, and though he is as far as possible from any design of exhibiting his own feelings, still it creeps out that he had a warm and generous heart. He could nobly forgive an injury—he sought to repay cruel tyranny and hard usage by seeking the eternal salvation of his master: and to his dying day he retained an affectionate remembrance of the dwellers on the skirt of the wood of Fochlut. Another thing we may be sure of, that, in spite of his lowly garb, for he was clad in the coarse dress of a slave employed in menial country work, and of his youth, for he was barely twenty-one years old, there was in his bearing and behaviour something that at once won kindly feelings from others, and also insured respect. Tradition tells us that, when a mere child and placed out at nurse, his foster-mother became so attached to him that she could not bear to have him out of her sight, and he repaid her love by constantly being on the alert to give her pleasure or save her trouble. His watchfulness and care for his little sister Lupita are minutely dwelt on by his biographers. His grief at being separated from his family and country often breaks out unwittingly in his writings, and he laments that he had become a stranger to them. His relations showed their estimation for him when they earnestly besought him to remain with them when he once more returned to the banks of the Clyde. Later on, during his long preparation in Gaul to fit him to become the Apostle of a great nation, he always met with friends who became deeply attached to him; and when at last he found his vocation, and became, indeed, the preacher of the Gospel and the converter of the heathen, the charm of his manner and presence was such that, on first sight or hearing of him, children would leave their homes and follow him, and courtiers would renounce their worldly prospects and become his disciples.

And now the Saint has arrived at the end of his weary journey, and he stands upon the sea-shore looking out upon the broad Atlantic. How his heart would beat as his eyes gazed at those mighty waves crested with foam and swelling on the deep blue surface of the ocean. For those surging waves were to carry him back to the land of his birth. But where was the ship on which he was to embark? The answer shall be given in the Saint's own words: "The day on which I arrived the ship had moved out of her place, and I asked to go and sail with them, but the master was displeased, and answered, angrily, 'There is no use in asking to go with us'". No doubt the appearance of the intending passenger gave little promise of payment. He had no money to offer: his solitary garment, a tunic of sheepskin coming down to the knees, and his primitive footgear tied with leathern thongs, bespoke his lowly condition. The young man bore the refusal meekly. "When I heard this," he continues, "I left them to go back to the shed where I had received hospitality, and on the way I began to pray. Before I had finished praying, I heard one of the sailors crying out loudly for me, 'Quick, come along, for they are calling for thee!' I made haste to return to them, and they said, 'Come, and as we receive thee in friendship, do thou be with us a friend'." (*Conf.*, pp. 388-9.) Of the nature of the ship and its crew he tells us little, except that the latter were heathens. In those days it would be a large vessel which could carry fifty men, and such would be used only in war. Ships belonging to private individuals were much smaller, and possessed only the rudest accommodation for passengers. They drew so little water that there was no room for a cabin. They used a rude sail, but relied for the management of the ship chiefly on their oars, especially when they neared the land.

St. Patrick is now on the blue waters of the wide Atlantic; a favourable breeze is wafting him to his home in Britain, and his heart bounds with joy at the thought that his captivity is come to an end, and that a few days' sail will bring him in sight and in touch of his native land. He is at an age when the blood flows briskly through the veins, when the spirits are buoyant, and when hope is fresh and unchilled in the soul. His life's purpose has been made known to him, and he braces himself up to a steady and diligent preparation for it. His youth has not been crushed nor soured by misfortune, or hardship, or privation; on the contrary, his hardy, abstemious, laborious life has made him superior to the hundred wants which a condition of ease and prosperity entails on those who are born in palaces and halls. He can bear fatigue, and hunger, and cold, if need be; and so he contemplates his task without fear whatever its carrying out may cost him.

CHAPTER IV.

HIS RETURN TO DUMBARTON AND ARRIVAL AT TOURS,
394. FROM MARCH TO DECEMBER.

ST. PATRICK'S *CONFESSIO.* HIS LITERARY STYLE. HIS VOYAGE FROM KILLALA BAY TO MORECAMBE BAY. HIS LANDING AT HEYSHAM. CONDITION OF LANCASHIRE AT THE TIME. ST. PATRICK'S WELL AT SLYNE. ST. PATRICK IN PATTERDALE. ARRIVAL AT DUMBARTON. HIS VISION IN WHICH HE HEARS THE VOICE OF THE IRISH. HE SETS OUT FOR TOURS. LANDS AT BOURDEAUX. ST. PATRICK'S THORN TREE ON THE BANK OF THE LOIRE. REACHES MARMOUTIER.

THE principal authority for the life and character of St. Patrick is, of course, to be found in his own writings. There still remain to us two works which are admitted by the weightiest critics, of both ancient and modern times, to be the genuine products of his pen: his *Confessio* and the *Letter to Coroticus.* They are brief, and do not pretend to give anything like a narrative of the saint's life, but they are eminently characteristic; they give us an insight into the mind of the writer, which no words of others could have supplied. In them he appears before us as he really was; unconsciously he exhibits his intimate thoughts and feelings, and enables us to form an estimate of his inner soul, which would have been simply impossible without them. Besides, they give us the most certain account of many of the incidents in his very wonderful career. For my own part, I must confess that much of my admiration for Ireland's great Apostle has sprung from repeated perusals of his *Confessio*.

It will not then be out of place to give some account of this very ancient monument of Ecclesiastical History. It is comprised in six folio pages of the Bollandists. Their copy was made from a Manuscript belonging to the Monastery of St. Vaast at Arras, which has since disappeared, having been lost in the troublous times of the French Revolution; a still more famous Manuscript is yet preserved in the Library of Trinity College, Dublin, and forms a part of the far-famed Book of Armagh. The history of this Manuscript is especially interesting, and it affords us the strongest assurance of its genuineness. It was copied from an older Manuscript supposed to have been the original by St. Patrick, for it contains these words: "Hucusque volumen, quod Patricius manu conscripsit suâ". (So far the volume which Patrick wrote with his own hand.)

Of course it is possible that this supposed original may have been taken from a still older Manuscript. The copy now at Trinity College was made during the short episcopate of Torbach, Archbishop of Armagh, in 807, by a scribe of the name of Ferdommach, and so belongs to the very beginning of the ninth century. Besides the *Confessio*, the volume contains, amongst other things, some account of the Saint's Life, the New Testament, and the Life of St. Martin of Tours, by Sulpitius Severus. It has ever been held in the highest veneration in Ireland, and oaths in matters of great importance were often taken upon it. It was styled the Canoin Phadraig or Patrick's Canon, and in the year 907 was enclosed in a case by Donough, the son of the King of Ireland. This case is supposed to be the leathern satchel still preserved with it, and which is of very great antiquity. A keeper of this much revered treasure was appointed, named Moyre ; his family became its hereditary guardians, and an endowment of eight townlands near Armagh was provided to ensure the fulfilment of the trust. In the seventeenth century Florence M'Moyre proved unfaithful, and sold his charge to a Mr. Arthur Brownlow for the paltry sum of five pounds. In 1858 the then Protestant Primate, Beresford, purchased it for three hundred pounds, and placed it in the

Library of Trinity College. (O'Hanlon's *Lives of the Irish Saints*, March 17, page 401.) Miss Cusack, in her *Life of St. Patrick*, has supplied us with an accurate copy of the Latin text, and a carefully executed translation into English.

St. Patrick's thoughts evidently flow too fast for his pen to record them, and he frequently bursts forth into expressions of his faith in God, his burning love for Him, and his eager desire for martyrdom. In this way the regular narrative is frequently interrupted, and it is often difficult to ascertain the proper sequence of events. He seldom gives us names of places or persons, and it is at times impossible to fix the dates of most important matters. Still, throughout the whole composition there shines forth a truthfulness and force which compel the admiration and belief of the reader.

The following extract gives us, in his own words, his motive for writing: "Therefore I cannot and ought not to be silent concerning the great benefits and graces which the Lord has bestowed on me in the land of my captivity, since the only return we can make for such benefits is, after God has reproved us, to extol and convey His wonders before every nation under Heaven". (*Confessio*, p. 581.) Yet he is conscious that his task is a difficult one to him. He says: "Although I thought of writing long ago, I feared the censure of men, because I had not learned as others who had studied the sacred writings in the best way, and have never changed their language since their childhood, but continually learned it more perfectly; while I have to translate my words and speech into a foreign tongue" (p. 584). It was in extreme old age that he took up his pen to make this permanent record of his gratitude to God for that wonderful Providence which had guided his extraordinary career. But his mastership in composition was not equal to the intensity of his wishes. It is not an easy production to read, and, even to a careful student, many parts of it remain obscure and barely intelligible. Yet to those who are anxious to have an insight into his interior, it is simply invaluable. It opens to them the hidden motives which ruled his life; it shows the lofty spirit in which he acted on all occasions, and, above all, the profound humility which made him always lowly and contemptible in his own estimation of himself.

St. Patrick does not tell us in his *Confessio* what was the destination or occupation of the ship in which he took passage, and we are left to guess whether the voyage was undertaken for commercial or other purposes. At first the weather was favourable, and they crossed the Bay of Donegal, making for the bold headlands of Carrigan and Slieve League, perhaps two of the most lofty, precipitous, and picturesque mountains of that most picturesque coast. They were not very bold navigators in those days, and, as a rule, they kept as much as possible within sight of land. However much St. Patrick might admire the magnificent outline of the mountains, he had, at the time, a more serious object in view, and he turned his attention to the crew of the ship. Though they were heathens, he spoke to them of the religion of Christ and of the power and goodness of God, and his words fell on no unfruitful soil. The men gazed with wonder on this poor, forlorn youth, who, having nothing, and even craving a favour at their hands, still spoke to them as one having authority and claiming their reverence and obedience. As they rounded the northern coast of Ireland they would have other natural wonders to observe, and the basaltic rocks about the Giant's Causeway, and the perpendicular cliffs of Fairhead, would compel their admiration while they exercised their skill in the steering of their craft.

Everything seemed to promise a prosperous voyage, for the shores of Britain were already full in sight; but it is evident that the wind must have changed to the north-west, for, instead of reaching the mouth of the Clyde, they were driven southwards. Local tradition tells us that their vessel ran on a sandbank at the mouth of the Duddon. The rising tide would free them from this peril, and we find them landing on the Lancashire shore of Morecambe Bay, near Heysham. But as just opposite this spot, at a distance of two miles from the shore, is a rock called in the Ordnance map St. Patrick's Sker, it may be that their vessel ran against it and suffered serious damage. However, they managed to reach the shore at Heysham, and all the circumstances point to the conclusion that they were there wrecked: for we find that the whole crew abandoned their vessel, and when St. Patrick set out by land to reach his home they accompanied him. The spot at which they gained the land was subsequently marked by a small chapel built on the highest point of a rock overlooking the sea, and it is still known as St. Patrick's Chapel.

It is very difficult to give an Englishman of the present day anything like an adequate idea of the condition, at the end of the fourth century, of that part of Roman Britain which constitutes the modern Lancashire. Now within its irregular borders it contains the largest population of any county in England, amounting to not less than three millions and a half. Its great cities and towns are numerous, and of these Liverpool and Manchester rank next to the Metropolis. Its industry and its commerce are household words throughout the habitable world. But when we go back 1,500 years and come to the year 394 we find a very different picture presented to our eyes. In the first century the most powerful of all the British tribes, the Brigantes, occupied the country north of the Mersey and the Humber, and they yielded only after a stubborn and prot longed resistance to the might of Roman arms' But their submission was complete, and during the rest of the Roman dominion in Britain we hear of Lancashire only as the camping ground of detachments of horse and foot soldiers. Of these military stations Bremetonacæ or Ribchester on the north bank of the Ribble was the chief, and of the others I need mention only Mancunium (Manchester) and Coccium (Wigan). There was a station on the Lune, on the site of the modern Lancaster, but the allusions to it in the ancient Chroniclers and Geographers are so scanty and obscure that the learned are still undecided as to its name. One of the latest writers on the subject, and at the same time one of the mos-

cautious, thinks it may have been Longovicum.[1] Of course it cannot be expected that much can be known of the history of a place whose very name is uncertain, and yet a few facts have been ascertained. The Romans erected a fort on the summit of the hill, on which the modern castle stands, a tower in it is called Hadrian's Tower, and this takes us back to the beginning of the second century. Milestones bearing the names of the Emperors Philip and Decius have been found in the immediate neighbourhood. An inscription, assigned to the date 222, records the renovation of a basilica which had fallen into decay. A monument already alluded to speaks to us of a cavalry officer, a native of Tréves, who died here. Abundant remains of tile and pottery have been found at Quernmore, a few miles from Lancaster, proving that a considerable manufacture was there carried on. Coins in great numbers have been discovered from time to time within the city boundaries, reaching down from early Roman times to the reign of the Emperor Theodosius and his sons Arcadius and Honorius. The occasional occurrence of the name Windy Harbour tells us that farm-houses and villas

---

[1] Probably the original name used by the native Britons was Lone-wick, the village on the Lone or Lune; and Longo-vic-um is merely a Latinised form of it.

were scattered over the country. Of the existence of Christianity there is no documentary evidence, but the names compounded of Eccles to be found in North Lancashire suggest that there must have been communities of Christians who made use of this word to designate the buildings they used for Divine worship. Two places at no great distance from Lancaster are called Ecclesrigge, " the church of the ridge or hill ": of these one is near Ulverston, and the other near the head of Windermere, close to Ambleside. They are both in the near neighbourhood of a Roman road, and it cannot be a very bold supposition to maintain that Eccles is as sure a sign of an old Roman church as Castra is of a Roman camp, or " street " of a Roman strata, via, or road. But whatever progress Roman civilisation had made in Lancashire at the period in question, it was near its end, and had already received some rude shocks. For many years the inroads of the Picts from Caledonia and the Scots from Ireland had spread desolation and ruin throughout the land, and of course the north-western coast was specially exposed to their depredations. St. Patrick's father had taken no unimportant share in the expedition of Theodosius against them: though they were beaten back for a time their inroads were constantly renewed, and Calpurnius had himself, as is well known, fallen a victim to a raid by the Scots on the banks of the Clyde. The sense of security by residents in the open country was thoroughly destroyed, and what had been smiling tracts of corn land or pasture, carefully cultivated by the skill of the Roman husbandmen and retired veterans, were fast becoming mere deserts, roamed over by vast herds of wild swine and infested by wolves and foxes. But bodies of troops were still kept at the military stations, and there can be no reasonable doubt that a troop of horse would occupy Longovicum at the time of our Saint's landing at Heysham. Indeed the name occurs in the " Notitia Imperii," which was composed about the year 401, and which professes to give us a detailed account of the functionaries of the Empire, military and civil, and of the forces stationed at each depôt. The date of the work is only seven years later than 394, the year of St. Patrick's return to Britain, and consequently we may take the statements of the " Notitia " as giving a faithful description of the condition of things in Roman Britain at the time. From it we learn that the " Dux Britanniarum," who held the chief military command in the island, resided at York (Eboracum), that he was surrounded by a numerous staff of officers, and held there a petty court. The immense bulk of the forces was, indeed, stationed at Dumbarton and along the Antonine Wall, but the military posts scattered over the country were duly maintained and enough troops were stationed to preserve good order.

We must now return to St. Patrick, whom we have left on the rock of Heysham, with the shipwrecked crew of the abandoned vessel gathered round him. He was in a very awkward position. Had he been alone, it would have been natural for him, the son of an officer of rank, and a distinguished magistrate, as soon as he found out his whereabouts, to have proceeded to Longovicum—the nearest Roman station—to make himself there known to the authorities, and to have requested advice and assistance to enable him to reach his home. But his companions in misfortune had learnt to look up to him as their resource in every difficulty; he could not separate himself from them, and he would not desert them. This apparently simple resolve involved him in serious difficulties. The sailors were by race Scoti: no name was more dreaded in Britain than this: in their present helpless condition they had to fear for their liberties and their lives if they presented themselves before a Roman fort, or even fell in with a file of soldiers. Apparently they had lost all that they possessed, and it was no easy task to conduct them a distance of over a hundred and sixty miles to a spot to which the Roman power did not reach. However, saints are not easily daunted. Already the young man of twenty-one years had found in help from above the resources which enabled him to overcome all obstacles, and, strong in his faith, he fearlessly undertook to lead the forlorn party.

There is no record of what took place on that desolate rock of Heysham previous to their departure, but the memory of their presence still lingers about the spot, and when in after years the renown of St. Patrick's marvellous career filled the western world, when the old Celtic inhabitants of North Lancashire recalled his landing on their coasts, they showed their veneration for their illustrious countryman, a Briton as themselves, by erecting a rude but massive chapel in his honour. It is the most ancient building still standing in Lancashire. It dates from a time when the Angle had not crossed the Yorkshire hills to settle in Lancashire. It belongs to a period when the Celts dominated our western coasts, and when they obeyed a Celtic bishop and a Celtic chief. The tradition is still fresh in that primitive district, for even now it bears unmistakable old-world characteristics, and the people, the guide-books, and the county historians talk about St. Patrick's Chapel at Heysham. It is true that there are gathered on that desolate rock, exposed to every wind of heaven, other monuments of later date —of Saxon, of Danish, and Norman times; but we may well ask ourselves, what peculiar attraction the place possessed, so that for nearly a thousand five hundred years men of such different races were drawn to it? The most extraordinary of these monuments are the tombs hewn out of the solid rock, in the shape of open coffins. Surely some strong religious motive must have existed to create so great a desire to be buried in this unusual manner in such a place. Yet beyond the tradition of St. Patrick's presence here, we know of nothing else to account for it. Grant that St. Patrick landed on this remote spot, then the religious veneration of a simple people for the very foot-prints of a saint solves the whole difficulty; on the other hand, deny that he was ever here, it will become impossible to give an adequate account of this and other local traditions.

For Heysham is not the only place in North Lancashire whose name is inseparably linked with that of St. Patrick. It seems that when the crew had had time to consider their position, and to recover from the alarms and dangers of the shipwreck, and, further, to ascertain where they were, they resolved on making for the north, not following the great Roman road, but going across country as best they could, and thus avoiding the risks of meeting with a band of Roman troops. They were only poor geographers at that period, but it may easily have been that some of the crew may have known the country, and in any case we may be sure that the instinct of a sailor would guide them correctly. They proceeded five miles on their journey; they were perishing with thirst; meeting a woman of the country, St. Patrick asked her for some water. Whether she was frightened at the wild appearance of the strangers, or did not understand what they wanted, she made no reply. St. Patrick and his companions were in the utmost need; human aid seemed to fail them. A feeling that God was his only resource, and an assurance that His help would not be wanting, filled his soul; he boldly told the woman to take care what she was about, for he had but to strike the ground with his staff and a spring would rise at his command. He did so; to the wonder and amazement of the onlookers an abundant flow of water issued forth from the ground, and the thirst-stricken crew drank eagerly of the refreshing waters.' That spring has never ceased to flow: it flows yet, and is known to all the country-side as St. Patrick's well. It rises in the midst of a field, sloping towards the west, and can easily be seen by a traveller on the North-Western line of railway going northwards, on the right-hand side just before reaching Hest Bank Station. It has never been known to fail: it has never been frozen up. A wall has been built around it, and its solid construction tells us of the pious zeal of its builders; but it is now unfortunately in a ruinous condition. The well is highly reverenced throughout the whole country-side, and its waters are credited by Catholics and Protestants alike with many virtues. Legends of course have gathered round its history. One of these tells us that a former tenant of the neighbouring farm, wearied of the concourse of visitors to the well, had it filled up. From that time nothing prospered with him—his cattle died off, his crops failed, he was forced at length to give up his farm, and died in poverty. His successor profited by his example; he opened out and cleaned the well, he allowed free access to it, and his reverence was rewarded with abundant prosperity. My readers may smile at the story, but, true or false, it illustrates my position, that a religious veneration is to this day shown by the non-Catholic inhabitants of North Lancashire to the well hallowed by the name of St. Patrick.

The following narrative is, however, no legend: the person to whom it happened is well known, and there are many witnesses of the reality of the facts described. In the year 1875 there was a lad of Irish parentage residing in the town of Lancaster, and attending the school there, who had the misfortune to injure his foot so much that he became a cripple, and was obliged to use a crutch. He was for a time under medical treatment, but without being cured. At length his grandmother was advised to take the boy to St. Patrick's Well at Slyne. Accordingly she took him on a Sunday, and he bathed his injured limb in the clear water. He felt instantaneous relief, and returned on the following Sunday to try the waters again. He was so much better that he was able to go home with the help of a stick. He came a third Sunday, and again after bathing his foot in the well he was able to dispense with his stick. He is now a fine, healthy, young fellow, walking without limp or pain. The facts are perfectly notorious. I have spoken to the schoolmaster who remembered him quite well leaning on his crutch, and who asked him on his return to school what he had been doing.

and was told that he "had been to the Holy Well". The priests now at Lancaster have conversed with the young man and heard from him the tale that I have told. It is not for me to decide what was the cause of this cure. It may have been an answer to the strong faith of the child's friends; it may have been an instance in these prosaic days of the abiding influence of the great St. Patrick with God. In any case it proves the point that I am now trying to establish, that there is a deep-rooted conviction in the minds of the people in the neighbourhood that St. Patrick is in some way connected with the place and the well, and that the power of his intercession may be relied upon by those who ask it in simplicity of heart.

Nothing could have happened better calculated to strengthen the influence which St. Patrick had now gained over his strange following. From this time they confided entirely in him, and obeyed his slightest directions. The next stage in his journey is not so distinctly supported by tradition; but the party seems to have crossed the sands, and reached the firm land again at Allithwaite. Here again we find a Holy Well dating from Roman times, so Camden the historian, writing in James I.'s reigns, tells us—the name is probably derived from "hallow" and "thwaite," a field, and means holy field. Their route northwards soon brought them to the head of Lake Windermere to the foot of Kirkstone Pass, and so into the wild, desolate valley of Patterdale.

But here I cannot do better than give St. Patrick's own account of his journey. In his *Confessio* he says, "After three days we reached land, and for twenty-eight days we journeyed through a desert. And their provisions failed, and they suffered greatly from hunger. And one day the master began to say to me, 'What sayest thou, O Christian? Your God is great and all powerful. Why canst thou not then pray for us, since we are perishing from hunger, and may never see the face of man again?' And I said to him plainly, 'Turn sincerely to the Lord my God, to whom nothing is impossible, that He may send us food on our way, until ye are satisfied, for it abounds everywhere for Him'. And with God's help it was so done, for lo! a herd of swine appeared before our eyes in the way, and they killed many of them, and they remained there two nights much refreshed, and filled with their flesh, for many of them had been left exhausted by the wayside. After this they gave the greatest thanks, and I was honoured in their eyes" (*Conf.* 589-90). It will be observed that the saint mentions no names of places, and to learn his real route, we must have recourse to other means of information. But when we have it well fixed in our minds that he was bent on returning to his home on the banks of the Clyde, the dates he gives us quite harmonise with the view I am now maintaining. Three days are sufficient for his sea voyage from Killala Bay, round by the north of Ireland, to Morecambe Bay; and twenty-eight days are not too much for his journey through a wild district from North Lancashire to Dumbarton.

A little westward of Kirkstone Pass is Grisedale Beck, which empties itself into Grasmere Lake. The dale took its name from the herds of wild swine that frequented it, for Grise is the old local word for a wild pig. There could not, therefore, be a more appropriate spot for the incident just recorded to have taken place.

The saint goes on: "They also found wild honey, and offered me some of it. And one of them said, 'This is offered in sacrifice, thanks be to God'. After that I tasted no more. But the same night, whilst I was sleeping, I was strongly tempted by Satan (of which I shall be mindful as long as I am in the body), and there fell a great stone upon me, and there was no strength in my limbs. And then it came into my mind, I know not how, to call upon Elias, and at the same moment I saw the sun rising in the heavens, and while I cried out 'Elias' with all my might, behold the splendour of the sun shone upon me, and immediately shook from me all heaviness. And I believe that Christ my Lord cried out for me." (*Conf.*, p. 290.)

What more fitting scene for the contest with the power of the evil one can be conceived than the weird, rock-strewn Patterdale? There is no spot that I have ever visited in which man feels smaller in presence of the grand, mighty and awe-inspiring works of God. Man, in that bare, desolate valley, shut in by the eternal hills, feels himself to be nothing in the presence of the Great God of heaven and earth. St. Patrick had just been honoured as more than human by those whose wants he had so wonderfully supplied, and now he was made to feel that it was by no power of his that he had done this deed, but that in very truth he was, when left to himself, only poor and blind and naked like the rest of men.

There would be but few inhabitants in that barren valley in those days, and yet the wonderful and supernatural is sure to be noised abroad, and to make a deep impression. And the dalesmen gazed on that slender youth in his rude, uncouth, sheepskin tunic, and marvelled at the power given to him. As time went on they or their children heard of the extraordinary conversion of a whole nation wrought by his preaching; they longed for a share in the blessings God gave through him, and they noted carefully each spot hallowed by his presence. Well has the memory been treasured up, the church, the well, nay, the dale itself, are all associated with his name, for Patterdale is nought but Patrick's dale, and the church is dedicated in his honour. Up to five years ago there was a very ancient yew tree growing in the churchyard, nigh unto the spring, whose years were to be counted not by centuries but by over a thousand years; but, alas! the storms of the winter of 1886 brought it to the ground, and it is now nothing more than a memory.

St. Patrick thus proceeds with the account of his journey: "Soon afterwards I was taken captive. And on the first night I remained with them I heard a Divine response saying, 'You shall be two months with them'. And so it was. On the sixtieth night the Lord delivered me out of their hands. And on the road He provided for us food and fire and dry weather daily until, on the fourteenth day, we all reached our journey's end. As I have before mentioned, we journeyed twenty-eight days through a desert, and on the night of our arrival we had no provisions left." From this it appears that they were taken prisoners on the fifteenth day of their march. Who were his captors he does not say, but probably they were troops enlisted under the Roman banner, who dismissed them when they found them harmless, and perhaps because they could gain no spoil from them. It is not unlikely that this imprisonment was at Carlisle, where the Romans maintained an important military station.

The new assurance St. Patrick received from God, that he was under His special protection, must have been a great comfort to him. The fact that the last fourteen days of his long travel were favoured with dry weather suggests that he must have left his master's house in Antrim in the early spring. We may allow him at least a fortnight to cross Ireland to the west coast, and his journey by sea and land and his captivity altogether occupied three months, so it may be that he arrived at his home in August or September of 394.

The memory of this journey has been carefully preserved. When, by St. Patrick's preaching and miracles, the Irish had become a Christian people, they ever turned with gratitude and love towards their great apostle. His words were remembered and quoted: his wonderful acts were celebrated in prose and verse, and his very foot-prints became sacred. The affectionate interest of a whole people traced out every spot where he had been and followed him in every journey. The country he had traversed in his way from the north bank of the Lune to Dumbarton on the Clyde became in the eyes of the Irish of the sixth and seventh centuries holy ground, and it was not long before devout pilgrims began to tread in his footsteps. I have already spoken of the little church at Heysham, which still bears the name of St. Patrick: at Kilpatrick an hospital was founded for the reception of pilgrims who came to visit his birth-place. The whole distance between these two hallowed spots became the scene of a pilgrimage in his honour, which continued for nigh a thousand years, until the ruthless hand of Henry VIII. destroyed alike the devotion and the institutions it had produced. Kuerden, the diligent antiquarian of James I.'s reign, tells us of a deed anterior to the Reformation conveying a messuage in Lancaster for the use of pilgrims to the chapel of St. Patrick at Heysham. Heysham and Dumbarton thus became the outermost links of a chain stretching through North Lancashire, Westmoreland, Cumberland, and the south-western counties of Scotland. From time to time all along the route we come across mementoes of St. Patrick's presence. Rock and dale, church and well, by their names speak to us still of the lowly traveller of the fourth century. Let any one who calls this in question try to account for the existence on our north-western coasts of such names as St. Patrick's Sker, St. Patrick's Chapel, St. Patrick's Well, on the shores of Morecambe Bay—as Patterdale, or St. Patrick's Dale, and Preston Patrick in Westmoreland, and Kilpatrick in Dumfriesshire. The numerous and continued pilgrimages gave rise to the dedication of churches and dales in honour of St. Patrick; but what was the cause and origin of the pilgrimages themselves? What other reason can be assigned than the entire belief of the pilgrims that their dear saint had once been in those very places and made them for ever holy in the eyes and hearts of his children? And the tradition abides still; though the Catholic Church has for the most part lost its hold upon the people in those parts, the memory of St. Patrick is still fresh, and forms a cherished part of the folklore of the district. In the most unexpected places—by the lonely sea-shore, in the rock-strewn dale—the same holds good; and the country people who know little of the successive waves of British, Saxon,

Danish, or Norman occupation can still talk of St. Patrick travelling their way as if it were a thing, not of fifteen centuries ago, but of yesterday. Traditions in thinly inhabited districts are tenacious of existence. And though the district of which I am writing is as Protestant as Protestant can be, it still cherishes the memory of a saint as Catholic as was St. Patrick.

But what sort of a home did St. Patrick find? We know his father and mother had been slain in the great expedition of 388. But it seems that relations of at least one of his parents escaped the misfortunes of that disastrous year, and still remained in the neighbourhood. Probably a brother of Calpurnius was enlisted in the legion of the Batavi, had accompanied it to Theodosia, and, like many another Roman veteran, had in his maturer years turned his hand to the plough. St. Patrick gives the following account of his reception: "So again after a few years I was with my relations in the Britains (Britannis), who received me as a son, and earnestly besought me that then at least, after I had gone through so many tribulations, I would go nowhere from them" (p. 591). His hospitable relative must have been well advanced in years, or this language would not have been applicable to him. The saint's affectionate nature must have been greatly soothed by this kindness of his friends, and he must have found an exquisite satisfaction in revisiting the loved scenes of his youth. At the same time a deep sadness would fill his soul as he gazed again on the spots made memorable to him for ever by the slaughter of his parents and his own and his sister's capture. Probably his father's villa at Bannaven would long have been a ruin, and abandoned as no longer offering a secure abiding place. The blackened walls might still remain standing, but the roof would have fallen in. Weeds would be growing in the court-yard, and the once trim garden would be given up to desolation. Indeed, though the Roman garrison was still maintained at its old strength of near 10,000 men, horse and foot, the former sense of the irresistible might of Roman arms was gone, and a feeling was creeping over men's minds that the world-wide Empire of Rome, unconquered and unconquerable, as they loved to style it, was nearing its end. In the camp there might be the old pomp of war, but in the suburbs the display of patrician wealth and taste was fast dying out.

What effect the warmth of his welcome by his relatives might have had on his mind under other circumstances we cannot tell, but now his resolve was already taken. He had offered himself up to the conversion of the Irish nation, and he could not turn back. And God was not long in making known clearly to him His will. St. Patrick continues his narrative thus: "And there in the dead of night I saw a man who appeared to come from Ireland (Hiberione), whose name was Victoricus. And he had innumerable letters with him, one of which he gave to me. And I read the commencement of the letter, containing the voice of the Irish (Vox Hiberionacum). And as I read aloud the beginning of the letter, I thought I heard in my mind the voice of those who were near the wood of Focklut, which is near the western sea. And they cried out: 'We entreat thee, O holy youth, to come and walk still amongst us'; and my heart was greatly touched, so that I could not read any more, and so I awoke" (p. 592).

From this time he had no further doubt. Though, as he says, "Many gifts were offered to me with sorrow and tears, and I offended many of my seniors against my will, but, guided by God, I yielded in no way to them" (p. 598). He remained proof against the suggestions of flesh and blood, firmly resolved to leave his country and his relations. His stay at Dumbarton was marked by many other supernatural sign and visions from God. He says: "On another night, whether in me or near me God knows, I heard eloquent words which I could not understand until the end of the speech, when it was said: 'He who gave His life for thee is He who speaks in thee'. And so I awoke full of joy" (p. 592). "And, again, I saw one praying within me, and it was as it were within my body, and I heard, that is above the inner man, and then he prayed earnestly with groans. And I was amazed at this, and marvelled and considered who this could be who prayed in me. But at the end of the prayer it came to pass that it was a Bishop, and I awoke. And I remembered that the Apostle said: 'The Spirit helpeth the infirmity of our prayer, for we know not what we should pray for as we ought, but the Spirit Himself asketh for us with unspeakable groanings, which cannot be put in words'." (*Rom.* viii. 26 (p. 592).)

Altogether, his visit to his home was, in many ways, remarkable. After years of separation from religious persons and offices, he was once more in a Christian community. He could again join in the offices of the Church, and converse with her ministers. As his absence had been only six years, he may well have met with some survivors of the priests who had known him as a youth, whose advice he accuses himself as having thought so lightly of at the time. And they would wonder at the exalted degree of sanctity to which he, a mere youth and a layman, had attained.

Though he was led by an interior light, and directed by a voice from above, still it was not merely a comfort, but a great gain to him, to open his heart to a priest and receive from him human guidance and sympathy. Above all, it must have been an immense satisfaction to him to assist once more at the daily Mass and receive the Holy Sacraments. All this, however, had no effect in inducing him to settle down quietly at Dumbarton amongst his friends: there was a voice perpetually reminding him of his high vocation, and urging him to take steps to carry it into effect. Yet how was this to be done? Who was to assist him to acquire the necessary education for his great and hazardous mission? The remembrance of his great uncle St. Martin had never faded away from his mind. When tending his sheep on the slopes of Mount Slemish he had thought of the words in which his mother had described this great servant of God. He loved to think, in his own utter desolation, of the virtues which adorned St. Martin, of the influence he exerted over others, and of the reverence in which he was held. All these thoughts now returned upon his mind in full flow, and he soon formed a resolve to leave Britain, to make his way to Gaul to the banks of the Loire, to throw himself at the feet of his venerable uncle, and beg him to be his guide and his helper.

There were, of course, many difficulties to be overcome. A long journey had to be undertaken. Travelling, except to persons of abundant means, was tedious, wearisome, and hazardous. It is true that Britain, for a time, enjoyed comparative peace under the firm rule of Theodosius. After defeating Maximus, six years before, he had placed as Vicar in Britain an officer from the East, Chrysanthus, who protected the island from external foes and established internal peace. On leaving Britain, Chrysanthus was next made Governor of Constantinople, and then became a Bishop. This is a striking instance of the hold that Christianity had gained over men in high station at the end of the fourth century. We here see an official of the very highest rank exchanging his secular dignities for the work of a Bishop. I may advert to another fact illustrating the same point. When, a few years later, Constantine the Briton assumed the purple, and was hailed in Gaul as Emperor of the West, he took his son, Constans, who had become a monk, from the cloister, and placed him at the head of an army he sent into Spain. These facts prove, beyond a doubt, that, at the time of St. Patrick's visit to Dumbarton, Britain was, to a very great extent, Christian. The sixth legion had its headquarters still at York, and the second had been removed from Caerleon in Monmouthshire to Richborough in Kent to confront the Saxons, who were yearly becoming more formidable. To St. Patrick, who had already traversed the wild country of the West of Ireland and the desert that lay between the Lune and the Clyde, the journey through Britain was not very formidable. But to reach his uncle's abode he had to cross the sea, and make a long journey by land through a district which was fast slipping away from Roman rule and Roman civilisation. On this occasion he would have no reason to avoid the Roman roads or military forts, and probably he would travel southward, on the great Antonine road called the Tenth, which would bring him to Bremetonacae (Ribchester), through Mancunium (Manchester), to Deva (Chester). Thus he would pass through Lancashire a second time. St. Patrick gives no details of this journey, but a passage of Probus seems to refer to it. "After twelve days in the company of the Gauls, he reached Brotgalum, going on from thence to Trajectus. Here, by the aid of the Christians, the blessed Patrick obtained his liberty, and, having escaped, he arrived at Tours and joined Martin the Bishop." (*Trias Thaumaturg*, p. 48.) If this passage really refers to the journey of St. Patrick to Tours, and it is difficult to see to what else it can belong, it would appear that the saint spent twelve days at sea in a vessel manned by Gallic sailors. The port of embarkation is not mentioned, but as the voyage was of twelve days' duration, this would fall in very well with the supposition that he started from some port on the north-western coast, such as the Portus Setantiorum in Lancashire, or Deva in Cheshire. He finally reached the coast of Gaul at Bordeaux (Brotgalum or Burdegala). This is very much out of his direct course, being 200 miles more to the south than the mouth of the Loire; but this can be easily accounted for. It may be that the captain of the ship refused to land him at the former place; or, what is quite as likely, that the winds and waves of the Bay of Biscay made it more convenient for the ship to enter the Gironde and not the Loire. The saint seems to have journeyed eastwards to Trajectus, situated on the Dordogne, about sixty miles from Bordeaux. He appears to have been under restraint, for Probus speaks of him making his escape from his companions, and then striking northwards for the city of Tours.

Again local traditions come to our aid, and associate in a most charming way the name of our saint with a well-known spot in western France. About twenty miles westward of Tours he reached the Loire. Here, on the slope of a hill not far from the Chateau de Rochette, is to be found the Commune of St. Patrice. Its inhabitants record an ancient tradition, which, in its simplicity, is full of freshness and poetry. I am quoting from what might be supposed a most prosaic document, *The Annals of the Society of Agriculture and Science of the Departement of Indre et Loire*, vol. xxx., 1850, p. 70. It is given in the appendix to Fr. Morris' excellent *Life of St. Patrick*, and runs as follows: "St. Patrick being on his way from Ireland to join St. Martin in Gaul, attracted by the fame of that saint's sanctity and miracles, and having arrived at the bank of the Loire, near the spot where the church now bearing his name has been built, rested under a shrub. It was Christmas time when the cold was intense. In honour of the saint the shrub expanded its branches, and shaking off the snow which rested on them, by an unheard of prodigy, arrayed itself in flowers white as the snow itself. St. Patrick crossed the Loire on his cloak, and on reaching the opposite bank another blackthorn under which he rested at once burst out into flowers." Since that time, says the chronicle, the two shrubs have never ceased to blossom at Christmas in honour of St. Patrick (p. 172).

The authority I have cited vouches sufficiently for the existence of the tradition, and it also gives a detailed statement of what occurs annually to this day at Christmas-time : and it appeals to the testimony of thousands who at the end of December in each year are eye-witnesses of its repetition. The writer, Mgr. Chevallier, President of the Archæological Society of Touraine, says : " We have lately verified this circumstance with our own eyes, and we can vouch for its truth without fear of contradiction". . . . " The circulation of the sap, which should be suspended in winter, is plainly revealed by the moist state of the bark, which easily separates from the wood which it covers. The buds swell, the flowers expand, as in the month of April, and cover the boughs with odorous and snow-like flowers, while a few leaves more timidly venture to expose their delicate verdure to the icy north wind. The tree is the Prunus Spinosa, the blackthorn commonly called the sloe. This singular growth of flowers has been repeated every year from time immemorial. The oldest inhabitants of St. Patrice have always seen it take place at a fixed period of the year, no matter how severe the season may be; and such has also been the ancient tradition of their forefathers. This year the flowers were in bloom from Christmas to the first of January, that is, at a time when the thermometer was almost always below freezing point. Although growing on the slope of a hill, this shrub is in no way sheltered from the north wind; its branches are encrusted with hoar frost, the icy north-east wind blows violently amongst them, and it often happens that the shrub is loaded at one and the same time with the snow of winter and the snow of its own flowers."

The local devotion to St. Patrick is, as we might naturally expect, no new thing. We can trace it back to early in the eleventh century, and as it was not then introduced for the first time, we may reasonably suppose that it has existed ever since the saint's days. By a charter dated 1035 a nobleman named Archambauld makes over to the monks of the Abbey of Noyers "a house and land adjoining the Church of St. Patrick, with all his rights as patron of the church and cemetery". This was before the invasion of England by William the Conqueror. Many years afterwards, in 1069, Archambauld had accompanied Foulque, Count of Anjou, in a military expedition, and he was mortally wounded in an attack on the Castle of Trebas. The brave, old man was anxious that his pious gift to St. Patrick might stand good, and in his dying presence his son Andrew solemnly confirmed the donation. The style of the church tells us that it dates from the tenth or eleventh century.

It is truly wonderful that the footsteps of this lonely wanderer in strange and far distant lands should have thus impressed themselves on the very soil; and that in countries as diverse as the shores of North-west Lancashire and the banks of the Loire memorials should tell us of the Divine might that directed and guarded this chosen vessel of God. When St. Patrick found himself on the northern bank of the Loire he was on the Great Roman road from Angers to Tours (via maxima), and had but twenty miles to journey before reaching his destination. He arrived at length, perhaps footsore and toil-worn, at the precincts of the far-famed Monastery of Marmoutier on the Loire, not far from the city of Tours (Turones), the see of his renowned great-uncle St. Martin.

On his way he would be constantly sustained by the thought of his high vocation, and by the prospect of immediately entering on a direct preparation for it. No doubt it was late for him to resume the studies which had been so rudely interrupted, but he did not shrink from the drudgery of learning lessons which were familiarly known to most fairly-educated boys. We have already seen that he felt his deficiencies in book-learning to the end of his life, and that he never acquired facility in writing composition nor the power of telling a well-ordered narrative of events. But his sense of his deficiency only served to increase his desire to commence his training in literature and the practice of a religious life.

CHAPTER V.

SAINT PATRICK AT MARMOUTIER AND LERINS.

A.D. 394-418.

ST. MARTIN, BISHOP OF TOURS. ST. NINIAN AT MARMOUTIER ST. MARTIN'S DEATH. CONDITION OF THE ROMAN EMPIRE AFTER THE DEATH OF THEODOSIUS THE GREAT. ST. PATRICK AT LERINS. COUNT MONTALEMBERT ON LERINS.

THE reader who has kindly perused the previous chapters must have sympathised with me that I had to deal with such scanty materials, and, perhaps, may have set slight value upon the narrative as being drawn more from the imagination than from real historical sources. I must confess the actual facts have been few. Yet they *were* facts. After years of controversy between adversaries of no mean skill, and in real earnest, the statements on which I have rested my account of St. Patrick's birth and early life are generally admitted as all but certain. That they occurred in a country and at a time when history sheds a very uncertain glimmer is true, and my readers will share my own keen satisfaction that, in treating about St. Patrick's long sojourn in Gaul, we get into fuller light, and tread on more certain ground.

He now became the disciple of great saints, of men who, besides their episcopal dignity, are renowned as foremost in their age, for strong individual character and eminent virtue. He is in succession an inmate of the great Abbey of Marmoutier, of the far-famed school at Lerins, and of the palace of St. Germanus of Auxerre. He is no longer limited to such instruction as he could pick up at his mother's knee, or as it pleased the Holy Spirit to pour into his soul in the wild dales of Antrim; but he is brought in contact with some of the master minds of the age, who have held their own in the courts of the Emperor and in the schools of Rome, and whose treasures of wisdom and experience all contribute to form and strengthen his own character.

I will not attempt to describe the meeting between St. Martin, now a venerable old man of nearly 80 years, and his youthful grandnephew. The reader may picture this for himself. But we may be sure that our young Briton would find in the grand old man, the Bishop of Tours, all that his fondest dreams could have suggested. His uncle had been a soldier, and in spite of the burden of years there would be still the upright form, the firm tread, the attitude of resolute command. But the pomp of the soldier was not there, in its stead was the humility of the Cross. His clothing was not of purple and fine linen, but a rough, coarse habit of camel's hair. There was no attempt at conventional niceties, for he gave little care to his personal appearance, and his hair was matted and unkempt. But his looks showed that his thoughts were more bent on heavenly things than occupied with earthly affairs, and that he was accustomed to intercourse with the Angels and their Divine Master. At this period of his life he spent much time at his chosen retreat at Marmoutier, where he formed a monastery about two miles distant from Tours, on the northern bank of the Loire. I cannot do better than transcribe the passage from the biographer St. Sulpicius Severus. "So secret and retired was the place that he did not miss the solitude of the desert. On one side it was bounded by the high and precipitous rock of a mountain, and on the other the level was shut in by the river Loire, which makes a gentle bend. There was but one way into it, and that very narrow. His own cell was of wood. Many of the brethren made themselves dwellings of the same kind, but most of them hollowed out the stone of the mountain which was above them. There were eighty scholars under training of their saintly master. No one had aught his own; all things were thrown into a common stock. It was not lawful, as to most monks, to buy or sell anything. They had no art except that of transcribing, which was assigned to the younger, while the older gave themselves up to prayer. They seldom left their cell, except to attend the place of prayer. They took their meal together after the time of fasting. No one tasted wine except when compelled by bodily weakness. Most of them were clad in camel's hair; a softer raiment was a crime; and what of course makes it more remarkable is, that many of them were accounted noble who, after a very different education, had forced themselves to this humility and patience; and we have lived to see many of them Bishops. For what is that city or church which did not covet priests from the monastery of Martin! (*Vita Martini*, c. vii. Newman's *Church of the Fathers.*) Such was the school of perfection in which Patrick now found himself. Such were his companions in his life of preparation for his apostolate. And such was his new master in the supernatural life. St. Martin had himself been well trained.

Early in the fourth century the fame of the virtues and austerities of St. Anthony and his disciples, in the arid desert of the Thebaid, had been carried throughout the Eastern world. St. Athanasius, when banished from Alexandria to Trèves, brought with him an ardent admiration and love for the eremitical life, and his history of St. Anthony spread throughout the West the renown of these holy Anchorites. Every one is familiar with the beautiful passage of St. Augustine, in which he gives an account of the wonderful conversion of some courtiers at Trèves from a worldly life to one of seclusion and penance, brought about by accidently reading St. Athanasius's book. St. Martin was the first in the Western Church to spread far and wide the holy rule of the monks. Under St. Hilary, Bishop of Poictiers, he founded the first monastery in Gaul. From this beloved retreat he had, much against his will, been torn, to become the Bishop of Tours.

We must bear in mind that though in the fourth century many of the cities of Gaul had long enjoyed the light of the Gospel the country districts were, for the most part, Pagan—the faith had scarcely been preached in them, and the population still worshipped the old Celtic deities of their ancestors, or the less reputable gods and godesses of their conquerors. The zeal of the new Bishop was roused at the sight. In the words of Cardinal Newman, " Martin took upon him to enter and destroy the kingdom of Satan with his own hands. He went, unarmed, amongst the temples, the altars, the statues, the groves, and the processions of the false worship, attended by his monastic brethren ; he presented himself to the barbarian multitude, converted them, and made them join with him in the destruction of their time-honoured establishment of error. . . . In consequence of his triumphant exertions, he is considered the Apostle of Gaul." (*Church of the Fathers*, p. 330.) By his fearless labours among a heathen people he had become a fitting teacher for St. Patrick, the destined converter of a whole nation from darkness to light. For our acquaintance with the life and character of St. Martin we are indebted to St. Sulpicius Severus, one of his most distinguished disciples. Sulpicius had been a lawyer in lucrative practice, enjoying a great reputation for eloquence. Touched by the Gospel teaching, he had renounced all his worldly prospects, distributed his property amongst the poor, and become an humble but fervent disciple of St. Martin. I could not give a better proof than this act of Sulpicius of the high esteem in which the Bishop of Tours was held, or of the great advantage which his direction was to St. Patrick. Besides, it was at once a great pleasure and a great profit for the young monk, not merely to be under such wise rule, but also to have the companionship of such a brother as Sulpicius Severus. He was a cultivated scholar, a polished gentleman, as well as an ardent aspirant after religious perfection. Sulpicius's *Life of St. Martin*, when it was given to the world, was eagerly laid hold of by St. Patrick. When he entered on his great mission he took it with him, along with the New Testament, and to the day of his death he looked upon it as his greatest treasure. The book of Armagh still attests the veneration St. Patrick retained to his dying day for the saintly Martin and his fellow disciple.

One other distinguished saint whom he very probably met during his stay at Marmoutier may be mentioned here. I allude to St. Ninian, afterwards Bishop of Whitherne in Galloway. He was born in 360, and so was thirteen years older than our saint; the place of his birth was on the banks of the Solway Firth, as that of St. Patrick was on the Clyde. They were thus closely connected by the tie of a common country, being both natives of the Northern Province of Roman Britain. St. Ninian was of British descent, his father being a chief of high rank and a Christian, and he was brought up a devout believer in the Faith. Whilst still a youth, he thirsted for a fuller knowledge of Divine things than he could obtain in Cumbria, and he proceeded to Rome. He was fortunate in attracting the notice of successive Popes. He pursued his studies under exceptional advantages, and by his virtuous conduct he so far secured the esteem of St. Siricius that that holy Pope chose him to preach the Gospel to his countrymen, and with his own hands consecrated him Bishop when he was about 36 years old. In the year 397 St. Ninian was on his way from Rome to Northern Britain, and the fame of St. Martin attracted him to Tours. He was warmly welcomed by the aged saint. They held together many important conversations on the best mode of converting the heathen, and when St. Ninian took his leave he asked his host to send along with him some men skilled in the building arts to erect a church in Britain. We cannot doubt that St. Martin would introduce to his distinguished visitor his youthful nephew; St. Patrick had left North Britain only recently, and he could give much information about the people and the state of religion, which would be valuable to St. Ninian, who had been absent from the country for over twenty years.

In the young monk St. Ninian would see no mere inmate of the cloister, but a man already accustomed to face the difficulties of life; one who had, young as he was, learned the royal power of ruling others. His knowledge of the world and of men had not been gathered from books, but had been acquired in the hard school of experience. And St. Ninian, who himself had spent the greater part of his life in the schools and palaces of Rome, would be amazed at the shrewdness and soundness of his remarks. But he would see far more than this. In the course of conversation Patrick would most likely reveal much of his own history, and of his high aspirations to bring the Scoti to the faith, and the accomplished Bishop, fresh from the presence of the Pope, would recognise in him a spirit of zeal akin to his own. Besides, saints often possess a supernatural instinct by which they can detect the presence of sanctity in others; and we may well imagine that the meeting of the aged Apostle of Gaul with St. Ninian, so soon to be the Apostle of the Picts, would not be without its influence on the novice who had already been forewarned by heaven that he was to be the apostle of Ireland. We read in Bede that on his arrival in his own country St. Ninian set about erecting in Galloway, at Whitherne, a church of stone, an

unaccustomed mode of building in those parts, as
churches till then had been made of wood. Before he had completed it he became acquainted
with the death of St. Martin, and so fully convinced was he of the exalted sanctity of his friend
that he dedicated the new church under his
invocation. After a life of unceasing toil he
died full of years and honours about 430, and
was buried, as Bede assures us, in his own
church at Whitherne. He did not live to hear
of the wonderful work wrought in Ireland by his
young countryman, whom he had met at Marmoutier. But St. Patrick never forgot the illustrious visitor from Rome. He watched him
depart with the liveliest feelings of veneration
and interest, for he was going to his own native
land to preach and teach among his own people,
amongst whom he was born and brought up.
His own vocation was clear to him. He knew
he was destined for another mission in the land
of his six years' captivity; but his heartiest
sympathy and earnest prayers accompanied St.
Ninian. We know that in the sixth century this
name was so loved in Ireland that in the Martyrologies St. Ninian is mentioned under the name
Monennoc, "Mo" meaning "My," "Nenn" taking the place of "Ninian," and "Oc" being a
diminutive term of endearment, so that the

word may be properly translated, "My dear little Ninian". It is quite true that some distinguished Irish saints were brought up at Whitherne, but it is far more probable that the veneration rendered to St. Ninian in Ireland was owing to St. Patrick's love and reverence for him, and that during his apostolate in Ireland he taught his disciples to honour and love Saints Martin and Ninian.

And now the end is coming of that loving family under St. Martin's rule. He is still vigorous, and at the call of duty, he goes on a mission of peace to visit a neighbouring ecclesiastic. He is accompanied by his monks. The exertion is too much for him; it is his last effort, and he returns home to die. But in describing the last scene, I will again borrow the words of a Master. Cardinal Newman thus tells the story: "A fever had already got possession of him. He assembled his disciples and announced to them that he was going. They, with passionate laments, deprecated such a dispensation, as involving the exposure of his flock to the wolves. The saint was moved, and used words which have become famous in the Church—'Lord, if I be yet necessary to Thy people, I decline not the labour; Thy will be done!' His wish was heard, not his prayer. His fever lay upon him; during the trial he continued his devotions as usual, causing himself to be laid in sackcloth and ashes. On his disciples asking to be allowed to place straw under him instead, he made answer, 'Sons, it becomes a Christian to die in ashes. Did I set any other example, I should sin myself.' They wished to turn him on his side, to ease his position; but he expressed a wish to see heaven rather than earth, that his spirit might, as it were, be setting out on its journey. It is said that on this he saw the evil spirit at his side; and he addressed him in words expressive of his assurance that his Lord's merits were fully effectual for him, and his soul perfected. 'Beast of blood,' he exclaimed, 'why standest thou here? Deadly one, thou shalt find nothing in me: Abraham's bosom is receiving me.' With these words he expired." (*Church of the Fathers*, p. 348.) St. Martin was buried at Tours, and two thousand of his monks attended the funeral.

St. Sulpicius, in his second Epistle, tells us that he was absent at the time, but St. Patrick was still at Marmoutier, was present at the last sad scene, and was one of the mourners at his uncle's funeral. Probus tells us "that he remained with him for the space of four years, receiving the tonsure and admission into the clerical state, and he held fast to the doctrine and learning he had received from him". Probus further adds: "He passed his time in utter submission, with patience, obedience, charity, and chastity, and in all purity in soul and spirit, remaining a virgin in the fear of the Lord, and walking all the days of his life in holiness and simplicity of heart." (*Trias Thaumat*, p. 48.)

St. Patrick derived many advantages from his sojourn at Marmoutier: it is plain from his writings that his learning was more infused than acquired by study. In this he was like St. Martin, who, St. Sulpicius assures us, was unskilled in letters, but under his uncle he learnt to be obedient in all things, to despise the pleasures and vanities of the world, and to give himself more and more to the work pointed out by the Holy Spirit for him to do. One practice of the religious life cost him a severe struggle. In the northern climates in which he had been brought up, and in which he had lived up to reaching man's estate, he had been accustomed to use animal food. He found it difficult to give this up, and to be content with a mere abstinence diet. An amusing story is told by his biographers, how on one occasion "a desire of eating meat came upon him, until being ensnared and carried away by his desire, he obtained some swine's flesh, and concealed it in a certain vessel". The story goes on to tells us that he was reproved in a vision, and that he was filled with remorse. "Striking his breast with many strokes, he cast himself to the earth, and watered it with a shower of tears, as if he had been guilty of all crimes." When he arose from the ground, he utterly renounced and abjured the eating of flesh-meat, even through the rest of his life.

It is hard to account for St. Patrick's complete silence in his confession as to this part of his life. He never mentions Marmoutier nor St. Martin, and there is only one accidental allusion to his ordination to the Diaconate. As, however, this incident shows in a striking light his natural yearning for human sympathy, and the warmth and entire devotion of his attachments, I give it in his own words. "From anxiety, with sorrow of mind, I told my dearest friend what I had done in my youth, in one day, nay, rather in one hour, because I was not then able to overcome" (p. 594). This occurred before he was a deacon, and he fixes the date by remarking that it was thirty years before he was ordained Bishop, that is before 402. The memory of this youthful fault, committed when he was about fifteen years old, was a cause of deep sorrow to him for the whole of his life. At every great crisis in his life, it filled his soul with sorrow and anxious doubts, and we shall see later, that it again caused him serious trouble on his promotion to the Episcopate. Even in old age, he cannot allude to it without clearly showing how painful the recollection was to him.

It is time now to give a brief sketch of the march of political events, for they throw a strong light on matters which must have greatly influenced the actions and character of our saint. The Emperor Theodosius died in 395, when but fifty years old, the year after St. Patrick's escape from Ireland. Patrick would hear of his death with regret, not merely on public grounds, because the State had lost a wise and firm ruler, but also for more personal reasons. Calpurnius, our saint's father, had accompanied Theodosius the elder to Britain in 367, and the younger Theodosius, afterwards the great emperor, served in the army, and was his comrade in arms. Many a time must the boy Succat have heard his father talk of the cool courage and of the military skill of his commander's son. So when Theodosius became emperor, in St. Patrick's eyes he would not be a far-off stranger who was raised to the purple, but an old companion in arms of his father. On his death the empire of the east and west was divided between the two sons of Theodosius, Arcadius and Honorius, Arcadius taking the east, with Constantinople for his capital, and Honorius the west, who made Milan the seat of his Government. But the hands of Theodosius's sons were not those of the father. He had been a brave warrior and a great statesman. His sons inherited not his talents, and their reigns are little more than a record of disaster and disgrace. All the military skill of Theodosius had been taxed to keep at bay the barbarians from the north and east who now swarmed on the frontiers of the empire; and his utmost efforts had been needed to put down and crush insubordination amongst his ambitious courtiers and generals. It was not long after his strong hand had been withdrawn before attacks from without, and rebellions from within, prepared the way for the complete destruction of the empire. As long as Patrick was transcribing manuscripts, and pursuing the peaceful if austere life at Marmoutier, he would be little affected by the fears and alarms which agitated the world without. But the storm of barbarism which, under Alaric the Goth, spread desolation in Macedonia and Greece in 403, shortly after his being ordained deacon, burst upon Italy. The effeminate and cowardly Honorius fled from Milan to what he considered an impregnable retreat on the slopes of the Alps, in what is now Piedmont. Here he was in the utmost danger from the relentless pursuit of the enemy, and was only saved by the skill and valour of his great minister and general, Stilicho. Troops had been hastily summoned from the most remote districts of the empire to beat back the barbarians, and the legions guarding the Antonine Wall and Dumbarton took part in the great battle fought at Pollentia. In 406, only three years later, the wave of invasion burst over Gaul, and the Germans from the Rhine overspread and laid waste some of its fairest cities and most fertile districts. From these attacks no one was safe. In the words of Gibbon, "The consuming flames of war spread from the banks of the Rhine over the greatest part of the seventeen provinces of Gaul. That rich and extensive country, as far as the ocean, the Alps and the Pyrenees, was delivered to the barbarians, who drove before them in a promiscuous crowd the Bishop, the senator, and the virgin, laden with the spoils of their homes and their altars." This first invasion was not on so vast a scale as to produce great permanent effect in Gaul. The invaders secured their spoil and marched on : and the great bulk of the people continued Roman in institutions, in manners, in language, arts, and religion. It was soon to be succeeded by more serious assaults, before which civilisation, letters, and religion, all alike succumbed. Meanwhile, the weakness of the central authority in Italy made itself felt as far as Britain. The name of Honorius commanded no respect among the legions stationed in our island. The troops there, in all the insolence of irresponsible power, chose for themselves emperors for the hour, and on the first change of their caprice murdered the puppets they had created. In 406 they saluted as emperor a common soldier named Constantine. He was a man already past the prime of life, and was the father of two sons, one named Constans, who is said to have been a monk at Winchester. Whatever his origin and education may here have been, he proved a man of courage and determination, but unfortunately he was not content with rule in his native island, but aspired to dominion on the continent, and aimed at becoming Emperor of the West. His first efforts were successful. After being proclaimed Augustus, he led his troops to Boulogne ; with the assistance of some Roman corps which lay dispersed in the neighbourhood he cleared the province of the German barbarians. His success caused him to be received by the Gauls as a deliverer, and he was acknowledged Emperor of the West. I need not pursue his history further than to say that he took his son Constans from the cloister, conferred upon him the dignity of Caesar, and put him in command of an army despatched to subdue Spain. The expedition was successful, but the success was short lived, and Constans was put to death by Gerontius, one of his own generals, who rebelled against him. Meanwhile the father, Constantine, had fixed his seat of Government at Arles, a former imperial residence. He actually obtained from the weak Emperor Honorius a recognition of his title, but did not long enjoy his dignity, for in 411 Arles was besieged and finally taken by Constantius, a general sent by Honorius to re-assert his authority over Gaul and Spain. Constantine was taken prisoner, and on his way to Ravenna was privately put to death.

In the midst of these storms of foreign invasion and intestine war, our saint was quietly pursuing his preparation for his great undertaking. He had learned the practice of the monastic life at Marmoutier; he was still further to advance in virtue and learning at Lerins, a small island in the Mediterranean, about two leagues from the French coast, and not far from Toulon. Nearly all the ancient biographers speak of his sojourn on an island in the Tyrrhene Sea, where St. Fiacc tells us he meditated, and modern writers are unanimous in identifying this island with Lerins. Here St. Honoratus had founded his famous school and monastery about 410. As St. Martin died in 397, there is an interval of thirteen years to be accounted for, and probably St. Patrick spent these years in the monastery at Marmoutier.

There are few more interesting episodes in Church history than the rise in the early part of the fifth century of this celebrated seat of learning and piety. As it has been described in eloquent words by the illustrious Montalembert, it would be almost presumptuous in me to go over the same ground; and though the extract is lengthy, I trust the reader will be grateful for my quoting his glowing narrative.

" The sailor, the soldier, or the traveller who proceeds from the roadstead of Toulon to sail towards Italy on the East, passes among two or three islands, rocky and arid, surmounted here and there by a slender cluster of pines. He looks at them with indifference and avoids them. However, one of these islands has been for the soul, for the mind, for the moral progress of humanity, a centre purer and more fertile than any famous isle of the Hellenic Archipelago. It is Lerins, formerly occupied by a city, which was already ruined in the time of Pliny, and where, at the commencement of the fifth century, nothing more was to be seen than a desert coast, rendered unapproachable by the numbers of serpents which swarmed there. In 410 a man landed and remained there; he was called Honoratus. Descended from a consular race, educated and eloquent, but devoted from his youth to great piety, he desired to be a monk. His father charged his eldest brother, a gay and impetuous young man, to turn him from ascetic life; but, on the contrary, it was he who gained his brother. After many difficulties he at last found repose at Lerins; the serpents yielded the place to him; a multitude of disciples gathered round him. A community of austere monks and indefatigable labourers was formed there. The face of the isle was changed, the desert became a paradise: a country bordered with deep woods, watered by beneficent streams, rich with verdure, enamelled with flowers, embalmed by their perfumes, revealed the fertilising presence there of a new race. Honoratus, whose fine face was radiant with a sweet and attractive majesty, opened the arms of his love to the sons of all countries who desired to love Christ. A multitude of disciples of all nations joined him. The West could no longer envy the East; and shortly that retreat, destined, in the intentions of its founder, to renew upon the coasts of Provence the austerities of the Thebaid, became a celebrated school of theology and Christian philosophy, a citadel inaccessible to the waves of barbarian invasion, an asylum for literature and science which had fled from Italy invaded by the Goths; in short, a nursery of bishops and saints, who were destined to spread over the whole of Gaul the knowledge of the Gospel and the glory of Lerins. We shall soon see the beams of that light flashing as far as Ireland and England by the blessed hands of Patrick and Augustine. There is perhaps nothing more touching in monastic annals than the picture traced by one of the most illustrious sons of Lerins, of the paternal tenderness of Honoratus for the numerous family of monks whom he had collected round him. He could read the depths of their souls to discover all their griefs. He neglected no effort to banish every sadness, every painful recollection of the world. He watched their sleep, their health, their food, their labours, that each might serve God according to the measure of his strength. Thus he inspired them with a love more than filial: 'In him,' they said, 'we find not only a father, but an entire family, a country, the whole world'. When he wrote to any of those who were absent, they said, on receiving his letter, written, according to the usage of the time, upon tablets of wax: 'It is honey which he has poured back into that wax, honey drawn from the inexhaustible sweetness of his heart'. In that island Paradise, and under the care of such a shepherd, the perfume of life breathed everywhere. These monks who had sought happiness by renouncing secular life felt and proclaimed that they had found it; to see their serene and modest joy, their union, their gentleness, and their firm hope, one could have believed oneself in presence of a battalion of angels at rest. The churches of Arles, Avignon, Lyons, Vienne, Troyes, Riez, Frejus, Valence, Metz, Nice, Venice, Apt, Carpentras, and Saintes borrowed from the happy isle, as it was everywhere called, their most illustrious Bishops. Honoratus, taken from his monastery to be elevated to the metropolitan See of Arles, had for his successor, as Abbot of Lerins, and afterwards as Bishop of Arles, his pupil and relative, Hilary, to whom we owe the admirable biography of his master. Hilary, whom the gentle and tender Honoratus had drawn from worldly life after a desperate resistance, by force of entreaties, caresses, and tears, retained in the Episcopate the penitent and laborious life of the cloister of Lerins. He went through his diocese and the neighbouring country always on foot and barefooted, even in the snow. Celebrated for his eloquence, his unwearied zeal, his ascendency over the crowd, and by the numerous miracles which he worked, he was once at variance with the Pope, St. Leo the Great, who deprived him of his title of metropolitan to punish him for certain uncanonical usurpations; but Hilary knew how to yield, and after his death the great Pope did him justice by calling him *Hilary of holy memory*. Amongst this harvest of saints, prelates, and doctors, which Lerins gave to Gaul and to the Church, there are still several whom it is important to indicate, because they are reckoned among the Fathers, and illuminated all the fifth century with their renown. Holding the first rank amongst these was the great and modest Vincent de Lerins, who was the first controversialist of his time, and who has preserved to posterity the name of the isle which had been the cradle of his genius. He composed the short and celebrated work which has gained him immortality in 434, three years after the Council of Ephesus, and on occasion of the Nestorian heresy which that council had condemned. He would not put his name to it, and entitled it humbly, *Remarks of the Pilgrim*, Commonitorium Peregrini. In this he has fixed with admirable precision, and in language as decisive as it is simple and correct, the rule of Catholic faith, by establishing it on the double authority of Scripture and tradition, and originating the celebrated definition of orthodox interpretation: *Quod semper, quod ubique, quod ab omnibus creditum est.* After having thus established the immutability of Catholic doctrine, he demands: 'Shall there be no progress in the Church of Christ?' 'There shall be progress,' he answers, 'and even great progress; for who would be so envious of the good of men, or so cursed of God, as to prevent it? But it will be progress, and not change. With the growth of the ages and centuries, there must necessarily be a growth of intelligence, of wisdom, and of knowledge for each man as for all the Church. But the religion of souls must imitate the progress of the human form, which, in developing and growing with years, never ceases to be the same in the maturity of age as in the flower of youth.' Vincent has inscribed at the head of his masterpiece, a testimony of his gratitude for the sweet sanctuary of Lerins, which was for him, as he says, the port of religion, when, after having been long tossed about on the sea of this world, he came there to seek peace and study, that he might escape, not only the shipwrecks of the present life, but the fires of the world to come. With Lerins also is associated the fame of Salvian, the most eloquent man of his age after St. Augustine, and surnamed the *Master of Bishops*, though himself only a priest. He passed five years at Lerins; he experienced there the charms of peace and solitude in the midst of the horrors of barbarian invasion, and that frightful corruption of the Roman world, of which he has traced so startling a picture in his treatise upon the *Government of God*. But the influence of the holy and learned Provençal isle shone still further than Lyons. Thence Troyes chose for its bishop that illustrious St. Lupus, who arrested Attila at the gates of Troyes, before St. Leo had arrested him at the gates of Rome. It was he who demanded of the king of the Huns, ' *Who art thou?*' and who received the far-famed response, ' *I am Attila the scourge of God*'. The intrepid gentleness of the bishop-monk disarmed the ferocious invader. He left Troyes without injuring it, and drew back to the Rhine, but took the bishop with him, thinking that the presence of so holy a man would serve as a safeguard to his army." (*Monks of the West*, Vol. I., p. 463-469 and 470.)

At Lerins St. Patrick made the acquaintance of these men so graphically described by Montalembert. But with St. Patrick to know persons whom he esteemed was to love them, and the companions of the day became the friends of his life. From intercourse with the polished scholars who were his fellow-companions in prayer, in labour, and in study, at Lerins, his own manner would gradually lose its rudeness, would acquire that indefinable charm which accompanies good breeding and refinement.

In this sanctuary of learning and religion, St. Patrick passed the years previous to 418, about which time he went to Auxerre to place himself under the direction of St. Germanus. Probably enough, he would make his acquaintance through St. Lupus, who was with him at Lerins. He could not be less than thirty-seven years old when he joined the community at Lerins, and he was more than forty when he came under the guidance of St. Germanus.

It may well be asked, what of Ireland during all these years? Had St. Patrick forgotten it? Did he in the repose of the monastic life shrink from the hardships, the toils, the disappointments of a missionary life? From time to time he would hear of the wild expeditions of Niall, king of Ireland, of the ravages he inflicted on the coasts of Gaul and Britain, and of the dread that the very name of the Scoti excited in the minds of men. Perhaps, too, he might hear of the violent death of Niall in the Iccian sea, now the English Channel, in the neighbourhood of Boulogne. Perhaps, too, the strange story of the death of Dathi, Niall's successor, at the foot of the Alps by a flash of lightning, might reach his ears. Such accounts might well stagger his purpose of preaching among such a people, had he been made of different stuff from what he was. But he neither hurried in the execution of his resolve, nor was he deterred from it by difficulty or danger. He waited for the divine voice to tell him when the time was come to set about the work of his life. That voice spoke not, till he was past the prime of life, and his hair was becoming tinged with grey. But his faith wavered not. In the meantime, he went on his way, perfecting himself in ecclesiastical learning and discipline; strengthening the deep foundations he had laid already, of patience, humility, and trust in God. In these days of haste, we cannot look back on the long preparation of well-nigh forty years of St. Patrick in Gaul without wonder and astonishment. But St. Patrick knew that he was under the guidance of the Holy Spirit, and that nothing was lost, but all was well —so long as he stood ready to act on the Divine admonition.

CHAPTER VI.

ST. PATRICK AT AUXERRE.

A.D. 418-429.

AUXERRE. GERMANUS, DUKE OF THE PROVINCE OF LYONS, CHOSEN BISHOP. HIS AUSTERITIES AND SANCTITY. ST. PATRICK BECOMES ONE OF THE CLERGY OF AUXERRE.

ST. PATRICK had been thoroughly trained in the exercises of a religious life at Marmoutier; and at Lerins he had acquired the literary and theological knowledge essential to one who was to speak with authority and give the law to a people. At Auxerre he was initiated in the art of administering a Diocese, and of dealing with the clergy and the flock. The authority of St. Fiacc establishes the fact of St. Patrick's being at Auxerre under the great St. Germanus. In his sententious, quaint way he says, "Over the sea, marvellous was his course until he stayed with Germanus in the south. . . . . He read the Canon with Germanus." (Verses 5 and 6, *Cusack's Life*, p. 559.)

Auxerre is a town of about 12,000 inhabitants on the banks of the Yonne, a small stream which falls into the Seine. It is 50 miles from Troyes, situated on that river, before its confluence with the Yonne. The basin of the Seine is separated from the watershed of the Rhone by the elevated plateau of Langres, the second highest city in France. Auxerre is thus described by the accomplished author of the life of St. German in the series of the *Lives of the English Saints*, undertaken at the suggestion of Cardinal Newman whilst he was still at Oxford. "No town in France," say the learned, "can boast of such a number of precious offerings. Yet there is nothing in the natural advantages of the place to raise it in men's consideration. To the mere traveller for pleasure Auxerre must appear very insignificant. The country around is uniform and tame. Its vineyards produce excellent wines, but vineyards are in reality not pleasant objects to behold. The river Yonne is large enough to supply the town with the necessaries of life, but too inconsiderable on the other hand to give much dignity to the walls it washes. The buildings are not of the most stately and attractive appearance. Many collegiate churches in France exceed St. Stephen's, the Cathedral of Auxerre, in architectural beauty. Yet, notwithstanding,

Auxerre has ever had more than the ordinary respect of Christendom, which is to be traced up to St. German, its founder and benefactor." Vol. i., p. 3.

St. Germanus was born at Auxerre in the year 378, and so was five years younger than St. Patrick. His parents held an honourable position in the neighbourhood, and gave their son an excellent education. From the schools of Gaul —and they stood in high repute in the 4th century—he passed on to those of Rome. He was destined for the bar, and paid special attention to the study of oratory. He made such solid progress that, on his return to his native city, he was soon employed as a pleader, and early advanced to a post in the government. His reputation rose higher and higher, and before long he was nominated Duke or Governor of the Province. At this time the Prefect of Gaul was the highest officer under the Emperor, and his jurisdiction extended over Spain, Gaul, and Britain. Under him were three Vicars, one for Spain, one for Gaul residing at Arles, and a third for Britain. In the third rank stood the Dukes, or Governors of Provinces, of whom there were 12 in Gaul; and Germanus was Duke of the Province of Lyons, though he resided at Auxerre or its neighbourhood. Gallia Lugdunensis was of immense extent, reaching from the Rhone to the shores of the Atlantic. It included a portion of the valley of the Saone, the valley of the Seine to the British Channel, and the districts inhabited by the half-subdued and half-civilised tribes of the Armorican Confederation, occupying the modern Normandy and Bretagne. The post held by Germanus was both important and dignified, and it brought him a handsome revenue. He married a lady of Auxerre, and led the life of a man of the world, seemingly engrossed in its cares and pleasures. Much of the leisure allowed him from the cares of Government he spent at his country house, and he indulged freely in the pleasures of the chase. In the midst of the city was an immense pear-tree held in great veneration by the townspeople on account of its size and age, and on this he was accustomed to exhibit the trophies of his sport, hanging up on its branches the antlers of the deer or the tusks of the wild boar. This practice, apparently innocent, brought him into collision with Amator, the saintly Bishop of Auxerre, and led to most important consequences. Some superstitious associations had gathered about the old pear-tree, and Amator requested the duke to discontinue the practice of hanging on its branches the spoils of the chase. The duke refused, and persevered in his custom. The bishop was determined to put an end to what was becoming a scandal, and taking advantage of Germanus' temporary absence he had the tree cut down to the roots and burnt, and the heads of the wild animals cast out of the city. This provoked the indignation of the Governor beyond all bounds; he was proud of his skill in sport, and he conceived that his authority as civil governor was set at naught. So great was his anger that he formed the idea of taking the life of Amator, and he set out at the head of a considerable force to carry out his rash purpose. But God had very different designs in his regard: He had chosen this very man, breathing blood and slaughter against one of His saintly servants, to be his successor in the See of Auxerre, and to be the greatest prelate of Gaul in his time.

Perhaps in the history of the Church there has been no more remarkable conversion since that of St. Paul on his way to Damascus. St. Amator received a revelation from heaven that his enemy was to be the future Bishop, and did not wait for his return, but set out for the neighbouring city of Autun, where Julius the Prefect of Gaul happened to be. To the amazement of that high functionary, he informed him that God had made known to him that he was speedily to die, and that Duke Germanus was to be his successor. Amator had so high a character for wisdom and sanctity that Julius made no objection to his petition that Germanus might be allowed to resign his post, and devote himself to the service of the Church.

On his return to Auxerre Amator summoned the townspeople to meet him in the hall of his house, and thus addressed them :—" My beloved sons, listen to me with attention ; what I have to communicate to you is of the utmost importance. By revelation from God I have learnt that the day of my departure from this world is at hand. I therefore exhort you all with one mind to enquire after the fittest person to be elected overseer of God's house."

The multitude remained silent, no one could speak for amazement. Amator did not await a reply to his unexpected announcement, but set out for the church. The multitude followed him. The whole town was now astir, and among the rest Germanus, with a large suite of attendants, was present. By this time his anger had cooled down, and animated by the general feeling of the townspeople, he was curious to see the end of this extraordinary scene. At the entrance of the church the Bishop paused, and bade the people lay aside their arms and staves, for they were about to enter the house of prayer, and not the camp of the god of war. His request was complied with, and the crowd poured into the church. As soon as the Governor had entered, Amator gave orders for the doors of the church to be closed and securely fastened. Then occurred this most astonishing incident. The venerable Bishop gathered round about him the clergy and the nobles present, and proceeding to the spot where Germanus was standing in the midst of his suite, laid hold of him. All eyes were fixed on the Bishop. No one knew what was coming next. He solemnly invoked the name of God, cut off the hair of the governor, stripped him of his rich, secular garments, and clothed him in the habit of an ecclesiastic. Apparently the amazed Germanus submitted without any effectual resistance; and the Bishop went on and ordained him Priest, addressing him in these words: "Labour you must, most beloved and revered brother, to preserve immaculate and entire the dignity which has been committed to you. Know that at my death God has willed that you should succeed to my office." Germanus listened to these words in amazed wonder. It was strange, wonderfully strange, that he should have entered that church the highest civil magistrate of a great province, with feelings far from friendly to Amator, and find himself now awed in his presence, and submitting to his decision as if he had no choice of his own. The multitude of citizens were simply stupefied at what had passed before their eyes. Their Duke, who had been so popular with them for his manly bearing, his power of command, and perhaps not least for his love of sport; who had been respected for his firm and upright administration of the law, and yet feared for his lofty mien and imperious temper, had bowed down before their aged Bishop, and taken upon him at his bidding the character of a priest. As they left the church their hushed voices found expression; some recognised in what had just passed a manifestation of the Divine Will, and rejoiced that God, when He was taking their saintly Bishop from them, so wonderfully pointed out to them his successor; while others would shake their heads and express their doubts as to the result of that wondrous day's proceedings.

As for Amator, he went to his home thanking God that his plans had so far succeeded, and that the first and most important step had been taken towards providing a worthy successor to his see. But what were the feelings of Germanus as he entered the Governor's palace? He was now 40 years of age, in all the vigour of his manhood. It was a period when a successful provincial governor might reasonably entertain hopes of rising to distinction. Men of attainments far inferior to his own had, by the caprice of a rebellious legion, or the favour of the Emperor, been able to make their way to the highest places in the state, and we may without rashness believe that Germanus was not insensible to such aspirations. His thoughts had not taken the direction of an ecclesiastical career, he had not sympathised with its spirit of zeal for the souls of men, nor its renunciation of the pleasures of the world. He was bound by many ties to his present mode of life, and at first it seemed impossible for him to break with them. He was married: could it be possible that he was called upon to renounce the affections of a life? Nay, was he not so bound by duty to another that he would be doing wrong in separating from the wife of his bosom? Yet there were the solemn words of Amator still ringing in his ear. He was to be Bishop of Auxerre. There was the holy rite of ordination to the sacred priesthood to which he had submitted, and which now seemed to be the Will of God in his regard. There was a struggle in his inmost soul between nature and grace. After all there were already new feelings rising in his heart, new aspirations springing up in him, and he was no longer the same man. A new view of life presented itself strongly, though vaguely, to his mind. He felt that God was calling him to His service; that the same Almighty Being, Master and Lord of the world and of man, was bidding him like Abram of old go forth from his father's house and be His servant to accomplish whatever work He might set him to do. And grace triumphed in that chosen soul. Then another thought presented itself: how could he, a mere man of the world, whose heart had been so set on earthly things, whose thoughts had been so engrossed in the wretched cares and business of the world, take in hand the affairs of God, and deal henceforth only with the eternal interests of the souls of men? He hesitated—he shrank from the task before him, but he awaited the further manifestation of the Will of God.

Scarcely had the holy Bishop Amator reached his own house when the syptoms of his last illness began to show themselves. He was in high fever. But he was all the more intent on his great purpose. He never lost an opportunity of urging those about him to elect Germanus as the future Bishop. In public and in private this was the theme of every discourse. The loss they were about to sustain brought tears into the eyes of his listeners, but they soon caught the infection of his eager desire, that Germanus should be his successor. On Wednesday the 1st of May, A.D. 418, Amator began to experience the agonies of death. In the midst of these he still continued to address words of consolation to all around. "Surely," he said, "these expressions of grief are ill-suited to your condition; you are about to obtain a bishop far better than I am. What poor services I may have been able to bestow he will greatly surpass." He then desired to be carried into the church, that he might die there, where he had so often celebrated the holy rites. Scarcely had he been placed in his Episcopal Chair, than in the sight of the multitude, he breathed out his soul to God.

It became the duty of Germanus, though still governor, to preside over the funeral of the venerable prelate. When this had been performed with all the solemnity due to one universally regarded as a saint, it became necessary for Germanus to resolve on his own course of conduct. It was a difficult point to determine. On the one hand were the plain words of the deceased bishop, and the unanimous feeling of the people, the nobles and the clergy, with whom at this time the selection of a bishop rested; on the other were the many ties which bound him to the world; how could he reconcile himself to accepting so responsible an office? He considered himself unfit for it by his previous habits of life; and he imagined that he did not possess the virtues nor the talents necessary for a due discharge of his duties. The ways of a lawyer, a courtier, and finally a civil ruler, were so different from those becoming a bishop. Aware, however, of the feeling of the town, he endeavoured to gain over to his views those who would exercise a powerful influence at the approaching election. But he now found that the sway he had been wont to possess over the minds of men was gone. His greatest friends turned against him, and when the day came there was but one voice from clergy and people, and that cry was, "Germanus Bishop". His reluctance was overcome; he could no longer oppose what was the universal wish, which had only grown in intensity during the interval which elapsed after the death of Amator.

And now appeared in his new manner of life the evidence that he had a true vocation. God had called him, in a wonderful, almost unheard-of manner, to His service, and it became plain to all men that He had poured out on His chosen servant a full measure of grace. From the day that he took on him the Episcopal office till his dying hour Germanus was an example of every virtue that should adorn a bishop. He devoted himself to prayer, to study, and eminently to a mortified and penetential life, the better to prepare himself to exercise power over the souls of men. He immediately resigned his office as governor, dismissed his numerous attendants, sacrificed the splendid and pleasant possessions of his wealth, gave away his substance to the poor, and enlisted himself in their company. His wife Eustachia became to him a sister, and from this time we hear no more of her. His table was seldom spread for himself, though towards others he exercised an unbounded hospitality. His days were given up to the pressing and unceasing duties of his ministry. His nights were spent in prayer and meditation. The account of his austerities almost takes away our breath. His clothing was the same winter and summer, and consisted merely of a tunic, a garment covering the whole person, and coming down to the feet, a hood for the head, ending in a point and falling down over the neck as far as the shoulders. But under these Germanus wore a hair-shirt which he never laid aside.

His abstemiousness in the matter of food was still more remarkable. He was so spare in his diet that he never ate wheaten bread, never touched wine, vinegar, oil, or vegetables, and never made use of salt to season his food. Christmas day and Easter Sunday he so far relaxed this rule as to allow himself one draught of wine, diluted so freely with water that it preserved but little of its flavour. Meat he never touched; what he did take was mere barley bread, which he had winnowed and ground himself. Severe as was this diet, it appears almost miraculous, when we are assured that he never ate at all but twice a week, on Wednesdays and Saturdays, and in the evening of those days.

His bed was even more uninviting. Four planks arranged lengthways contained a bed of ashes, which they kept together. By the continual pressure of the body they became hard, and presented a surface as rough as stone. On this he lay with his hair-cloth alone, and another coarse cloth for a coverlet. No pillow supported his head, his whole body lay flat on his uneasy couch. He rarely loosened his girdle or took off his shoes, neither did he ever part with a leathern belt which held to his chest a little box containing the relics of the Saints, namely, those of all the Apostles and of different martyrs. This, his only treasure, he valued above all earthly things. As we may imagine, his sleep was neither long nor uninterrupted. Often after the example of Our Lord, he would pass the whole night in prayer.

Well may the reader ask, did not his health

break down irretrievably under these unheard-of austerities? did he not render himself unfit for the discharge of his laborious duties? We know that he was of a sound, robust constitution, invigorated by sustained exertion in the open air; that he was about the medium height, and that when his tomb was opened many years after his death his head was discovered to be clothed with a luxuriant growth of long white hair. But this does not account for his being able to live for thirty years such a life as has just been described. He was leading the life of an angel, though clothed in a human body; he was dead to all the pleasures of the senses; and grace stepped in, and he was endowed with strength from above to triumph over the necessities and frailties of his mortal frame.

He at once applied himself to a diligent study of the Scriptures, and he became so imbued with their spirit and so versed in theological matters that he was looked upon as one of the doctors of the time. His reputation spread far beyond the limits of his diocese and Gaul, and his authority was reverenced in Italy and at the court of the Emperor in Ravenna. His was the age of the greatest doctors of the Church. The eloquence and learning of St. John Chrysostom had only just ceased to illumine the Church, for that great prelate died in A.D. 407. St. Jerome was still living at the time of Germanus' succession to the see of Auxerre, and from his retirement at Bethlehem he spread throughout all Christendom his love of the Sacred Scriptures; while his zeal for the purity of the Christian doctrine made him severe on every novelty of error, which was broached by the subtle and trained intellects of sophists and heretics. St. Jerome died in 420. But among a generation of great minds, that of St. Augustine, Bishop of Hippo in Numidia, towered like that of a giant, head and shoulders above his fellows. The writings of these great lights of the fifth century were spread throughout the Church. The scribes of Rome were kept busy in multiplying copies. The booksellers, whose shops adjoined the Forum, were unable to supply the demand. We are expressly told by St. Paulinus of Nola that the *Life of St. Martin* by Sulpicius Severus was so eagerly sought for as to produce a fortune to the copyists. Perhaps nowhere in the Church were the controversies then springing up debated with livelier interest than in Gaul. Italy was too much distracted with the invasion of barbarians carrying everywhere ruin and desolation, or with the endless and perplexing intrigues of a corrupt court, to have full leisure to give to theological matters.

The schools of Lerins were the great centre of intellectual activity in the early part of the fifth century. Here every point raised by the restless spirit of the age, every doctrine taught by the Church, and contested by heretics, every speculation started by the keen rhetoricians of Rome or Milan or Carthage, the maintainers of the old Pagan Philosophy, or the advocates of the new Christian Faith, were keenly scrutinised and discussed. We may be sure that each work of St. Augustine and St. Jerome was eagerly welcomed, and that their doctrinal and scriptural writings would be highly valued by teachers and their disciples.

Germanus had been well trained in the schools of Rome, and his mind had become acute and penetrating by the practice of the law, so he rapidly mastered the intricacies of theology. But what was of still greater assistance was the intense concentration of his mind on Divine truth and the power derived from his entire renunciation of earthly pursuits and aims. Besides, his bodily mortifications cleared away the clouds raised by the senses, and he gazed with undimmed eye on spiritual things. He began to be appealed to as an authority, and the greatest weight was attached to his opinions. " His own arguments," we are told, " were interspersed with revealed truth, and while he poured forth in torrents of eloquence the dictates of his conscience, he supported them always with the agreement of what he had read."

Meanwhile the administration of his diocese was his immediate care. He laboured incessantly in this himself. He was accessible to all. His house was open to every comer, and while he sat without taking a morsel, his board was abundantly spread for his numerous guests. But his zeal could not overtake the work before him, and he began to cast about for helpers in his task. To what place could his eyes so naturally turn as to Lerins, the great school of divines and bishops? He was familiarly known to St. Hilary, Bishop of Arles, and St. Lupus, who was soon to be elevated to the see of Troyes. Likely enough St. Patrick was recommended to him, in whom he soon found that he had a man after his own heart. He shared the zeal for souls, the courage in facing difficulties, the spirit of prayer and mortification of the holy St. Patrick. Nay, we may be sure that St. Germanus was not long in discovering his more wonderful gifts, and that he like himself held intercourse with Angelic spirits, and heard from God secret words, which it is not given to men to utter. In any case an intimate friendship was formed between the two men: for nearly fourteen years they were scarcely ever separated, and for thirty years, until St. Germanus' death in 448, St. Patrick looked up to him as his master in the spiritual life, and the most beloved of his friends. Each would have something to learn from the other. Germanus had all the culture of the time. His youth had been carefully trained in the best schools. His early manhood had been strengthened and refined by his practice at the bar, and his manners had been softened by intercourse with all that was intellectual and dignified in the land, while the period of his Dukedom had familiarised him with the rare art of ruling men. All these high qualities adorned him in his new station of Bishop, and elevated by the transforming power of divine grace, enabled him to exercise a sway over the minds of men which nothing could resist. And Patrick bowed before this all persuasive influence and became his fervent disciple. It is not difficult to imagine how his time was spent when under Germanus' roof. St. Fiace tells us he read the Canon with Germanus; another writer tells us that he was entrusted with the Ordo of the Church; it may be safely supposed that he was employed in the general work of the Diocese. He would learn the rules of ecclesiastical discipline observed at the time, and become familiar with the details of government of laymen, monks, and clerics. We may also remember that in the fifth century bishops held courts for the decision of secular causes. These courts were held in high estimation, partly from the high character deservedly borne by the judges, and partly from the assurance felt by the suitors, that their causes would be carefully examined into, and that a just sentence would be pronounced. As corruption prevailed in every branch of the imperial service, little confidence was felt in the administration of justice by a civil magistrate, and in important cases recourse was frequently had to the Bishop's Court. In the life of St. Augustine we read that he attached great importance to this portion of his duty. We have his own words for it that he sometimes gave whole days to the hearing of a case, and though he records his regret at having to give up so much time to secular matters, he considered himself bound by his Episcopal office to do so.

What was the case of St. Augustine at Hippo was that of St. Germanus at Auxerre. We may be sure that the court of St. Germanus would have the highest reputation throughout Gaul. His knowledge of the law, his absolute impartiality, his desire to do justice between the contending parties, and, his familiarity with the practice of the secular courts, made litigants anxious to have their causes heard by the tribunal over which he presided. When St. Patrick was again in Ireland his biographers tell us that he was a lawgiver as well as an apostle, and that his compilation of the Brehon laws was esteemed as of the highest authority throughout the island, and formed the standard to which for generations the Irish appealed in disputed cases. It was in the Bishop's Court at Auxerre that he acquired his knowledge of Roman law—sometimes he would listen to the decisions given by St. Germanus himself; and we cannot doubt that he would often act either as his assessor or his deputy. By ways unthought of by himself he was gradually led on to his great destiny, and formed for the execution of his task. He never lost sight of his mighty purpose, the purpose of his life. But he had learnt to wait; the Eternal Wisdom is patient in the execution of His plans, and He would have His servant wait until fully prepared, and until the hour fixed had arrived. From time to time circumstances would arise which would arouse a great yearning in St. Patrick's heart after the people he was to evangelise. When Constantine, the Briton, ruled the Western Empire from his city of Arles, he had amongst his troops a cohort recruited from various races, who owned not the Roman sovereignty, but who enlisted under its eagles for the sake of pay and booty. The cohort was honoured with the name of the Emperor of the West, and styled Honorius. Among them were two regiments of Scoti, or Irish. They were a brave if barbarous body of men, and they gave important aid in subjecting Spain to the dominion of Constantine. We can well imagine that the presence of troops from Ireland, or as it was then usually called Scotia, would familiarise the Roman government with this hitherto dreaded name, and associate more kindly sentiments with the word. It now appeared that if the Scoti had been fierce and restless enemies they could also be brave and faithful allies.

On the whole the years spent at Auxerre by our saint were happy years. In after-life he looked back upon them with fond recollections, and he assures us in his *Confession* that he often longed to re-visit his native country Britain, and Gaul, the land of his training in learning and religion. We may be sure that amongst the saints of Gaul of whom he speaks with such affection would be the friends he had made at Auxerre, and above all his beloved master St. Germanus. I may fitly conclude this chapter with the words of Probus: " He submitted himself in all things to the guidance of Germanus, living in patience, obedience, charity and chastity, in sanctity of heart and soul, preserving his virginity in the fear of the Lord, and living in goodness and simplicity during the whole period of his mortal career".

CHAPTER VII.

ST. PATRICK AND HIS AGE, 405-428.

PELAGIUS THE BRITON. CELESTIUS THE IRISHMAN. GREAT NUMBER OF CHRISTIANS. INTELLECTUAL ACTIVITY AMONG THE LEARNED. PELAGIUS HIGH IN THE ESTEEM OF ST. PAULINUS AND AUGUSTINE. IMBIBES THE DOCTRINES OF THEODORUS OF MOPSUESTIA. HIS REPUTE AMONG THE GREAT FAMILIES OF ROME. THE ANICII. DEMETRIAS. ALARIC TAKES ROME. DEMETRIAS AT CARTHAGE. ST. JEROME AT BETHLEHEM. SPREAD OF PELAGIANISM IN GAUL AND BRITAIN.

THERE was yet one more step to be taken in St. Patrick's thorough training as an ecclesiastic, and his preparation to become a nation's Apostle would be complete. He was to be associated with his saintly master, St. Germanus, in a contest with a specious and insidious heresy, which had laid fast hold on the minds of men: he was to take his share in a successful mission to put down a rising error, and he would then be a fit instrument for God's great design, to employ him to give the true Faith to Ireland. Perhaps

I may be pardoned if I give here as brief a sketch as may be of the condition of the religious world in the opening years of the fifth century.

By the conversion of Constantine, Christianity had become a great and acknowledged power in the whole Roman world. It was no longer obliged to practise its worship in secret, nor to hide in the catacombs. Its members were no longer the fervent few who clung to it in spite of persecution, and torture, and death. It became the religion of the State; the emperors were proud to proclaim themselves its disciples and its protectors. To profess Christianity was no longer a bar to distinction or preferment—it even became a recommendation. The generals of great armies, the leaders of the bar, the highest officials of the State were Christians. To be a Christian no longer meant renunciation of the world, or the pursuit of exalted virtue; for multitudes of people flocked into the fold of the Church, rich and poor, the inhabitants of cities and the country, learned and unlearned, good and bad, were now all members of the Church. We cannot wonder if so great an enlargement of its boundaries led to a relaxation of discipline, and also to an abundant growth of new ideas on points of faith. Many were Christians only in name, for it was not unusual for men to defer receiving baptism until a serious illness warned them of the danger of delay. The noble consular families brought their immense estates and almost unbounded wealth into the Church, and with them the habits of luxury and display ; while the leaders of intellectual thought, the rhetoricians and sophists of the day, when they became Christians, did not cease to exercise their busy, restless minds on all sorts of questions regarding divine and human things. They had been accustomed to the utmost freedom, nay, even licence, in their speculations ; nothing had been sacred in their eyes. They had valued themselves on taking nothing on trust, and plumed themselves on examining everything to the bottom. Yet out of these very men were often chosen the priests and bishops of the Church. On the other hand, those who had been brought up from infancy in the fold, for the most part were comparatively speaking untrained in the subtleties of philosophy, and inferior in rank and mental culture. We cannot then be surprised if at the commencement of the fifth century, whilst our saint was in the monastery at Tours, or the schools of Lerins, or the episcopal residence at Auxerre, novel opinions should be freely maintained in the great centres of intellectual activity, at Rome, or Constantinople, or Alexandria.

The Church had not defined her doctrine on many points in specific terms, and hence it was easy for a time, at least, to preach unsound doctrine without exciting attention or alarm. Often an erroneous doctrine had a specious appearance of truth: it seemed to be mainly advanced in opposition to an admittedly false doctrine; and thus it easily found advocates: and it depended on the skill, the boldness, and the good repute of its champions to make its way among the people. On the other hand, the Church often found its most able defenders amongst those very men who had been trained in the heathen schools. They had embraced the Faith with all their hearts; they had become little children in entering into her fold; and all their mental acquirements they devoted to elucidating her doctrines, and defending her decisions. Foremost among these were, in St. Patrick's time, St. Jerome in the East, and St. Augustine in Africa. Both had drunk deeply of classic lore; both had minds richly stored with all the learning of the times: and both placed at the service of the Church their accumulated treasures of knowledge. The Church still profits by their learned labours, and St. Jerome stands foremost as the translator and expositor of the Holy Scriptures; while St. Augustine is to this day honoured throughout all Christendom as the Doctor of divine grace. The names of both these great Doctors of the Church are inseparably linked with those of two wanderers from the British Isles, from Wales and Ireland, Pelagius and Celestius; and their heresy was, under God, the occasion of our saint's final mission to Ireland.

Of the early history of these two remarkable men we know but few details. The first-named, Pelagius, was a Briton; he was born about A.D. 370; his name was originally Morgan, meaning "born by the sea," of which his later name is a Greek translation. We are not informed whether or not he was of a Christian family, nor what it was which took him to Rome. It may have been with him as it was with his distinguished compatriot, St. Ninian, that he wished for a more thorough instruction in the Catholic faith than it was possible for him to get in Britain. The first we know for certain of him is that he was leading the life of a monk in the Eternal City, though not attached to any particular community. He never took orders to his dying day. He applied himself to the study of Greek, and he became so proficient in that language, that he was able some years later to converse and hold his own in argument with Greek bishops who knew no Latin. He also pursued with ardour the practices of a religious and an ascetic, and acquired a great reputation for holiness of life. St. Augustine, an unexceptionable witness, in his treatise *De Pecati Mercede*, speaks of him as an "eminently Christian man," and as "a Christian of no mean attainment in virtue". St. Paulinus of Nola became greatly attached to him, and looked upon him as a special servant of God. He had composed several works on theological subjects, such as on the Blessed Trinity, and on the Epistles of St. Paul, before he gained his unhappy notoriety for his errors on divine grace. He had the faculty of winning the confidence of youth, and he used his influence to lead them to the practice of a strict religious life.

Among his earliest disciples was a young Irishman, known to us as Celestius, but probably his name had been originally Nenn, meaning "heavenly," and he only followed a common custom in translating it into a Latin equivalent. We have already seen that even thus early the name of Scotus was becoming familiar to Roman ears. An Irishman was known even then as a bold adventurer and a brave soldier; but it was for Celestius to accustom the world to the idea that an Irishman, from the most remote known island in the western ocean, could be a subtle theologian and an acute reasoner. He was of noble birth in his own land, and with the adventurous spirit of his race he had crossed seas and continents until he found himself in the great capital of the world. At first he applied himself to the study of law; but becoming acquainted with Pelagius, he gave up the world, and devoted himself to a religious life. There was something in the character of the one which supplemented what was wanting in the other. Pelagius was grave and austere; Celestius confident and demonstrative. Pelagius sought to gain to his views by gentle persuasion and learned reasoning; Celestius, who was a tall, stout man, was often the spokesman of his friend in assemblies of bishops and clergy. Unfortunately for themselves and the Christian world, about the year 401 they made the acquaintance of Rufinus, a Syriac priest, a man trained under the influence of Theodorus, Bishop of Mopsuestia in Cilicia. The career of this remarkable man is a sad one. He was a fellow-townsman and school-fellow of St. John Chrysostom of Antioch. They became bosom friends, and were rivals only in the pursuit of learning and the practice of virtue. Theodorus gave himself with fervour to all exercises of a religious life. His days were spent in reading, his nights in prayer; he fasted much, he lay on the bare ground, he practised every form of ascetic self-discipline. But soon he was on the point of yielding to the fascination of a beautiful girl named Hermione, and it required all the entreaties and expostulations of his friend to prevail on him to be faithful to the life he had vowed. When later he became bishop, he laboured unceasingly for the conversion of the many heathens still dwelling in the city, and his eloquence in the pulpit was renowned far and wide. It is recorded that about the year 394, being at Constantinople, he preached before the Emperor Theodosius the Great: the sermon made so deep an impression on him that Theodosius declared "he had never met such a teacher". But his subtle intellect and his profound erudition did not save him from falling into serious errors against true doctrine. He allowed himself such a latitude in the interpretation of the Scriptures, and so much freedom in his philosophical speculations, that his writings have been deservedly branded as containing the germs of two heresies which have for centuries disturbed the peace of the Church, namely, Nestorianism and Pelagianism. He died, indeed, in the communion of the Church, retaining to the end of that saint's life the love and esteem of his early friend, St. John Chrysostom; but later ages are unanimous in condemning the tendency of the numerous works which he left behind him.

It was the ill-fortune of Pelagius and Celestius to suck in greedily the poison of his false doctrine about the power of unaided human nature to acquire salvation. From Rufinus they learned to call in question the transmission of Adam's sin to his posterity, and to deny the necessity of supernatural assistance from God to keep the commandments, and to avoid sin. They did not seek to set up a sect outside the Church, but they laboured assiduously and with only too much success to spread amongst the faithful the poison of their errors. At first their heresy did not attract any great amount of notice, but about the year 405 a bishop happened in the presence of Pelagius to quote with approbation the famous passage of St. Augustine's *Confessions:* "Da quod jubes, et jube quod vis". "Give what thou dost command, and command what thou wilt." Pelagius broke out in words full of indignation against what he held to be an intolerable disregard of the freedom of human action, making man a mere puppet in the hands of his Creator. This anecdote is told by St. Augustine himself in his book *De Dono Perseverantia*, c. 53. In the same year Pelagius wrote a letter to his friend, St. Paulinus, on nature and grace, and in it he dwelt almost entirely on the power and capacities of nature, referring only in the most cursory manner to divine grace, and that in such ambiguous terms that it was difficult to ascertain his precise meaning, and whether he really recognised a special influence of the Holy Spirit enlightening, vivifying, and strengthening the soul.

In truth, it was difficult for the orthodox writers of the time to put their finger on the exact teaching of these famous heresiarchs; and later on when confronted with bishops in Synod they often escaped condemnation by explaining away the obvious meaning of their words. This in great measure accounts for the long time that Pelagius continued to retain the esteem of such illustrious doctors of the Church as SS. Jerome and Augustine. One of his favourite modes of spreading his opinions was by letter-writing: of these he wrote immense numbers to persons scattered all over the Roman world, and even St. Jerome says of his early productions that they were "auriferus," full of gold. Another expedient was to insinuate himself into the favour of the great ladies of Rome, and whilst he impressed them with a deep sense of his exalted piety, he artfully taught them that their own virtues were the fruit of their natural powers, and that they stood not in need of any special grace from God.

One such household was that of the family of the Anicii, and this deserves a somewhat detailed description, as it well illustrates the secular and religious state of Rome before its siege and capture by Alaric, King of the Goths, in the year 410. The poet Claudian gives to the Anicii the first place amongst the illustrious families of the Roman nobility, and bids all others content themselves with ranking in the second grade. This occurs in a poem on the consulship of Probus and Olybius, the two sons of the house, "who in their earliest youth, at the request of the Senate, were associated in the consular dignity, a memorable distinction," remarks Gibbon, "without example in the annals of Rome". This name first appears in the year B.C. 249, when M. Anicius Gallus was tribune of the people; the family seems to have come to Rome from Præneste, and for the next seven hundred years, until the sacking of Rome by the Vandals under Genseric, it held a conspicuous and ever-improving position. One hundred and sixty-eight years before the Christian era, it was ennobled by the prætorship of Anicius, who gloriously terminated the Illyrian war by the conquest of the nation and the captivity of its king. Two consulships in the reigns of Nero and Caracalla marked the sustained eminence of the Anician line. The head of the family, early in the reign of Constantine, embraced Christianity, and he was the first of the Senate to do so. The family prosperity reached its height in Sextus Probus, who shared with the Emperor Gratian the honour of the Consulate, and exercised four times the high office of Prætorian Prefect. His immense estates were scattered all over the wide extent of the Roman world, and his generosity and magnificence won the gratitude of his clients, and the admiration of strangers. It is told by Paulinus in his life of St. Ambrose that two Persian satraps travelled to Milan and Rome to hear the eloquence of St. Ambrose, and to behold the grandeur of Probus.

The marbles of the Anician palace at Rome were used as a proverbial expression of opulence and splendour. Indeed, the residences of the highest nobles were extraordinary for their extent and magnificence. Gibbon says "that many of these stately mansions excuse the exaggeration of the poet, that Rome contained a multitude of palaces, and that each palace was equal to a city, since it included within its own precincts everything which could be subservient to use or luxury: markets, hippodromes, temples, fountains, baths, porticos, shady groves and artificial aviaries". To support such an establishment required immense revenues; but we are assured by Olympiodorus, the historian, in his account of the city at the time of its siege by the Goths, that several of the richest senators received from their estates an annual income of four thousand pounds' weight of gold, above £160,000 sterling, without computing the stated provision of corn and wine, which, had they been sold, might have equalled in value one-third more.

The accounts of the luxury of the great Roman ladies almost surpass belief. We read of a pagan matron of a senatorial family with her five hundred miserable slaves, all devoted to her personal service, and to the care of her ape, her parrot, or her lapdog; with earrings valued at £100,000; her dwarfs pressed out of human shape for the gratification of her morbid caprice; her pet philosopher as degraded in mind as was the poor stunted dwarf in body; and her fierce, unwomanly delight in the circus and gladiatorial shows. Even in the Christian household of Paula, though distinguished by spotless propriety in the midst of the prevalent corruption, and adorned by a tender charity and a deep humility unknown and unimagined by the most virtuous women of pagan Rome, there was a lavish display of magnificence. We learn from St. Jerome that like other patrician ladies she was carried by her slaves in a gilded litter through the streets of

Rome; that she feared to set her foot to the ground, lest it should be soiled with dust; that her silken robes were a weight almost too heavy for her slight form; and that she shrunk from the sunbeams that penetrated the thick curtains of her litter. She herself, in after days, reproached herself for the use of rouge, so common amongst women of her rank, and for the many hours wasted in the indulgence of the bath. What a change the advice, the example, the irresistible force of St. Jerome's influence wrought in that great house, is known to every reader of Church history of those times: how, from an abode of luxury and display, it became a house of prayer, of humility, of labour, and even austerity.

The palace of the Anicii was in no way inferior in its gorgeous splendour to that of Paula, and it, too, became under Christian teaching a home of every virtue. It pleased God to send upon it many afflictions. The wife of Probus became a widow; soon her son, Olybius, followed his father, and her daughter-in-law, Juliana, shared her widowhood. But one daughter, Demetrias, was left as the hope of the family, and it was in this household that Pelagius became a visitor and an adviser. But private misfortunes were not the only ones which tried the courage and endurance of this noble house. Public calamities fell thick upon the empire of Rome. The Emperor Honorius in his ignoble retreat at Ravenna by his feeble and uncertain rule provoked alike the ambition and vengeance of Alaric, the brave and skilful King of the Goths. In the year 408 Alaric overran Italy, and laid siege to the imperial city. For months he blockaded every approach by land or river, and by preventing the introduction of provisions into the city, he reduced its inhabitants to all the extremities of famine. For a time, indeed, the huge supplies accumulated by the foresight of a highly-organised municipal government gave hope to the Romans; but as months went on, first public, then private resources were exhausted. The rich who during the early months of the siege had liberally supplied the necessities of their poorer neighbours began to be in want themselves. They found that their costly palaces and rich furniture were of no avail, when they could not procure a loaf of bread. We read in particular of the unbounded charity of Laeta, the widow of the Emperor Gratian, but the Anician family, no doubt, had its full share in the good deeds and the sufferings of that terrible year. An ignominious peace secured only a brief respite for the unfortunate capital, and again in 409 Alaric threatened it with a siege. On this occasion, however, he was content with taking possession of the Port of Ostia, at the mouth of the Tiber, and so cutting off the great source of the supplies on which the population of Rome depended: and the fear of famine was sufficient to compel the Senate to submit to the terms of the conqueror, and receive an emperor at his hands.

Alaric withdrew his forces, but in the following year, 410, he again appeared in force before the walls of the city. The Senate this time made some show of courage, and prepared for a stout resistance, but they could not rely upon the fidelity of the motley population of the city, gathered from all the nations and peoples of the earth. At the dead of night the Salarian Gate, the most northern gate of Rome, was treacherously thrown open, and the hordes of barbarians from Germany and Scythia poured into the devoted city. The blast of the Gothic trumpet proclaimed to the bewildered and affrighted Romans that the glory of the imperial city lay at the mercy of an infuriated enemy. Through the streets rushed the exulting throng of warriors athirst for plunder and vengeance. The greatest gathering of the riches of the earth ever got together was to be had for the mere stretching out of the hand, and so they poured on. The palaces of the nobles were the special objects of their search, so woe was it to the sumptuous mansion of the Anicii.

St. Jerome in a letter written a few years after the event thus addresses Demetrias: "A while since thou didst tremble amidst barbarian hands, and didst hide thyself in the bosom and robe of thy grandmother and mother. Thou didst see thyself a captive, and thine honour not thine own. Thou didst shudder at the savage faces of the foe; didst see with silent groan God's virgins carried off. Thy city, once the head of the world, is the Roman people's grave." The unfortunate ladies, however, contrived to escape from the hands of their captors, and they took ship for Africa. From the deck of their vessel they could see the flames, which consumed the glories of Rome, redden the eastern sky. I need not tell how they found a refuge with St. Augustine; how Demetrias learned to despise the world, and aspire to a higher life. St. Jerome again thus described her life: "An incredible fortitude, amid jewels and silk, troops of slaves and waiting-women, the obsequiousness and attentions of a thronging household, and the refined dainties of a lordly establishment, to have longed for painful fastings, coarse garments, spare diet. . . . A trouble came upon that recruit of Christ, and like Esther a hatred of her apparel. They saw, who saw her and knew her . . . that at nights when no one knew, except the virgins in her mother's and grandmother's company, she was never clad in linen, never reposed on soft down, but on the bare earth, with her tiny haircloth for bedding, and her face bedewed with continued tears." The instructions and influence of St. Augustine finished the good work, and she resolved on solemnly consecrating her virginity to God. So secret was her wish, that her parents had arranged for her an honourable marriage. She must take a decisive step. Again I use St. Jerome's words : " She cast from her the ornaments of her person and secular dress, as if they were encumbrances to her resolve. Costly necklaces, precious pearls, brilliant jewels, she replaces in her cabinet. She puts on a common tunic and a more common cloak. Without notice she suddenly throws herself at her grandmother's knees, showing who she was only by weeping and lamentation. That holy and venerable lady was aghast, seeing the altered dress of her grandchild, while the mother stood astounded with delight. What they wished they could not believe ; their cheeks flushed and paled, they feared, they rejoiced, their thronging thoughts went to and fro. Grandchild and grandmother, and daughter and mother rush tumultuously on each other's lips. They weep abundantly for joy, they raise the sinking maid with their hands, they clasp her trembling form. They acknowledge in her resolve their own mind, and they express their joy that the virgin was making a noble family more noble by her virginity."

When St. Jerome wrote this letter he was eighty-three years old and in a far-off land at Bethlehem. But age had not chilled his exuberant feeling, and he bursts out: "All the churches throughout Africa almost danced for joy; not cities alone, towns, villages, even cottages were pervaded with the manifold fame of it. All the islands between Africa and Italy were filled with this news; it tripped not in its course, and the rejoicing ran forward. Then Italy put off her mourning garb, and the shattered walls of Rome in part recovered their pristine splendour, thinking that God was propitious to themselves in the perfect conversion of their nursling. The report penetrated to the shores of the East, and even in the inland cities the triumph of Christian glory was heard." St. Jerome then, mindful of his responsibility as an experienced director of souls, gives her grave and sobering advice, and, as if forewarned of the temptations to come, he bids her, "to humble herself under the mighty hand of God, and ever remember what is written: 'God resisteth the proud, and gives His grace to the humble'. Now where grace is in question there is not recompensing of works, but bounty of a giver, according to the apostle's saying: 'Not of him that willeth, nor of him that runneth, but of God that showeth mercy'. And yet to will and not to will is ours; yet not ours what is even ours, without God's showing mercy."

Pelagius had followed these noble ladies to Africa; his character was still unblemished, and even St. Augustine spoke of him in terms of great respect. What wonder then if he retained his influence in the house of Proba and Juliana, and if the latter appealed to him to write a letter of advice to her daughter, the now consecrated virgin Demetrias. Pelagius wrote accordingly, and his letter is still extant, having come down amongst the writings of St. Augustine. In it he gives her much good advice, but the poison of his errors on grace is easily detected, and he plainly implies that her virtues are her own: " Your personal nobility and opulence belong to your friends, not to you; but spiritual riches none but yourself can provide for you. In that is your right praise, your deserved preference, which cannot be except of thee, and in thee." So that St. Augustine indignantly exclaims: " Forbid it that a virgin of Christ should take pleasure in such words". The temptation was specious; it came from the pen of one who was highly esteemed in the Church. But it fell harmless: that inexperienced maiden was guarded by the watchful eye of the great Apostle of Divine Grace; and from him she learned that she must not admit the thought that she had anything which could give a title to glory in herself and not in the Lord. She persevered to the end of a long life, a submissive child of the Church, her life ever marked by generous benefactions to the poor and the Church. I have preferred to trace the career of Pelagius, and his constant disciple Celestius, by exhibiting it in the instance of this family, illustrious for its rank and its riches, but far more so for its virtues. Of Pelagius himself I need say little more. On leaving Africa he went to the Holy Land, and encountered the great St. Jerome himself. That vigorous writer, in his prologue to the third book of his Commentaries on Jeremias, thus indignantly describes the master and disciple: "The devil has not allowed me, content with a longed-for peace, to give my time to the explanation of the Scriptures, and to teaching to men of my own tongue the learning of the Hebrews and Greeks. But he labours day and night, openly and craftily, mixing up truth and falsehood, and deceitfully covering up lies with honey; so that he who hears the sweet words does not fear the fatal poison. He promises peace that he may wage the deadlier war. He laughs to be able to bite. He offers his hand that unexpectedly he may slay the unsuspecting Abner. . . . Here he is silent, in other places he makes injurious charges. He sends throughout the whole world letters like books, once good as gold, now accursed. He construes our patience, springing from the humility of Christ, to be a sign of a bad conscience. He himself remains dumb, but he barks through an Alpine dog, big and fat, who shows his rage rather with his heels than his teeth. For he is sprung from an Irish stock, from the neighbourhood of Britain, who, as the fables of the poets have it, like Cerberus, must be struck with a spiritual club, so that with his master Pluto he may keep eternal silence." Though neither Pelagius nor Celestius is named in the passage, they are plainly indicated and graphically portrayed. In a few well-chosen words he both compares and contrasts them.

It is evident from these words of St. Jerome that he, too, had experienced the fascination which Pelagius was wont to exert on almost all with whom he came in contact. The charm of his manner seems to have won all hearts; to see him was to be pleased; to hear him converse was to be convinced. The reserve and austerity of his behaviour inspired reverence, instead of repelling; and a feeling of entire trust and confidence in his goodness and rectitude took possession of the minds of his hearers. His thoughts seemed both subtle and profound; his learning was minute and extensive; and at first sight even St. Jerome took him for a great servant of God, and a deeply-learned theologian. He had that entire confidence in himself, that he never seemed to be in the wrong; and it was easy for others to share the same undisturbed trust in him. And when, under all these specious appearances, St. Jerome found that his whole doctrine on the necessity of divine grace was absolutely opposed to the teaching of the Church and the plain meaning of St. Paul's words, his indignation knew no bounds, and he broke out into the burning words just quoted. But the mind of Pelagius was set on maintaining his error, and spreading it by every means at his command; St. Jerome tried argument and failed; Pelagius remained unconvinced, and strove all the more assiduously to win disciples to his way of thinking. Even when he remained silent, his friend Celestius was loud in proclaiming his false opinions, and St. Jerome found himself compelled to leave the study of his beloved Scriptures to devote himself to the defence of the true Faith.

Meanwhile, the errors of Pelagius became widely disseminated throughout the Church. In Gaul, indeed, they obtained but little hold, thanks to the zeal and fidelity of the scholars of Lerins. There were some unfortunate exceptions; and one reputation otherwise brilliant in the Church was tarnished by some leaning to false doctrine. The famous John Cassian, founder of the Abbey of St. Victor at Marseilles, though he denounced the twin heresies of Pelagianism and Nestorianism, allowed himself to maintain some errors about Predestination connected with Pelagianism, which were condemned after his death. The most famous of the defenders of the orthodox doctrine, in the south of France, was St. Prosper, of Aquitaine, who, for many years, resided at Marseilles. He was quite a young man at the time, but he invoked the powerful aid of St. Augustine, then at the very height of his fame, though fast nearing his end; and that unwearied champion of the Faith replied in two books which have come down to us, *De Prædestinatione Sanctorum* and *De Dono Perseverantiæ*. But in Britain the case was far otherwise. We are not told whether Pelagius kept up any intercourse with his countrymen, nor whether any of his innumerable letters were addressed to friends or acquaintances in the island:

but his teaching was eagerly accepted in Britain, and spread from sea to sea. We may readily imagine that the Britons were proud of their able and accomplished fellow-countryman; that they heard with pleasure of his being on the most intimate terms with men of the highest attainments in religion and philosophy, and with families of the highest class. It was a constant theme of conversation among them, how an unfriended Briton, a simple monk without any ecclesiastical rank, by the sheer force of his own genius, his untiring industry and his indomitable energy, was acknowledged as one of the foremost thinkers and writers of the day. No wonder that they did not suspect that deadly error lurked under these fair appearances, and allowed national partiality to blind them to the dangers to faith and sound doctrine. Severianus, one of their Bishops, though we are not told of what See, is called by St. Prosper a Pelagian Bishop. He had a son named Agricola, and he is especially mentioned as having been active and successful in spreading the new opinions. The body of the Bishops remained faithful to the teaching of the universal Church, and beheld with dismay the spread of heretical doctrines amongst their flocks. All their efforts to stem the tide of error were unavailing, and in their extremity they requested the Bishops of Gaul to send them a man able and willing to refute the new heresy. As we shall see in our next chapter, this led to the mission to Britain of St. Germanus, the Bishop of Auxerre, accompanied by St. Patrick, as an important member of his suite.

CHAPTER VIII.

ST. PATRICK WITH ST. GERMANUS IN BRITAIN.

A.D. 429—430.

ST. PATRICK IN ARMORICA. THE EMPERORS HONORIUS AND VALENTINIAN. ST. CELESTINE POPE. ST. LUPUS, BISHOP OF TROYES. ST. GERMANUS SETS OUT FOR BRITAIN. MEETS ST. GENEVIEVE AT NANTERRE. STATE OF BRITAIN. GERMANUS AT THE SYNOD. AT ST. ALBAN'S. AT MOLD. THE ALLELUIA VICTORY. ST. PATRICK AT MANCUNIUM AND PATRICROFT.

It was about the year 418 that St. Patrick placed himself under the direction of St. Germanus at Auxerre. The great influence throughout Gaul which that distinguished man possessed prepares us to find that his zeal for souls was not confined to his own diocese. As former Duke or Governor of Gallia Lugdunensis his civil jurisdiction had extended from Lyons to the shores of the English Channel and the Atlantic. His reputation as a vigorous and able ruler survived his relinquishment of his rank and authority as Duke; and his aid as Bishop was eagerly sought by those who had felt the benefit of his civil rule. The Morini, a people dwelling on the sea-coast about Boulogne and Dunquerque, invoked his assistance. At the end of the fourth century Rouen had been blessed with a holy and active Bishop, St. Victricius. He was probably a Briton by birth, and had been a soldier in his youth, and his abandoning the military career had brought upon him much obloquy and suffering. He became the friend of St. Martin of Tours and St. Paulinus of Nola, and was raised to the Episcopate about A.D. 390. The Church of Rouen had been founded about the year A.D. 260 by Pope St. Stephen, who appointed as its first Bishop St. Mellon, a native of Cardiff in Glamorganshire. This Saint had journeyed to Rome on some business connected with the annual tribute paid to Rome by Britain; he had come under the influence of that saintly Pontiff and was baptised by him. Eventually he was raised to the priesthood, and finally sent into Gaul to found an episcopal see at Rouen. St. Victricius was the eighth Bishop, and under his vigorous administration the Church of Rouen flourished exceedingly. His reputation for learning and sound doctrine became so great that, in 394, he was summoned to Britain by the Bishops of that nation to assist them in appeasing the dissensions which even then prevailed in the island.

In his own city he obtained relics for the churches, instituted musical services, and trained widows and virgins in such perfection that Rouen, previously almost unknown, was spoken of in distant lands with reverence, and counted among cities famous for their sacred places. He died about 409. In the same year the Armoricans declared their independence of the Roman Empire; and the district soon fell into disorder in religious and civil matters. In these straits the inhabitants applied to St. Germanus for his help. That Saint had already discovered the abilities and zeal of St. Patrick, and he sent him to the sea-coast of North-Western Gaul.

The Rev. T. O'Hanlon, in his *Lives of the Irish Saints*, under the heading of St. Patrick, p. 519, quotes Malbranche, *De Morinis*, for the statement that St Germanus sent St. Patrick to preach to the Morini after the death of St. Victricius. He adds that Probus says that St. Patrick preached the Gospel and administered Baptism in Normandy; and that some popular traditions and even old chronicles record that he laboured in Boulogne and the adjacent territory. Perhaps the faint traces left of this apostolic journey, and the dim remembrance of St. Patrick's labours in what soon afterwards became known as Normandy, have contributed to the notion that he was connected with the district by birth. From this time forward he became a marked man. He had laboured with such untiring energy, and his mission had been crowned with such complete success, that men began to talk of him as destined to become a Bishop. The passage in St. Patrick's *Confession* is extremely obscure, but it seems to refer to the time succeeding his return from the Morini. " And I learned from certain brethren that before this defence, when I was not present, nor even in Britain, nor giving any occasion for it, he defended me in my absence. He had even said to me with his own lips, ' Thou art going to be given the rank of a Bishop,' though I was not worthy of it." (*Conf.* 595.) He alludes to a friend of his to whom he had made a confidence some thirty years before, and whom he describes as "his dearest friend, to whom he would have trusted even his life," and of whom we shall have occasion again to speak, when the question of his elevation to the Episcopate was seriously mooted.

We may now turn to the condition of Britain and Gaul in their political aspect. The wretched and effeminate rule of Honorius came to an end in 423. He had been a mere cypher in the government of the Empire of the West. Edicts had been made in his name, but others had dictated the policy of the empire, and directed the movements of the forces which contended with the swarms of barbarians, who from East and West were sapping the very foundation of the Roman power. The death of Alaric in 411 relieved Italy of a formidable enemy; but Ataulphus, his wife's brother, established himself in the south of Gaul, and he became sufficiently powerful to demand in marriage Placidia, the sister of Honorius, and to receive her as his bride. At this time the banks of the Rhine ever furnished new hordes of Franks and Burgundians to disturb the repose of Eastern and Northern Gaul. Honorius was followed by a successor, if not so contemptible as, yet still more detestable than, himself. Valentinian III. was but a baby when he ascended the throne: but as he advanced in years he became a monster of cruelty, treachery, and debauchery: he slew with his own hand Ætius, a brave soldier and a skilful ruler, who for many years by his energy and ability had maintained the honour of the Roman name; and he died by the sword of a patrician of Rome whose wife he had grossly outraged.

If we turn away in disgust from this shameful picture of imperial weakness and imperial wickedness we shall find in the bright examples of many holy Bishops a most refreshing contrast.

Amid the crumbling ruins of the old civilisation a poet like Claudian might revive in a measure the glories of classic literature, or generals like Stilicho or Ætius might almost rival the deeds of a Scipio or a Pompey; but for the true glories of the early part of the fifth century we must read the lives of the saintly Bishops of Italy and Gaul. Foremost amongst these towards the close of Honorius's reign was Pope Celestinus. He was of Roman birth, and was elected to the Chair of St. Peter in 422. In early life he had visited Milan and heard the great St. Ambrose preach. He had been deacon to Pope Innocent, and in his name had corresponded with St. Augustine of Hippo. His election was popular at Rome, and there was neither delay nor opposition to his succession. He found the Church greatly disturbed with disputes about the doctrine of Divine grace, in consequence of the teaching of Pelagius, and of Cœlestius, his principal supporter; the new Pope at once declared himself adverse to their doctrines, and he constrained Cœlestius to leave Italy and seek a refuge at Constantinople. But the new heresies had acquired too much influence to be easily put down, and during the whole of his reign, lasting eleven years, till 433, it required all the vigilance and energy of Celestine to guard the

Church from this dangerous error. One of his leading counsellors was Palladius, whom he had made deacon of Rome. Palladius was a man of great ability and zeal, and he appears to have taken special interest in the affairs of the Western Church. Gaul, Britain, and later on Ireland, were the chosen objects of his watchfulness and care. Pelagianism had made such progress in Britain by the year 429 that the British Episcopacy lost all confidence in their power to put it down; still they could not abandon the attempt without an effort, and they resolved on inviting their brother Bishops of Gaul to send them some able and zealous missionaries to refute the false teachers and confirm the shaken faith of the people. The news of this step was carried to Rome; the deacon Palladius took up the matter warmly, and St. Prosper (who somewhat later on was the Pope's secretary) tells us: "The Pope, through the action of Palladius the deacon, sent Germanus, Bishop of Auxerre, in his own stead to root out heresy and direct the Britons to the Catholic faith".

Of the accomplishments and virtues of St. Germanus I have already said enough. He stood foremost among the Prelates of Gaul. In spite of his years and many labours he accepted, without hesitation, the task imposed upon him by his fellow Bishops and by the Holy See, and set himself with characteristic ardour to seek such help as would ensure success. He chose as his colleague the Bishop of a neighbouring diocese, St. Lupus of Troyes. The career of the last-named deserves a brief mention. He was of a noble family of Southern Gaul, and when arrived at man's estate he was married to the sister of St. Hilary, Archbishop of Arles. After seven years of wedlock, with the consent of his wife, he separated from her to devote himself to a religious life. He followed Hilary to Lerins, then flourishing under the care of the founder, Honoratus; and was there joined by his brother, the great writer and controversialist, St. Vincent. Here he remained a year, and left Lerins to embrace the monastic state. Probably enough it would be at Lerins that he would first make the acquaintance of St. Patrick. In 426 he was, much against his will, prevailed upon to accept the Bishopric of Troyes. At a Synod, held at Troyes, he was recommended by the assembled Bishops as a fitting person to share St. Germanus's expedition to Britain, and he was at once accepted.

Amongst his own clergy St. Germanus had ready to his hand St. Patrick. He had known him intimately for eleven years, and had conceived the highest esteem for him; and, more than this, he had formed with him a solid friendship which was to last till his death. Naturally, the fact of St. Patrick's having been born in Britain would have its weight in the choice. To many of the Gaulish Bishops the language of the country people was familiar, and they thus possessed a fair knowledge of Celtic, a form of which was used in Britain. As for St. Patrick, we may reasonably suppose, in spite of his long absence from his native country, that he still retained a fair recollection of the language of his childhood. He must have heard with deep emotion that he had been selected by his beloved master to accompany him to Britain. It was his own country, it was endeared to him by the memories of his youth, and the graves of his father and mother were by the side of the swiftly flowing Clyde. Thirty-five years of his life had been spent in preparing to preach the Gospel to the heathen, the inhabitants of Hibernia or Scotia; and now he found himself by the act of his superiors brought one step nearer to his long cherished desire.

It is not necessary for me to record all the incidents of the journey of his apostolic company. But one deserves notice. As they made their way down the Seine they came to Nanterre, four miles from Paris, and here occurred a notable event. I cannot do better than describe it in the words of Alban Butler (vol. i., p. 17):—

"The inhabitants flocked about them to receive their blessing, and St. Germanus made them an exhortation, during which he took particular notice of Genevieve, though only seven years of age. After his discourse he inquired for her parents, and addressing himself to them, foretold their daughter's future sanctity, and said that she would perfectly accomplish the resolution she had taken of serving God, and that others would imitate her example. He then asked Genevieve whether it was not her desire to serve God in a state of perpetual virginity, and to bear no other title than that of a spouse of Jesus Christ. The virgin answered that this was what she had long desired, and begged that by his blessing she might be from that moment consecrated to God. The holy Prelate went to the church of the place, followed by the people, and during long singing of psalms and prayers (says Constantius), that is, during the recital of None and Vespers (as the author of the *Life of St. Genevieve* expresses it), he held his hand on the virgin's head. After he had supped he dismissed her, giving a strict charge to her parents to bring her again to him very early the next morning. The father complied with the commission, and St. Germanus asked Genevieve whether she remembered the promise she had made to God. She said she did, and declared she would, by the Divine assistance, faithfully perform it. The Bishop gave her a brass medal, on which a cross was engraved, to wear always about her neck, to put her in mind of the consecration she had made of herself to God; and at the same time he charged her never to wear bracelets or necklaces of pearls, gold, or silver, or any other ornaments of vanity. All this she most religiously observed, and considering herself as the spouse of Christ, gave herself up to the most fervent practices of devotion and penance."

The extract is long, but it furnishes us with a beautiful instance of the spirit of the times, of the high esteem in which holy virginity was held, and of the power often possessed by Saints of penetrating into the secrets of holy souls. Besides, St. Patrick was afterwards to become the trainer of almost countless virgins, who under his guidance and stimulated by his exhortations dedicated themselves entirely to God's service. And it may be that the action of St. Germanus towards the little Genevieve was to him a model and an encouragement. He had been an interested spectator of the scene, and had noted the bright face of the saintly child looking up into the eyes of the venerable Bishop with unbounded trust; and it was to him an experience which in after years was to bear abundant fruit in his own training of the great Saint Bridget.

A few words will describe the state of Britain, to which the steps of this holy company were directed. In the year 410 the formal connection of the island and the Imperial Government was severed. The Emperor Honorius addressed letters in that year to the cities of Britain, bidding them provide for their own security; and in the year before, the last of the Roman legions had quitted our island to join the fortunes of Constantine, whom they had elected Emperor. However the Britons might for the moment rejoice at their recovered liberty and independence, they soon found that it was a perilous boon. Dangers from without, from the sea-rovers, the Saxons, and from the ever restless and savage tribes of Caledonia, the Picts, pressed upon them: and there seems to have been no spirit of union or organisation to oppose them. A rivalry sprung up between the towns where the old Roman municipal institutions still prevailed, and the chiefs, who on all sides rose up to press their own claims as the representatives of the natives of the soil. The result was inevitable; and Britain, unable to offer any effectual resistance to the barbarous races which swarmed from north and south, was gradually and surely occupied by a conquering race. It is not difficult to guess what were the results of such a state of things in the religious condition of the island. Christianity had slowly followed the steps of the Romans. Before the time of Constantine religion had made much progress, and after his time the country gradually assumed a Christian character. Wherever Roman troops were established there would be sure to be Christian soldiers, and priests were found to minister to their wants. Places of worship, sometimes of a very humble character, and built for the most part of wood, were to be seen in the neighbourhood of the camps. The faith slowly penetrated among the native Britons, and many of their chiefs became faithful and zealous followers of the Cross. We have on record the names of three episcopal Sees, York, London, and a third, supposed by Lingard to have been at Lincoln. The Bishops of these Sees were present at the Council of Arles, held in 314, but they were representatives of a much larger number. The poverty of these Bishops was so marked at the Council that supplies were granted to them from the Imperial treasury. At the time of St. Germanus's visit the British Episcopate did not contain one man of sufficient mark for his name to have been handed down to us; and their application to the Gaulish Bishops, to St. Victricius in 394, and to St. Germanus in 429, to compose differences and oppose heresy, shows what a modest opinion they had of their ability and learning. Severianus, a Gaulish Bishop, and his son Agricola had been driven from the Continent by the decrees of Valentinian III. against the professors of Pelagianism; and they had sought a more hopeful field for spreading their errors in Britain, and so successful had been their efforts that the appeal to the Synod of Troyes in 429 seemed the only means of stopping the evil.

It was not that Britain at this time was altogether destitute of schools of learning. Faustus, afterwards Abbot of Lerins and Bishop of Riez, is an instance of this. Tillemont is of opinion that he was a native of Britain; for he is styled a Briton, and the modern Bretagne did not get its name till towards the close of the fifth century. Of him we read that his mother was a woman of remarkable character, impressing all who came in contact with her with a deep sense of her piety and her real worth. Her son studied Greek philosophy, though in a Christian spirit. He became a proficient in rhetoric, and is said to have pleaded at the bar. About 426 he retired from the world and entered the monastery of Lerins, then presided over by St. Maximus. There he became a thorough ascetic, and a great student of Holy Scripture. But his leaving Britain before the arrival of St. Germanus prevented his taking a part in the controversy against the Pelagian teachers. There was also at this period in the far north-west of Britain a great and shining light, St. Ninian, Bishop of Witherne, in Galloway. For upwards of thirty years he had laboured unceasingly and with conspicuous success in preaching the Gospel, first to the scattered Christians in what is now Cumberland and the south-western counties of Scotland, and later on to the southern Picts who had settled to the south of the Antonine Wall after the Roman garrison had been withdrawn. He is deservedly reckoned as the Apostle of the Picts; though after his death some of the converts returned to their ancient superstition, and are with justice styled by St. Patrick at a later period, "the apostate Picts". But two centuries after his death we still find the fruits of his labours in the Christianity and religious establishments on the banks of the Forth, and the Monastery of St. Serf was the guardian and trainer of the great St. Kentigern, first Bishop of Glasgow. But in 429 there was little communication between the people of South Britain and their far-off neighbours living near the Roman Walls of Antonine and Hadrian: and St. Ninian took no part in the missionary journey of St. Germanus. Indeed he was fast nearing his end, and died full of virtues and honours the following year. He had built churches, founded religious communities, kept fresh in the hearts of the scattered Faithful the truths of religion, and converted multitudes of the wild and all but savage Picts to the practice of Christian virtues. The thought of St. Ninian must have occurred often to the mind of St. Patrick when he landed on British soil, and he must have longed to see again the great Saint and missionary whom he had seen at Marmoutier just before the death of his uncle, St. Martin. But it was not to be, and the Apostle of the Picts and the future Apostle of Ireland never met again in this life.

It seems probable that, on leaving Nanterre, which is lower down on the Seine than Paris, St. Germanus and his party would pass through the forest, now known as the Forest of St. Germain, on their road to Rouen, where St. Victricius had been Bishop, and thence proceed to Havre at the mouth of the Seine. Here the Channel is about 120 miles across. When the travellers reached the coast, winter had already set in, and their voyage across the Channel was a dangerous one; and Constantius, the biographer of the Saint, gives us a lively description of the passage. At first, indeed, they had a fair wind and smooth sea, but a change took place in the weather when they had lost sight of the Gallic coast, and Constantius tells us of the gathering storm, the rising gale, the darkening clouds, and the swelling foam-capped waves. The passengers cowered with fear, and even the sailors, overcome by the violence of the tempest, abandoned their labours in despair. The ship was out of sight of land, it lay powerless in the trough of the sea, and all hope seemed at an end. St. Germanus, during all this crash of the elements, was sleeping peacefully. Worn out by previous fatigue he had laid himself down to rest, and a deep sleep had settled upon his exhausted frame. His companions and the crew turned to him as their only chance of escape from immediate death. He arose calm and undismayed. He called upon the name of Christ and bade the sea be still, and taking some oil he sprinkled some drops upon the raging waves, invoking the most Blessed Trinity. His prayer was heard, the fury of the storm began to subside, a favourable change in the direction of the wind took place, and the ship pursued in safety its voyage to the British coast.

It was not the first time that St. Patrick had been at sea. In early life he had crossed the Irish Sea in one of the small rude boats used by the pirates of Ulster; his return voyage to his own country near Dumbarton had been a stormy one, and in all probability ended in the destruction and abandonment of the vessel on the shores of Morecambe Bay. Again, he had had a painful experience of the perils of the ocean when he travelled from Dumbarton to Bordeaux, encountering on his way the gales and storms of the Bay of Biscay. But perhaps he had never been in more imminent peril than in his voyage across the British Channel, and never had he seen more visibly the Divine protection extended to the servants of Heaven.

On arriving in Britain they received a most hearty welcome. Their progress inland was marked by an almost enthusiastic greeting. The country people, on hearing of the approach of the illustrious visitors, left their rude ploughs and clumsy mattocks and crowded the roads by which they were to pass. And many a time did the kindly Germanus bid his followers stop, and go himself into the fields to address the assembled rustics, who greedily drank in the words which fell from his lips.

It is not necessary for me here to describe

at length the great Synod of Bishops, clergy, and people in which St. Germanus confuted the Pelagians, but I may call attention to the closing incident. At the end of the sitting a person of high military rank (he is called a Tribune by Constantius, though at that time there were no Roman troops in Britain) presented to the Bishops his little daughter, who was blind, begging they would implore the Divine mercy in her behalf. St. Germanus referred the case to his adversaries, but they shrank from the ordeal and even joined their entreaty to that of the afflicted father, begging the Saint to do what he could for the blind girl. On this he uttered a fervent prayer to the Blessed Trinity, and taking from his breast the little box of relics he always carried about with him, he applied it to the eyes of the child. Her sight was immediately given to her. It was impossible to give to the awe-stricken crowd a more convincing proof on which side lay the truth of God than by this miracle.

The direct purpose of the mission was now mainly accomplished, and the heresy of the Pelagians effectually confuted. But St. Germanus had his own private devotion to satisfy, and he lost no time in setting about it. One of the feelings which most occupied his soul was a profound veneration and an intense love for God's holy martyrs. He never parted with the box which contained their relics; night and day it always rested on his breast. Now Britain contained one shrine whose fame had gone through Christendom, and at Verulam rested the body of St. Alban. To this spot of all Britain St. Germanus now directed his steps. The courage, the fortitude, the triumph of the martyr of Christ had made holy the spot on which his blood had been shed; and St. Germanus longed to tread that sacred ground. The people were summoned to the grave of the Saint, a solemn service was performed, and the Bishop ordered the tomb to be opened. He reverently placed within it some of the relics he had brought with him, and took up from the place where the blood of the martyr had been shed some earth still bearing a red stain. This precious treasure he carried back to Auxerre with him, and placed in a new church which he built there in honour of St. Alban.

The winter was now far advanced, but the holy company did not return to Gaul, and we next find them in North Wales, at the little town of Mold, in Flintshire, not far from the river Allen, an affluent of the Dee. We can readily imagine that the Pelagian heresy had laid a strong hold on the minds of the people there. Pelagius had sprung from that neighbourhood, and his countrymen were proud of the fame he had acquired. Besides, his exaggeration of the power of the will, unaided by Divine grace, to win salvation, fell in with the old teaching of the Druids, and the half-instructed Britons eagerly embraced his doctrines. It is not, then, to be wondered at that the zeal of St. Germanus for sound doctrine induced him to cross over the midland counties and devote himself to the reclaiming of these wandering souls. As it happened, the inhabitants of North Wales were early in the spring of 430 suffering from another calamity—one of those incursions of savage barbarians which were only too common in the fifth century. The untamed and restless Picts had now free play for indulging their predatory habits, when the Roman legions were withdrawn from Britain: the deserted Wall of Antoninus could no longer restrain them in their barren hills and sterile moors, and they were ever ready for a raid on the cultivated regions of Southern Britain. Apparently on this occasion no effectual opposition was made to their progress through Cumberland and Lancashire: even the fortified camp of Chester they either found deserted, or they evaded by a flank movement. On the banks of the Dee they found unexpected auxiliaries. A band of Saxon pirates had pushed their way up the stream, and uniting their forces with the Picts, they harried at pleasure the fertile valleys about Mold. The terrified and helpless Britons had abandoned all hope, when hearing of the approach of the missionaries, they sent an urgent message to bid them come to their assistance. Their request was at once complied with, and St. Germanus and St. Lupus came as messengers of Heaven to revive their drooping spirits. It was now the season of Lent, and the saintly Bishops set themselves vigorously to work to renew the spirit of religion in the souls of these fear-stricken multitudes. They preached every day to the people, and it says but little for the state of religion at the time in the district, that finding many of them had never been baptised, they administered that sacrament to great multitudes, baptising them in the waters of the Allen. On March 30th fell Easter Day, and the Bishops and people prepared to celebrate the festival with all possible solemnity. They erected a temporary church of the branches of trees, and had scarcely concluded the devotions of the day when word was brought them that the Picts and Saxons were advancing upon them. These vigilant enemies had received intelligence of what was going on in the British camp, and thought it a favourable moment for making an attack. But a sufficient watch had been kept by the Britons for them to receive timely warning of the approach of the enemy. The religious exercises in which they had been engaged had animated their minds with an overpowering enthusiasm, and they stood ready to resist with their lives. St. Germanus put himself at the head of some lightly armed troops and proceeded to survey the country. His military skill enabled him to select an advantageous position. The enemy must necessarily advance along a valley embosomed in high hills. Here he posted the bulk of his force: and as the Picts and Saxons entered the valley, unconscious of the presence of the foe, a sudden shout of "Alleluia" burst forth from the throats of the Christians, resounding through the mountains and gathering volume as it was re-echoed from side to side. The effect was marvellous. The advancing force was seized with consternation. They imagined that the rocks overhead were ready to fall and crush them. A universal panic fell upon them and they turned and fled. They threw away their arms and whatever could impede their flight, and many of them perished in the river. The Britons had an easy task to gather up the spoils, and it was with grateful hearts that they thanked God for so glorious and seasonable a deliverance. The memory of this battle is still treasured up in the local traditions of Flintshire. The spot where the barbarians were routed is still pointed out by the inhabitants as Maes-Garmon, or the field of German. It is about a mile from Mold, and the mountainous district afforded a convenient situation for the ambuscade and the success of the stratagem.

That St. Patrick was an interested spectator of these events in the mission of St. Germanus cannot be called in question; but we have written authority in an ancient Irish writer for the next incident which I am about to record, in which his share is clearly mentioned. The author of the preface to St. Fiac's hymn to St. Patrick, writing in the seventh century, says: " In a city where their preaching was unsuccessful, St. Germanus took counsel with St. Patrick as to the course they should pursue. The Saint answered: 'Let us for three days observe a rigorous fast at the city gates, and then let us leave the matter in the hands of God'. This counsel was followed, and their preaching was crowned with complete success." (Cardinal Moran, *Essays on the Early Irish Church*, p. 18.) There are good reasons for believing that the city alluded to by the Irish scholiast is Manchester, and that the place where the fast was observed was Patricroft. Manchester is about fifty miles from the scene of the Alleluia victory. It was an important military station of the Romans, and continued to be a considerable municipality after the withdrawal of the Imperial troops. It had enjoyed in its near neighbourhood the advantage of a Christian church, for the very name of Eccles tells us of an ecclesia, or place of assembly for Christians; hence it was natural for St. Germanus to direct his steps thither At Mancunium he met with a most uncourteous reception, but following the advice of St. Patrick he had recourse to prayer and fasting. He seems to have retired to Eccles, and there along with St. Patrick to have joined preaching and administering the Sacraments to his devotions. Such was the impression made on the popular mind that the spot received the name of Patrick-cruagh, the hill of Patrick, and it retains the name to this day under the name of Patricroft. The brook that runs through the township is styled Gildea, the servant of God, and evidently records in the name the labours of these two great servants of God. In those days it often happened that a Christian preacher could find no other pulpit from which to address the people than some rising ground, round which the congregation gathered, and a river or brook had to supply the place of a baptistery. But God blessed their prayers and evangelical labours; on their return over Salford Bridge on the Irwell, the city gates were thrown open and the missionaries received a hearty welcome. To the close of Queen Elizabeth's reign a curious monument of this incident survived on the road between the bridge and the old wall of Roman Mancunium. It was known as Patrick's Stone, and no doubt St. Patrick preached from it to the Manchester men of that day. So well known was this stone as St. Patrick's, that in the proceedings of the Manchester Court Leet held on October 5th, 1592, it is mentioned as a landmark along the road, familiar to every one. A second entry, under date October 8, 1618, gives us later and more precise information about this venerable monument of our Saint. It runs thus: "The jurye findeinge that John Valentine and some others, occupiyenge upper rowmes anendste ye Patrick Stone, beinge an ordinarye waye boathe to Church and Marketplace do power oute and down from their said habitaçons, suddes, filthye and noysome waters . . . doe order," &c. From this it is evident that the stone stood in the neighbourhood of church and market-place, and a skilled local antiquarian should have little difficulty in approximating to its true position. At the time of our Saint's visit, Manchester was not a city of upwards of half-a-million of inhabitants, but consisted of a few houses that had gathered round the walls of the Roman camp, settled on the tongue of land formed by the junction of the Irwell and the Medlock. The occurrence of places with St. Patrick's name attaching to them for upwards of a thousand years, through all the diversified fortunes of the district, affords a strong presumption that he once honoured South Lancashire with his presence, and won the enduring love and veneration of its people; and I invite those who brush away this narrative as unworthy of credit, to supply some better explanation of undoubted facts.

It was not the wont of writers of those rude times to fill in their narrative with the names of places, or with the minute particulars with which modern authors elucidate and illustrate their works. To them the character of their heroes was everything. They recorded faithfully their labours and their sufferings in the cause of Christ; they especially dwelt on the miraculous events with which God sanctioned their careers; but they took no pains to describe the localities of these wonderful deeds, or to detail the incidents or dates which we so much value. Constantius thought only of the virtues and labours of St.

Germanus, and his object was that his readers should learn from his pages to honour his memory and value his intercession. When Constantius was a boy the renown of St. Germanus filled all Gaul, and in later life he sought to put down in writing a record of his acts and his virtues. But Britain was to him an unknown land, and it never entered into his head to give us an account of its cities and of its inhabitants. The scholiast of St. Fiac's hymn was equally innocent of any idea of illustrating the history of Britain, but he eagerly recorded the fact, so honourable to his national patron, that St. Patrick had been a trusted adviser of the great St. Germanus, the legate of Pope St. Celestine to our island. But the names have remained rooted in the memories of the inhabitants—they survived after the traditions of the missionaries from Rome had been lost—but they are full of meaning and of life to those lovers of Lancashire sacred history who give their attention and their best endeavours to revive the holy memories of the past. Patrick's Hill, Patrick's Stone, and Gildea Brook are part of the history of Lancashire : to some they have no meaning, but to others who have given themselves to the work they are full of significance and tell of the presence in our county of great servants of God.

There is little else to tell of this great missionary expedition to our island. It had been eminently successful. The deadly heresy of Pelagianism was effectually put down in Britain. The saintly missionaries returned to Gaul in the course of the year 430, and most historians say that St. Patrick accompanied St. Germanus back to Auxerre. St. Patrick's share in maintaining the true faith among his countrymen in Britain was another important stage in his preparation for his greater enterprise of the conversion of Ireland.

CHAPTER IX.

HOW HE RECEIVED HIS COMMISSION TO PREACH THE GOSPEL TO THE IRISH FROM ST. CELESTINE, AND SAILED FOR IRELAND.

430—433.

If the year 430 was fortunate for Britain, it was also memorable in the annals of the Church, and it proved an important stage in the life of our Saint. In Britain the heresy of Pelagius had met with a severe check. At the same time, the Western and Eastern Churches were preparing for the conflict, which Nestorius had provoked by denying that our Blessed Lady could be rightly styled the Mother of God. When St. Germanus, with St. Patrick in his suite, returned to Auxerre, he was welcomed with enthusiasm by the citizens. They found that the whole religious world was alive with rumours concerning the General Council which was about to be held at Ephesus. But for the moment, the minds of the Bishop and his confidential adviser would be occupied with cares more immediately pressing in the diocese itself. Whilst they had been absent in Britain the political situation in Gaul had changed for the worse. On all sides the barbarians were pressing on the remnants of the Roman Empire. In Toulouse a powerful Gothic prince had established himself as Master of South-Western Gaul. The Burgundians ruled in the Eastern provinces, and the Frank held possession of the North-Eastern corner, while in Armorica the Bacaudae were in open revolt. Only the long strip of central Gaul, from the British Channel to the mouths of the Rhone, paid a forced and unwilling obedience to the Imperial authority. Well might their loyalty to Rome be severely shaken, for misgovernment and oppression everywhere prevailed in what was left of Roman dominion in Gaul. The Government made incessant demands for men and money to repulse the attacks of its numerous enemies, and its exactions became at length intolerable. The administration was corrupt to the last degree, and the taxes, which might have been borne had they been fairly levied on rich and poor alike, became unendurable when they were used as fresh pretexts for extortion. The amount of tribute to be paid by towns and districts was fixed by officials at headquarters, often only imperfectly acquainted with the resources of the locality, and so it was in many instances excessive; and as for the mode of collection, it was unfair and unequal, allowing the rich and powerful to escape their due share and placing a double burden on the needy who were least able to bear it. A demand for a considerable sum had been made on the city of Auxerre, and the inhabitants were filled with alarm and uneasiness. Their only hope of escape lay in the influence which their saintly Bishop might be able to exert on the central authorities at Arles, and they had no sooner welcomed him among them than they begged him to present their earnest petition for a remission of the impost. The good Bishop recognised the justice of their plea, and at once resolved on setting out in person to urge upon Auxiliaris, the Prefect of Gaul, then residing at Arles, to comply with the prayers of the towns-people. This journey was successful, and the Prefect, out of respect for their distinguished envoy, granted their request. As there is no mention of St. Patrick accompanying St. Germanus to the south of Gaul, we may suppose that he remained at Auxerre attending to his duties in the cathedral church and the administration of the diocese.

While Gaul was thus distracted with war and smouldering discontent, the Imperial power of Rome experienced another rude blow in the invasion of Africa. From the Straits of Gibraltar to the mouths of the Nile, along the southern shores of the Mediterranean, a civilised and Christian community had flourished for many centuries. It had attained a high degree of prosperity; some of its highest officials had aspired to and won the Imperial throne, and the Church numbered amongst its clergy some of the greatest thinkers and writers of their time. St. Cyprian and Tertullian had distinguished themselves by their vigorous controversial treatises. St. Athanasius had become illustrious by his unwearying and triumphant defence of the Divinity of Jesus Christ. And during the first thirty years of the fifth century St. Augustine of Hippo had held the foremost place among the Doctors of the Church as the defender of her doctrine on divine grace. To St. Patrick his writings had been familiar from the time when he had studied in the schools of Lerins. In the recent expedition to Britain his chief, St. Germanus, had successfully taught the doctrines of St. Augustine, which were the teaching of the Church, and its venerable head, St. Celestine. They looked up to St. Augustine as a most powerful and persuasive expounder of this doctrine, and though he was now in his seventy-sixth year they still regarded him with confidence and reverence.

It would then be with profound grief that, in the early autumn of 430, they heard the news that Genseric, with a band of Vandals, had crossed from Spain and spread his devastating hordes over the rich lands of the African sea board. Never were more ruthless invaders. Before them the land lay blooming like a paradise: behind them it was a howling wilderness. They made war even on the works of Nature, and not an olive tree nor a vine was left standing. At the end of May, 430, they invested the city of Hippo by land and sea. The city was crowded with refugees from the neighbouring country, and they had sad tales to tell of the ferocity of the invaders, and the destruction which dogged their footsteps. In the third month of the siege the saintly old man, St. Augustine, Bishop of Hippo, was prostrated by sickness; grief at the sights and sounds of woe and misery filled his soul. His country in ruins, the faith in danger, calamity present and in future—such was the prospect ever present to the mind of one who had been for thirty years the father of his people. From the first he accepted his illness as his last, and devoted all his energies to making a worthy preparation for his end. That end came on the 28th of August, while the besieging forces were still gathered round the devoted city. All Christendom mourned over the news, for a great light had been extinguished, a valiant champion of the faith had fallen. At Auxerre the sorrow was deep and lasting: SS. Germanus and Patrick had been brave soldiers in the fight for true doctrine, but St. Augustine had been their leader. We, too, in our generation have known what it is to lose a great doctor in the Church; the recent sorrow we experienced when Cardinal Newman was taken from us prepares us to realise the grief that spread throughout Christendom on hearing of the death of St. Augustine.

But in the changeful history of the Church disaster in one region of the earth has generally been the signal for renewal of its beneficent action in another. If Africa was to be blotted out of Christendom, a new kingdom in the far West was to be added to its empire. The news of the successful mission to Britain was nowhere hailed with greater joy than in Rome; to one person in particular it proved the turning-point in his career. Palladius, Archdeacon to Pope Celestine, had already shown himself deeply interested in the conversion of the Celtic nations. By some he is supposed to have been of Celtic origin, and to have been born in Gaul or Britain; but of one thing we are certain, that he set himself earnestly to work to counteract the spread of the pernicious doctrines of Pelagius and his friend Cœlestius. We have already seen how he was instrumental in sending St. Germanus to Britain, and we may be sure that he would be filled with joy when the news of the complete success of the enterprise reached Rome. But he was not content with the triumphs of others, and he conceived the project of offering himself to the work of converting souls, and that in the still more distant island of Ireland. When we consider the circumstances of the man, and of the task he contemplated, it is impossible not to be struck with profound admiration at his zeal and self-sacrifice. We must remember that he had reached almost the topmost rung in ecclesiastical preferment. He was Archdeacon of Rome, second in rank and authority only to the Holy Father, the Pope. He was the trusted counsellor of St. Celestine, and many important steps in the government of the Church had been taken on his advice. To leave Rome and make a missionary expedition to Ireland would appear to his friends a wild and extravagant project. He was throwing up the most brilliant of prospects, for might he not in due time aspire to be a future Pope? The Archdeaconry of Rome had been to many, and was to be to many others, a stepping-stone to the throne of St. Peter.

Ireland, at the early part of the fifth century, was a country little known, and that little was unfavourable. It was a barbarous land beyond the limits of the Roman Empire when at its height. Its inhabitants were known as the fiercest of pirates and the greediest of spoilers, and the extraordinary intellectual energy of Cœlestius had been a thorn in the side of the Church for many years, and so would not help in producing a more agreeable opinion of his countrymen. But Palladius was nothing daunted by the unpromising nature of the task set before him. The success just achieved by SS. Germanus and Patrick in Britain fired his imagination. They had restored an island to the obedience of the Holy See and to the profession of the true Faith, and that greatly through his instrumentality; why should not he have the Divine blessing on a bolder effort to spread the Faith in a barbarous and heathen land? That friends should express their astonishment and regret at his resolution, and that Pope Celestine might feel deeply the prospective loss of so trusted and sagacious a counsellor, we need not doubt, but Palladius was not to be turned aside from his heroic purpose, and he won the consent and approbation of the Holy Father. However, nothing could be done that year; the time and attention of the great officials of the Church were engrossed with the doings of the Council of Ephesus; Palladius could only nurse his project in his own mind and make such preparations as might be to ensure its success.

As the heresy of Nestorius gave rise to one of the great intellectual movements of the age, as it brought into clearer and more precise relief the teaching of the Church on the all-important doctrine of the Incarnation, as it greatly impressed and influenced the minds of the leading ecclesiastics of the early part of the fifth century, a brief notice of it may be here given. In our own time we have witnessed the profound impression produced on the whole Christian world by the doctrinal pronouncements of the Holy See, and we may fairly measure the effects of similar decrees on the Bishops and Faithful of the times of St. Patrick. When Pius IX. declared in 1854 the dogma of the Immaculate Conception of our Blessed Lady, the whole Church hailed it, not as a new belief, but as an authoritative declaration of what had always been held. "Quod semper, quod ubique, quod ab omnibus." And many a pious mind rejoiced with exceeding great joy that what it had always believed and cherished had been stamped as true by the infallible voice of Peter's successor. Again, when in 1870 the

Vatican Council, summoned by the same great Pope, and presided over by him, proclaimed the truth that the decrees of the Holy Father in matters of faith and morals were to be received by all the Faithful with the same authority as those of the Universal Church, its utterances were welcomed, not as anything new in substance, but as a distinct and clear definition of an ancient and undoubted truth. Many can still remember the hopes and fears that animated their breasts during the weeks that immediately preceded these important declarations, and the sense of relief that accompanied the hearing of the good tidings that they had at length been formally placed on the great statute book of the Universal Church.

Similar hopes and fears agitated the breasts of Christians in the years 430 and 431. The great doctrine that God had become man, " that the Word had become flesh," that the Godhead and manhood had been united in the one person of Jesus Christ, true God and true man, had severely tested the submission of the haughty and subtle intellects who in the reigns of Theodosius and Valentinian abounded in the great cities of the East. They shrank from openly attacking the received doctrine, but they sought to minimise it and explain it away. Theodore of Mopsuestia had been the restless exponent of these rationalising tendencies. We have seen how his teaching had laid the foundation of the Pelagian heresy, and in Nestorius a second equally fundamental error found a champion. Nestorius was early in the fifth century a monk in the convent of St. Euprepius, near the gate of the city of Antioch. He was a clever student and became a brilliant orator, being possessed of a fine voice. At the death in 427 of the Patriarch of Constantinople great difficulties arose in the appointment of a successor, as the city was broken up into factions, and the Emperor Theodosius, in the hopes of restoring peace, recommended the monk Nestorius. The Emperor's hopes of an assuagement of the bitter religious quarrels in his capital were speedily and grievously disappointed. In his first sermon the new Patriarch showed what manner of man he was, and thus addressed the Emperor: "Give me, my prince, the earth purged of heretics, and I will give you heaven as a recompense. Assist me in destroying heretics, and I will assist you in vanquishing the Persians." Every one who opposed his ideas was fiercely assailed, and before long this *malleus haereticorum*, this pounder of heretics, became himself a heretic. A priest of Antioch, Anastasius by name, a man of similar character to Nestorius, had been summoned to Constantinople to assist him in the government of the diocese. This man in a sermon electrified and scandalised his audience by saying: "Let no man call Mary Theotokos (God-bearing), for Mary was but a woman, and it is impossible that God should be born of a woman". This statement shocked the faith and feelings of the people, and when it was discovered that the Patriarch himself, in a series of set discourses, maintained the same false doctrines, the excitement and indignation knew no bounds.

I need not pursue the details of the controversy that raged for the next three years. Suffice it to say a General Council was summoned, and met at Ephesus. Ephesus is well known to readers of old classical lore and the pages of the New Testament, and the Fathers often mention it. The student of Herodotus will remember its being taken by Crœsus, of Lydia, who offered costly presents to the temple of Artemis. This temple, after the time of Alexander the Great, became the grandest and greatest in the Pagan world, and in the times of St. Paul, Diana of the Ephesians was the object of enthusiastic if interested worship. The city was chosen by St. John for his abode, and here for many years he gave shelter to the Mother of Jesus, whom his Divine Master had given to him in those memorable words: "Behold thy Mother". And so it was not an unfitting place to be chosen as the seat of the Council of Bishops summoned to vindicate her honour as Mother of God. Now, the student may look in vain for the name of Ephesus in the map of Asiatic Turkey: the harbour has been choked up, and has become a swamp. The ground is covered with mounds, the sole remains of temple and theatre, and with rank vegetation. Antiquarians have a difficulty in fixing the site of the great temple, and the place is known only as Ayasaluk. The Council held its first session on the 22nd of June, 431, and the seventh and last session on 31st August; 198 Bishops subscribed its decrees. The two heresies of Pelagius and Nestorius, after disturbing the peace of Christendom for so many years, were now finally condemned, and from this time forward we hear little of Pelagius and his Irish fellow-heretic, Cœlestius. They did not return to the West, but died in obscurity. The fate of Nestorius was even more lamentable. At first he retired to his convent at Antioch, but his presence after a time gave umbrage to the Bishop, and he was sent to a remote place of banishment, exposed to the incursions of the Arabs, into whose hands he fell. He was delivered from them, only to fall again under the suspicion of the authorities, and he died worn out with disappointment and ill-usage.

Meanwhile Palladius, having received the approbation of the Pope, diligently set about preparations for his journey. He received consecration as Bishop from Celestinus. He gathered together books and relics; and we have the names of two of his companions, Silvester and Solinus. The *Tripartite Life* tells us that Celestinus gave him twelve men to go with him to instruct the Gaiedhel (p. 377). It is not improbable that on his way to Britain he passed through Auxerre, and conferred with St. Germanus. To St. Patrick it must have been a trying occasion. He knew that the conversion of Ireland was destined by God to be his work. Yet he beheld it entrusted by the Vicar of Christ to another. But that marvellous patience of his, that trust that God in His own good time would accomplish His purpose in spite of delays and arrangements that seemed to give his special task to others, failed him not. And when Palladius, with his company of holy missionaries, departed for Britain, he followed them with sincere prayers for their success. For himself, he still waited in calm contentment for the manifestation of the Divine will.

I need say little more about this expedition. It met with scant success; and St. Palladius, after a short time spent in Wicklow, being opposed on all sides and disheartened by the death of his faithful fellow-missioners, set sail to return to Rome. His ship was driven northwards, and he landed in North Britain, to die amongst the Picts. His name is commemorated on 6th July. It may be that he did not possess the qualities to succeed in the extremely difficult task he had set before him. His talents had enabled him to climb to all but the highest place in the Christian Church, but they were better suited to the circumstances of a great city, of a world cultivated and refined, than to confront the hardships and perils of a distant and barbarous land. The task which fell from his hands was to be taken up by another. A rougher hand and a more robust will succeeded where the sprightliness of the Celt and the polish of a high Roman dignitary proved unavailing. But even at this distance of time we ought not to forget the brave spirit, the self-forgetting disposition which led St. Palladius from his antechambers of the Lateran to face the wintry cold of a northern island, and to deal with the rude manners of a wild and uncivilised tribe. His memory should always be held in honour as the first missionary of Christianity in Ireland.

The sad news of the death of St. Palladius was brought to Auxerre by some of his disciples who were in Britain. The names of two of them are given us by Probus as Augustine and Benedict (*vita* Quinta). There was at least one person who was most profoundly affected by the intelligence; to St. Patrick it was like a distant voice from heaven summoning him to his work. He was now past the prime of life, being fifty-eight years of age, but he was hale and vigorous; it had been the dream of his life to go to convert Ireland to the faith; angelic voices had whispered in his ear that the children of Ireland were calling out to him to go and preach to them the way of life. He may sometimes have been tempted to think that an opportunity would never come of realising this dream. But now the time had come. The Father of the Christian world had undertaken the work; what did it matter if the first attempt had failed and the first instrument had broken in his hand? Could not he offer himself to take up the interrupted work, and perhaps, late as it was, he might be accepted? When the matter was communicated to St. Germanus he seems to have shown no hesitation in making up his mind. He knew St. Patrick thoroughly; he had found in him a most able assistant. His experience had taught him that he was equal to the most difficult tasks. Every commission in which he had employed him had been crowned with success, and he had found in him in times of difficulty and uncertainty a wise counsellor and a courageous helper. Other things too pointed him out as well fitted for the task. He knew the people of Ireland well; he had lived amongst them, and was well acquainted with their feelings and their language. More than this, he had a deep-seated love for them, and longed to be to them the messenger of the good tidings of the Gospel. And so St. Germanus determined on giving St. Patrick's proposal every aid in his power.

But an obstacle arose from an unexpected quarter. The fault of St. Patrick, committed when he was a mere boy, which seems to have been a momentary yielding to some sudden and unexpected temptation, was again to cast a shadow over his path. The saint, before he was ordained deacon, had confided his secret to a friend, in whom he had the most implicit trust. This person had continued to show himself as animated with the most kindly sentiments towards St. Patrick, and in his absence on some of his missionary journeys before he was in Britain had defended him before others. He had even said to the saint: "Thou art going to be given the rank of a bishop". What occasioned a change in his feelings towards his friend of nearly thirty years we are not told, but in his *Confession* St. Patrick bitterly complains that "before all persons, good and bad, he detracted him publicly, when before he had freely and gladly praised him". This treacherous friend betrayed St. Patrick's confidence, and it became a question of serious consequence for the responsible authorities to decide upon. "His elders," the *Confession* says, "spoke of his sin as an objection to his laborious episcopate." St. Patrick felt the charge very acutely. He says: "I was on that day strongly driven to fall away here and for ever. But the Lord spared a proselyte and a stranger for His Name's sake, and mercifully assisted me greatly in that affliction, because I was not entirely deserving of reproach."—(*Confession*, p. 593.) The decision was favourable to St. Patrick, and Germanus not merely recommended him to Pope Celestine as a fit person to take up the unsuccessful mission of St. Palladius, but sent with him to Rome Segetius, one of the worthiest and most venerable of his priests, to bear testimony to his high appreciation of the candidate for the Irish Apostolate. Probus puts into his mouth the following prayer, uttered before he started for Rome: "O Lord Jesus Christ, lead me, I beseech Thee, to the seat of the Holy Roman Church, that receiving authority there to preach with confidence Thy sacred truths, the Irish nation may, through my ministry, be gathered to the folds of Christ ".—(Probus, *Trias Thaumaturgus*, p. 48.)

As to the time of this journey to Rome, that it was after Patrick had heard of the failure of St. Palladius's mission we have the high authority of the *Tripartite Life*. This life is attributed to St. Evin, an author of the sixth century; and O'Curry says of him that he had probably seen St. Patrick and conversed with him. There are no dates given by the ancient authors, and so we can only conjecture at what time of the year St. Patrick set out on his arduous journey, for arduous it must have been, as he had to cross the lofty mountainous chain of the Alps. If the death of St. Palladius was on the 6th of July, 431, the news could scarcely reach Auxerre before August or September, and as some time must be allowed for the inquiry made into the antecedents of St. Patrick, this must have caused further delay, and it seems improbable that he could begin his pilgrimage so late in the year, but would wait until the following spring, when the melting of the snow would make the passes of the Alps practicable. There can be little doubt as to his route; he would descend the Rhone as far as Vienne, then gradually ascend the valley of the Isère until he reached the pass of the Little St. Bernard. This pass was well known to the Romans; most authorities now agree that it was the one chosen by Hannibal. Though it was considered one of the easiest of the passes, it reaches a height of 7190 feet. On the Italian side of the Alps the path descends into the Val d'Aosta, and following the course of the Doria Baltea, reaches Ivrea, the ancient Eporedia. The route then crosses the great plain bordering the north bank of the Po.

It would appear that at Ivrea he and his companions met with a most kindly reception. A simple monk and an aged priest would not journey in any great state in those days, and the rough mountain roads amid everlasting snows and far-spreading glaciers must have sorely tried our travellers. But the old town of the Salassi, Eporedia, with its old Roman bridge, spanning the river with its single arch, and its cathedral built on the foundations of a former temple of the sun, offered them a much-needed rest. They were kindly welcomed by its saintly Bishop, who was named Amatorix. Probus tells us that he was a man of wonderful sanctity and a chief Bishop in the north of Italy. The letters of St. Germanus would be to him a sufficient warrant of their character and mission. And when he heard the errand on which they were bound, he entered warmly into their project. There are no records of what passed between the Bishop and his guests, but it is not hard to imagine that St. Patrick would tell him of his wish to go to Ireland; of the incidents in his early life which first enkindled in his heart the burning desire to devote himself to the conversion of the island, and of the angelic voices which at intervals during forty years had reminded him of the work to which he had been called. He would add that it was now his intention to proceed to the feet of Pope Celestine to crave his approval. Amatorix was at once attracted to his saintly visitor, and he encouraged him in every way in his power. From the choice that St. Patrick made of him to be his consecrator, it is probable that this matter was discussed by them on this occasion, and that there was an understanding arrived at that the consecration should take place at Ivrea, if the Pope's sanction should be obtained. As Ivrea was on the great Roman road from the Alps to Rome and also to Ravenna, its selection for the place of consecration was perfectly suitable and convenient.

Refreshed and encouraged, the travellers pursued their way, and in due course reached Rome At this period the Popes resided in the palace adjoining the Church of St. John Lateran. This magnificent building had been given in 312 to

Pope Melchiades by Constantine the Great, the very year of his great victory near Rome, at the Ponte Molle, over Maxentius, and it continued to be the Papal abode until 1377, when on the return of the Popes from Avignon, Gregory XI. fixed his residence at the Vatican. The Quirinal was not built until the sixteenth century, when the present edifice was commenced by Gregory XIII. in 1574. I can give no particulars of their stay in the Eternal City. But there cannot be doubt that their arrival would be welcome to the Papal Court. The Popes have always displayed a marked pertinacity in prosecuting any undertaking which they have once commenced. Celestine had despatched Palladius to Ireland with that full hope of success which good men feel when engaging in an effort to spread Christ's kingdom on earth. It had been a bitter disappointment when the sad news arrived of the complete failure of the mission and of the deaths of its chief and the principal members of his suite. At first the outlook was gloomy enough: the times were perilous, the Pope was growing old, no one offered himself to replace the heroic Palladius. When, then, Patrick and his companions presented themselves in audience before the Holy Father, and he read the letters in which St. Germanus commended the bearers to His Holiness, his heart must have leaped with joy. Germanus was too well known for his high character and sound judgment to allow of any doubts as to the fitness of the new candidate for a difficult and dangerous work. He had known Patrick for upwards of fourteen years; he had ever found him a model of every priestly virtue; he had availed himself of his counsel in moments of perplexity, and found him full of courage and resource. He had employed him on missions of high moment, and never had occasion to repent his confidence. The appearance, also, of St. Patrick was in his favour. He was grave in his manners, resolute in his carriage, winning in his conversation. The project of converting Ireland was to him no whim recently or lightly taken up. It had been the aim and object of his life. If to try the stuff of which he was made the Holy Father pointed out to him the laborious nature of the mission, his answer was the frank one that for more than forty years he had given himself to the work, and for forty years had been waiting patiently for the Divine Will to enable him to carry it out.

A long-standing tradition of Rome tells us that the question was submitted to the assistant clergy of the city, and after carefully weighing the matter they all declared of one accord, that for the mission to the Irish people no one was so well suited as St. Patrick; and at the same time they declared him to be "a man of religious life and sanctity, of angelic aspect, adorned moreover with heavenly wisdom, and enriched with every virtue".—(*Officium Canonic, Lateranen, Antiquiss*, printed in 1622.) Everyone knows the end. The Pope granted the request of the missionary. He bade him go in peace; he bestowed upon him the blessing of St. Peter, and he conferred upon him all the powers necessary for the religious administration of the people he should convert. Before his departure the aged Pope gave the saint the name by which he is now universally known, for up to this time he had been called Succat. Patricius was at one time a title of high distinction, but Gibbon tells us (*Decline and Fall*, viii. p. 300) that in the fifth century the illustrious name of Patricius was assumed by the meanest subjects of the Roman Empire. He also supplied him with many things necessary or useful for his mission, and, amongst the rest, with relics of the holy martyrs.—(Moran, p. 28.)

It was the last great act of the Pontificate of Celestinus. A week after he died, on August 1, and was succeeded by Pope Xystus. Celestine had been a vigorous Pope. He had been a steady supporter of St. Augustine both in his administration of ecclesiastical affairs in Africa, and in his uncompromising defence of the Church's doctrine as to the necessity and efficacy of Divine grace. He was equally zealous in Gaul. In his letter to the Gaulish Bishops, he says: "By no limits of place is my pastoral vigilance confined; it extended to all places where Christ is adored". He also adopted St. Cyril, of Alexandria, as his spokesman on the unity of the Divine and human personality in Jesus Christ, and had the happiness of seeing the heresy of Nestorius condemned in the Council of Ephesus. St. Prosper (in his book *Contra Collatorem*, xxi.) sums up the evidences of his zeal for the true Faith in these words: "While the Pope laboured to keep the Roman island Catholic, he made also the barbarous island Christian by ordaining a Bishop for the Scots". His ancient epitaph in the cemetery of St. Priscilla testifies that he was an excellent Bishop, honoured and beloved of everyone, who for the sanctity of his life now enjoys the sight of Jesus Christ and the eternal honours of the saints.

St. Patrick would leave the eternal city with feelings of profound thankfulness, and his first thought was to hasten back to Eporedia, to beg at the hands of the Bishop the grace of consecration. In that old Celtic town of the Salassi, in its grey-towered cathedral, Amatorix the Bishop imposed his hands upon him and sent him forth on the mission which has influenced the history of the world. Probus tells us that some other clerics were ordained to the office of minor degrees, on the same occasion; and that the Canticle of the Psalmist was appropriately sung by the choir of clerical chanters: "Thou art a priest for ever after the order of Melchisedech".—(*Colgan*, p. 40.) The *Tripartite Life* gives us the names of two of those then ordained—Auxiliaris and Esserinus—and speaks of others also. It would be with a light step and a joyful heart that the new Bishop commenced the ascent of the southern slope of the Alps. His life had been a strange one. His purpose had been early formed, but for well nigh forty years he had waited for an opportunity to carry it out. He was now a Bishop with full powers from the Vicar of Christ, and he must not lose an hour in commencing his work. He returned to Auxerre, where we can well imagine the enthusiastic welcome he would meet with, but he tarried there no great length of time. The meeting between the two saints, Germanus and Patrick, we can easily imagine. They were never again to see each other in this life, but their hearts were ever knit together by the closest ties of affection and esteem, and to the death of St. Germanus in 448 he was the object of the tenderest regard on St. Patrick's part.

Leaving Auxerre, he hastened to cross the English Channel, and we find him again in Britain, in the autumn of 432. As we have seen, he brought some companions from Italy; others would join him in Auxerre, but it was in Britain that he trusted to find his most useful auxiliaries, and he devoted the winter months in seeking them among the British monks and priests. It is to this period of St. Patrick's life that we must ascribe the many traces of his presence in Wales and Cornwall. Borlase, in his *Antiquities of Cornwall*, tells us that "by persisting in their Druidism the Britons of Cornwall drew the attention of St. Patrick that way. About the year 432, with twenty companions, when on his way to Ireland, he halted a little on the shores of Cornwall, where he is said to have built a monastery. This was at Padstow. Usher (*Premord*, p. 842) says that St. Patrick, after visiting St. Germanus, stayed some time amongst the Britons in parts of Cornwall and Wales."—(Anderton's *Britain's Early Faith*, p. 163.) At Llaniltyd, on the coast of Glamorganshire, we find many traditions of the saint. It would be in 432 that the saint visited this spot; but the Welsh chronicles give a different version of his connection with the place, viz., that while staying there as a youth he was carried off by pirates. It is said that as a consequence of St. Patrick's presence here it has never been known that a spider's web has been found in the church. Our saint was eminently successful in gaining associates for his mission. Jocelyn tells us that he found "many learned and religious men from whom he afterwards promoted thirty to the rank of Bishop".—(*Montalembert*, iii. 79.) One of these, who became the first Bishop of Louth, became an attached friend of our saint, and made with him the following bargain: " If I shall leave the light before thee I commit to thee my community". And Patrick replied : " I too commend mine to thee, if I go before thee to the Lord".—(*Ibid.*) Another Welsh monk, named Carantoc, who followed St. Patrick, is described in the Cambrian legend as a strong knight under the sun, wonderful, spiritual, a chief abbot, patient, a teacher of faithfulness, a herald of the Celestial Kingdom (p. 80).

Whether it was that at this time the connection of St. Patrick with Liverpool took its rise I cannot clearly learn. It is certain, however, that a cross was there erected in very remote times by the scattered inhabitants of the north bank of the Mersey in his honour, and was known down to post-reformation times as St. Patrick's Cross. The street in which it stood is called Crosshall Street, and evidently took its name from Cross

Hall, the seat of the Crosses from the time of King John. Probably the family took its name from the cross, as many family names were assumed about that time, and were often suggested by some striking object in the neighbourhood. Leland speaks of the cross as existing in his day, and marks its site on a map drawn up at the time. And, again, in the time of the Civil Wars the cross is marked on a map prepared for the use of Prince Rupert in some military manœuvres he was contemplating. As in 432 Lancashire was as Celtic as any other part of Britain, there is nothing strange in St. Patrick seeking for missionaries on the north as well as on the south of the Mersey. I know of no other incident in his career which accounts satisfactorily for the choice of Liverpool as the site of a monument in his honour. There can be scarcely a doubt that the cross dates from a period long preceding the Saxon, Danish or Norman settlements of Lancashire, and belongs to the time when the Celts were undisturbed masters in the land, and so to the age of St. Patrick himself. If it be objected that Liverpool was out of the way the saint would naturally go, the answer is very easy. In the first place, he was seeking for helpers in the work of preaching the Gospel, and would go wherever he heard of a prospect of success; and, secondly, we may observe that from the moment of receiving the Apostolic mission at the hands of St. Celestine he seems to have been animated with an insatiable desire of work and a restless, untiring energy. No labours seem to have wearied, no difficulties to have daunted him. The obscurity of his early life, his many years of humble submission, his hard, abstemious, studious career in monastery or bishop's house, had stored up within him a boundless amount of fervid energy, and he threw it all into his great work.

As for the Britons at this time, they too seem to have exulted in a newly-born sense of freedom and life. For centuries every exercise of liberty had been denied them. The Romans had for nearly 400 years crushed every national aspiration under an ever-abiding irresistible power of arms and laws. That power was now at an end, and the Briton was his own master, a free man in his own land. Unfortunately there was no political centre round which they could gather. Every petty community aimed at an independent existence. The local chiefs being free from the foreigner strove only to extend their own authority and power. Thus Britain fell ingloriously before the hordes of barbarian invaders from east and north and west. But they clung tenaciously to their faith, and cherished the Christian glories of their country. But such was their hatred and scorn for the savage men who had murdered their countrymen and occupied their lands that the desire of their conversion never entered their minds. To the Saxon and the Pict they would not preach the Gospel; with them they would hold no intercourse except at the point of the lance. When then the majestic figure of St. Patrick appeared amongst them, when in their own language he talked to them of the neighbouring island of Erin, and announced his commission from the Common Father of the Christian world to convert its people, they were ready and eager listeners. He communicated to them some sparks of the fire which burned in his own breast, and they joyfully offered to follow his lead. What was the Saxon's loss was the Irishman's gain. The stormy sea which separated them from Ireland had no terrors for them, and they turned from the advancing waves of Saxon settlement, and confronted boldly the billows of the Atlantic, chafed into fury as they rolled between the rocky headlands of Wales and the coasts of Wexford and Wicklow. Their zeal, their intrepidity, their devotion has been well repaid. If they helped in the great work of the conversion of Ireland in the fifth century, and again in the sixth fanned its smouldering embers into new and vigorous life, the benefit has been abundantly repaid in the constant interchange of good offices in that and the succeeding centuries, and the new Apostolate of the Irish race in this the nineteenth century to the Welsh of this day, robbed as they have been of their faith in the true Church.

But we must return to St. Patrick. His labours had been most successful; he had secured the willing and eager assistance of some of the brightest and best of the British clergy; but his faith was to undergo another trial. He was walking along the rocky shore of the promontory, now called St. David's Head, revolving the prospects of his mission. He had reached the spot, which long bore the name of St. Patrick's Seat, when in vision he saw the whole island of Ireland stretched out before his eyes. The sight appalled him; for a moment he felt overwhelmed with the magnitude and difficulty of his task. His heart for once seemed to fail him, and he was discouraged and filled with despondency. It was but a passing trial. The dark cloud began to lift, and he beheld the island dotted all over from end to end with monasteries; he saw it peopled with men and women, faithful followers of Christ, earning for itself the title of Island of Saints and

Doctors. He returned from his walk by the sea-beaten cliff, encouraged and consoled, and lost no time in pushing forward preparations for his great expedition.

The winter had now nearly passed; the year 433 was fairly commenced, and St. Patrick set sail in command of a numerous company on a voyage which is one of the most memorable and most momentous in the history of Christendom. The green seas bore him to the shores of Wicklow. He strained his eyes to catch the first glimpse of land, and watched the sugar-loaf mountain come in sight. Round its base the river Dargle winds its way to the sea at Bray, and at its mouth St. Patrick landed, raising the standard of the cross on its pebbly banks. What memories would fill his soul as he trod again the soil of Ireland. Forty-five years before when he was a boy of fifteen years old, helpless and unfriended, he was brought to these shores to be sold into a barbarous land to a heathen master. He had trembled before the fierce and passionate Milcho, and shrunk from his blows and stripes. And now he came with a message to kings and princes, which they must needs obey, with power given him from above before which their trustiest weapons dropped from their hands. He came, the herald of the Great King of Heaven and

Earth, to preach the Faith of Jesus Christ; his work was to gather force and volume as the ages rolled away, and after more than fourteen centuries it still stands and grows. Perhaps amongst God's saints he symbolises and personifies more than any other a nation's faith and a nation's love.

APPENDIX I.

NOTE TO CHAPTER I.

On St. Patrick's Birthplace.

It is very curious that it should be necessary to say anything in support of the statement that this great saint was born at Kilpatrick, near Dumbarton, on the north bank of the Clyde; for there is literally nothing to be said in defence of any other theory as to his birthplace. Had the case to be argued in a court of law, with counsel engaged on either side, in which the plaintiff represented the opponents of Kilpatrick's claim to this honour, and the defendants had to plead the arguments in its favour, it would be quite within the range of possibility that after having heard the plaintiff's learned counsel, the judge, without calling for the statement of the other side, would interrupt the pleadings, and say that the plaintiff had no case, and that it would be unnecessary for him to hear the rebutting arguments. We must remember that it is merely a dry point of history that is before us, and that sentiment or prejudice has no place. It is not a question of liking or disliking; still less of right or wrong. It is a mere question of evidence, and, as a matter of fact, the evidence is all on one side, and there is absolutely none on the other.

Regarding the precise date of our saint's birth, there may be some slight diversity of opinion among the learned as to the exact year, but all agree in this, that he was born in the last quarter of the fourth century. If then we wish to arrive at the truth we must go back to those authors who lived and wrote nearest to those times, and we must accept their witness as decisive of the point. I shall not weary the reader with giving just now the evidence of the opposing side, but will deal with it later. I will proceed to summon the witnesses for the defence in the order of time in which they lived, and will in entire confidence abide by the verdict of an intelligent public.

My first witness shall be the great saint himself, and his testimony judged by the state of things in his time will alone be sufficient. I may, however, premise that the saint in his writings was, as far as it is possible to conceive, innocent of any idea of giving an answer to the question before us. He wrote from the fulness of his heart to express his gratitude to God for His merciful guidance of his path through life, and it is only incidental allusions, dropped without design, that help us in any way in our inquiry. I will first quote the passages in which he speaks of his native country, and then those which point to the actual place of his abode when in his father's house.

I. As to his country, St. Patrick says in his *Confession*, c. x.: "Thus then after a few years I was again in the Britains with my kindred, who received me as a son". NOTE.—" Et iterum post paucos annos in Britanniis eram cum parentibus meis qui me ut filium susciperunt."

Again, in c. xix., he says: " Wherefore though I should have wished to leave (them) that I might go unto the Britains, a journey most desirable to me as unto my country and kindred, and not thither only, but that I might go as far as the Gauls to visit my brethren and to see the face of the Saints of the Lord". NOTE.—" Unde autem etsi voluero amitter illas, et ut pergens in Britannias, et libentissime paratus eram, quasi ad patriam et parentes: non id solum, sed etiam usque ad Gallias visitare fratres, et ut viderem faciem sanctorum Domini mei."

Finally, in his letter to Corotic, the British chieftain,

who had carried off some of his converts into captivity, he says : " For them I have given up my country and my kindred. . . . I have written . . . this letter . . . to be forwarded to Corotic ; I do not say to my fellow-citizens, nor to the fellow-citizens of the Roman saints, but to the fellow-citizens of demons through their evil deeds, . . . companions of the Scots and apostate Picts."

NOTE.—" Pro quibus tradidi patriam et parentes . . . Scripsi verba ista . . . Mittenda Corotici, non dico civibus meis neque civibus sanctorum Romanorum sed civibus dæmoniorum ob mala opera ipsorum. . . . Socii Scotorum atque Pictorum apostatarum." " I was of noble birth according to the flesh, my father being a decurio." " Ingenuus fui secundum carnem ; decurione patre nascor."

The saint could not express in plainer terms his nationality ; the Britains were his country and that of his kindred ; he longed to go to the Britains to see his country and his kindred, and that country was at the time in the hands of men whom he would not call countrymen on account of their crimes and their friendship with the Scots and apostate Picts. But our opponents say that the Britains here spoken of were not the island of Great Britain, but the land of Bretagne in France. Let us see if this contention can bear examination. We must remember that twenty-seven years of St. Patrick's life belonged to the fourth century and that the Roman Empire counted " the Britains " amongst its provinces until 410. Again, the word used by St. Patrick to designate his country was " the Britains," and he nowhere uses the singular form " Britannia ". Speaking then the language universal in his time, he says that his country was " the Britains," and when he particularises his countrymen, he speaks of them as having become " the companions of the Scots and apostate Picts ". This description exactly fits the inhabitants of the banks of the Clyde, for a band of Scots had settled in the Mull of Cantyre as early as the fourth century, and at the time the saint wrote the Picts converted by St. Ninian had in great measure relapsed into Paganism.

Do even our opponents state that the country now known as Bretagne was ever known as "the Britains" at any time previous to the sixth century? I am not aware that a single passage from ancient writers has ever been cited to support this view; on the contrary, whenever the writer has used the word in the plural form he has uniformly and expressly meant Great Britain.

There is another consideration which tells convincingly against our opponents. The ancient name of the north-western coasts of Gaul was not Britannia but Armorica. From the time before Cæsar this word had been in common use; in the time of St. Patrick it was still the universally used name. When we read of the rebellion of Armorica against the Roman general Aëtius in the time of St. Germanus the rebels are not called Britons but Bacaudæ, and in truth the name of Britannia was not given to it until the fifth century was reaching its end, and the fugitives from the island of Britain seeking to escape from the cruelties of the Saxons settled in great numbers on the other side of the Channel. The landing of Hengist and Horsa is usually assigned to the year 449; it took them thirty years to make good their hold on the single kingdom of Kent, and as late as 520 King Arthur and his Britons inflicted a severe defeat upon the invaders at the battle of Badon Hill. The emigration was at first slow, but, as the Saxon power extended, it increased in volume, and British influence became so dominant in the westernmost province of Gaul that it acquired the name of Britannia. You may look in vain in Smith's magnificent classical atlas for the name of Britannia on the map of Gaul, but in Spüner's atlas of the Middle Ages the name is duly marked in the map of France which corresponds with the accession of Clovis, 487. St. Patrick would no more have used the word "the Britains" to designate the present Bretagne, than a writer of the nineteenth century would employ Scotia as the name of Scotland in the fifth century. As a matter of fact Bretagne did not get its modern name till after his time, just as Scotland was not used for North Britain until the eleventh or twelfth century.

Cardinal Moran on this point says (p. 301, *Dublin Review*, 1880): "It remains true that it was only at a comparatively late period that the name Britannia began to be applied to any part of the continent". The learned Benedictine Lobineau affirms "that it was only after the middle of the fifth century that this name began to be used to designate a portion of the Gaulish territory". "About the year 458," he writes, "the inhabitants of the island of Britain, flying from the swords of the Saxons, gave to a portion of Armoric Gaul the name of Bretagne (*Histoire de la Bretagne*, vol. i. p. 5). Even then, however, the plural form of the name continued to be restricted to the island of Britain, and there is no example of its being used in reference to Bretagne in France until the close of the sixth century." If then we are to accept St. Patrick's own statement of his nationality we can come to no other conclusion than that he was undoubtedly a native of Great Britain.

As to the minor point, the precise locality of his birth, the testimony of St. Patrick points clearly to its belonging to the region defended by the great Roman wall. Here are his words: "I, Patrick, a sinner, the most unlearned, and the least of all the faithful, and held in contempt by very many, had Calpurnius, a deacon, for my father, . . . who lived in the village of Bannavem, Taberniæ. He had close by a small villa where I was made captive." NOTE.—"Ego Patricius peccator, rustissimus et minimus omnium fidelium et contemptibilissimus apud plurimos, patrem habui Calpurnium diaconum . . . qui fuit vico Bannavem Taberniæ. Villulam enim prope habuit, ubi ego in capturam dedi" (*Confessio*, p. 1).

These names do not tell their own story as plainly as

the word "Britanniæ" does, and it will require some explanation to enable us to identify them with any modern place. The word Bannavem, or, as it is spelt, Banavem and Bonaven, is composed of two Celtic words, Ban or Bun, meaning mouth, and Avon a river, and the whole word means "river mouth". It is evident that there may have been many "river mouths," just as in modern times there are many Bartons or Claughtons, and the saint adds the word "Taberniæ" to distinguish the village in which his father resided from other places of the same name. Tabernia is but an abbreviation of the word "Tabernaculorum," and the writers of the Second, Third, and Fourth Lives given by Colgan say he was born in the "Campus Tabernaculorum" or "Magh Tabern," near the city of Nemthor. The plain was so called from having in Roman times been the site of a great encampment, and was in very truth a field of tents. The *Tripartite Life* identifies Nemthur with Alclyde, another name of Dumbarton, in the following words: "Patrick was of the Britons of Alcluaid by origin. . . . In Nemthur, moreover, the man St. Patrick was born." It adds that "St. Patrick was brought up in Nemthur," and that he and his nurse "were ordered to clean the hearth of the royal house at Al-cluaid". These very ancient Irish writers then fix for us the site of Bannavem Taberniæ as close to the great Roman wall terminating at Nemthur, or Alclyde, or Theodosia, or Dumbriton, or Dumbarton. The reader will observe that St. Patrick names Bannavem Taberniæ as the village near which his father possessed a small villa, and where he was residing at the time when his son was taken prisoner. The other writers quoted speak of the Magh Tabern as the place in which the saint was born, and say it was near Nemthur, and identify Nemthur with Alclyde, the modern Dumbarton.

It may be objected that the many names of Dumbarton are very suspicious, or at least that they tend to introduce an element of doubt. It is not difficult to give a satisfactory answer to this objection. The remarkable rock on which the town now stands naturally attracted the notice of the earliest inhabitants. Objects of nature were greatly reverenced by the Celtic races, and wherever the Druidical worship prevailed they were invested with a peculiar sanctity, hence the great Tor at the junction of the Clyde and Leven early acquired the name of the Holy Rock, or Nen-tor, variously spelt by the ancient writers as Nentur, Nemthur, Nemther or Emptor. From another point of view, as a conspicuous landmark on the north bank of the Clyde, it acquired the name of Alclyde, the Rock of the Clyde. For a short period after the campaign of Theodosius, during the remainder of the Roman occupation, it was called after its conqueror Theodosia, but the name was short-lived. The poet Taliessin, in celebrating the exploits of his hero Rederech who sailed from Wales to recover the kingdom of Strathclyde from which some years before he had been expelled, describes him as landing at Nevthur (another reading gives Nenthur), and on the banks of the Clyde fighting the battle which recovers for him his inheritance. NOTE.—(The Black Book of Caermarthen, the most ancient manuscript of Wales.) Venerable Bede speaks of "the Clyde which in former times divided the Picts from the Britons . . . where to this day stands the city of the Britons called Alcluith" (*Eccles. Hist.* i. 5), and elsewhere he says that Alcluith signifies "the Rock of Cluith" (i. 12). Finally, Camden (in his *Britannia*, p. 666) says: "This, formerly Alcluid, began to be called afterwards by the Britons, who held it for a long time against the Scots, Dun-britton, that is the city of the Britons". It is an axiom as old as Euclid that things equal to the same thing are equal to each other. If then Nemthur according to the *Tripartite Life* is the same as Alclyde, and Taliessin says the same; if Alclyde according to O'Flaherty and Camden is Dun-britton; and if Dunbritton is the same as our modern Dum-barton, as everybody allows, we may conclude with the

APPENDIX I.

certainty of one of Euclid's problems that the Nemthur of old, the birthplace of St. Patrick, is the Dumbarton of to-day. It may be a reproach to a man to bear many aliases; it is no reproach to a city, whose history extends over fifteen hundred years, that it bore different names under the different conditions of time through which its history ranges. It does not make history doubtful to know that Dublin was once called Eblana, that Chester was known as Deva, or Preston as Asmundesham. There is no confusion in the fact that Troy is sometimes called Ilium, or that Constantinople was once Byzantium. The change of names makes it no more doubtful that Nemthur is the present Dumbarton, than the fact that the El-Kods is the only name of Jerusalem now in use amongst the native races of Palestine, causes any uncertainty about the identity of the Holy City. The case may be summed up in the formula: Nemthur = Alclyde, Alcylde = Dunbritton, and Dunbritton = Dumbarton, therefore Nemthur = Dumbarton. Q. E. D.

Ancient Irish historians, old Welsh bards, mediæval biographers, and modern geographical authors, without any previous concert, and having widely divergent motives, agree in the conclusion just arrived at.

What link is wanting in this chain of evidence? The witnesses are unexceptionable; and I may add the name of St. Fiacc to those already given. He states that in so many words, that St. Patrick was born at Nemthur. His evidence is highly important, for he was a contemporary of St. Patrick. According to Dr. Todd, the year 418 is about the year of his birth; and, as he survived St. Patrick, he may have lived to eighty or ninety years of age. He was made Bishop by St. Patrick, and was the first Bishop in Leinster, and his holy master gave him a box containing a bell, a reliquary and crozier, and a book-satchel. He was about fifteen years of age when St. Patrick landed in Ireland, and he had the best opportunities for knowing the truth about St. Patrick's birthplace. We see from what I have said above that he was in the confidence of the saint, and may easily have learnt that he was born at Nemthur from his own lips. The hymn in which he records the events of St. Patrick's life is the *Vita Prima* of Colgan, and its authenticity is now universally admitted. What he says is confirmed by the statements of the saint himself, and subsequent writers repeat it as an admitted fact. Is a writer of the nineteenth century, however learned, and however great an adept in the art of ingenious reasoning, to be accepted as having better means of information or greater desire to tell the truth?

The *Vita Septima* of Colgan, or as it is also called the *Tripartite,* is commonly ascribed to St. Evin, and O'Curry tells us that he was living in 504, only eleven years after St. Patrick's death, and that he probably had seen and conversed with him. This life is highly valued by critics, and is especially emphatic in identifying Alclyde as St. Patrick's birthplace.

Need I summon any more of these old writers to give their witness? So far as I know only one names Tours as the place of St. Patrick's birth, and as he stands absolutely alone, and his statement is not followed by subsequent biographers, his testimony may be set aside without further notice. In the later middle ages Marianus Scotus, who died at Mayence in Germany in 1082, unhesitatingly says under date 372, "St. Patrick is born in the island of Britain". And to conclude the mediæval writers, Jocelyn of Furness, who wrote towards the close of the twelfth century, speaks of Calpurnius as "dwelling in the village called Tabernia situated in the Campus Tabernaculorum, so called from the tents that the Roman army had erected there near the town Empthor, bordering on the Irish Sea". This place is further identified in the eleventh chapter, where it is said that there stood on a certain promontory, rising above the said town Empthor, a fortification of which some ruins remain. This place is famous, situated in the valley of the Clyde, and called in the language of that country Dunbreaton, that is, the rock of the Britains. Every one of these witnesses was Irish, and yet they record it as an historical fact that their patron saint was thus born in the island of Britain.

To come somewhat nearer our own times. Colgan, the industrious collector of lives of our saint, who flourished in the seventeenth century and from whose labours so much of what we know about St. Patrick has been derived, says plainly: "The true and common opinion of both our domestic and foreign writers is that St. Patrick was born in Greater Britain". NOTE.—Verior et communis nostrorum domesticorum et exterorum scriptorum est, S. Patricium in Majori Britannia natum esse.

O'Flaherty in his *Ogygia*, written in the reign of Charles II., says: "From this river (Cluide, called Glotta by Tacitus) Dunbriton was formerly called . . . Alcluid, that is, the rock of the Cluid; . . . below Dunbriton is the plain of Taburn on which the town Nemther stood, which gave birth to the illustrious missionary St. Patrick, and there he spent part of his youth, as we are assured by the ancient writers of his life" (Hely's Trans., p. 317).

I also give the statement of a learned priest of the eighteenth century, whom Cardinal Moran calls the illustrious Innes: "It was about this time when the Romans, by the erection of the new province of Valentia, were in possession of all betwixt the walls from Northumberland to the Firths, that the holy bishop, St. Patrick, apostle of Ireland, was born upon the confines of the Roman province at Kilpatrick, near Alcluyd or Dunbriton in the north of Britain, as the learnedest among the Irish, as well as other foreign writers, do now agree (*Civil and Eccles. Hist. of Scotland*; Spalding Club, p. 34).

Finally, I will conclude with the testimony of the great Cardinal Moran, who now rules over an important diocese in Australia, and whose literary labours are highly valued by the learned. He has written in the January number of the *Dublin Review* for 1880 an elaborate article setting forth his matured conviction that St. Patrick was a Briton, born on the banks of the Clyde; and he adds that those great masters of Irish literature in our own day, Petrie, O'Donovan, and O'Curry, are of the same opinion. He goes through the whole range of ancient Irish authors who in any way refer to the subject; beginning with St. Patrick himself and SS. Fiacc and Evin his disciples, he goes through the successive lives of the saint, he weighs every allusion to the subject found in sermon or hymn or occasional tract, and he brings his work to a close by affirming his entire and profound acceptance of the proposition I have endeavoured to set forth. It was this very article of Cardinal Moran which first drew my attention to the matter, and I should be ungrateful if I did not acknowledge how deep my obligation is to him. I have derived equal advantage from his other important work, *Essays of Early Irish Church History*, in elucidating the facts which make up the history of St. Patrick.

Among the witnesses I have called as to the birthplace of St. Patrick all are Irish in birth, in feeling and in aspiration, with the exception of two. One of these is St. Patrick himself, and the other the famous Scottish historian Innes; and certainly no one will ascribe an anti-Irish feeling to either of them. St. Patrick's testimony carries all the more weight because it was utterly unintentional, and the words are recorded by his pen because they were the truth; and no reader of Innes can doubt that he diligently and laboriously sought the truth, and told it because it was the truth. When Fiacc and Evin, Probus and Jocelyn, wrote down in prose and verse that St. Patrick was born at Nemthur, otherwise Alclyde, surely their sole motive for so doing was that in their very hearts they thought they were recording the simple historical truth.

But the advocates on the other side say persistently that their national saint was born in Gaul, because he was mixed up with Gaul, and spent so long a time in it. Surely this is no reason for assigning to him Gaul as a birthplace. We may just as well say that Pelagius was not a Briton or that Cœlestius was not an Irishman, because they spent their whole lives in Italy and the East, and never revisited their native land. In the fourth century the Roman Empire was the one great country; Italian, Gaul, Spaniard, and Briton were all alike Roman citizens, and they were at home alike in the Imperial city or the most distant province, and their nationality was Roman. St. Patrick's father was a Frank from beyond the Rhine, and his mother Conchessa was a Gaul; but Calpurnius was a soldier, and the chances of a soldier's life brought him and his family to the banks of the Clyde. There was nothing strange in this, but it would have been indeed strange if, when St. Patrick returned to Dumbarton to find his home broken up and the country in a state of peril and confusion, he, with his earnest desire to become a priest, had remained there in circumstances which rendered impossible the fulfilment of his wishes. All his hopes were centred in his venerable uncle, St. Martin of Tours, now indeed an old man, but still in the very height of his reputation. To Gaul then he went, and we cannot wonder, when we consider the unsettled state of the times and the confusion which reigned in political matters, that he did not visit again the place of his birth. Marmoutier became to him a home, and, when his uncle died, he had formed attachments which kept him in Gaul. At Lerins he found a second home, and from that time forward it was in Gaul he found all he wanted—friends, occupation, and subsistence. His friendship with St. Germanus formed a new tie, and whether he was serving in the church at St. Auxerre or preaching the Gospel in Armorica it was still in Gaul that his interests and his time were employed. Nobody calls in question his intimate and prolonged connection with Gaul, but how does that affect by a hair's breadth the place of his birth?

But our opponents urge that the disordered state of

APPENDIX I.

North Britain at the time was such that it is impossible to reconcile with it the facts which St. Patrick himself mentions. He tells us that his fellow-captives were numbered by thousands, and they say this could not have been in a locality so desolated by invasion and inroads. My answer is complete and destroys every atom of force this objection at first seems to have. The region of Dumbarton was not abandoned by the Roman legions until many years after the date of St. Patrick's captivity, but continued to be occupied by a large force. Of this there is unquestionable proof. There is preserved to us a valuable document of those times which gives the real distribution of the Imperial army in Britain. It is a, comparatively speaking, rare book, but it was well known to Gibbon, who makes frequent use of it; and it is equally familiar to those scholars who, in our own age, seek to ascertain the real condition of things in Britain at the close of the fourth century. It is styled *Notitia Imperii*, and was drawn up early in the reign of the Emperor Honorius about the year 401. It professes to give an official list of the dignitaries of the Roman Empire and the number and the distribution of the Roman troops. From its very nature it is a thoroughly dry book, and no one would think of reading it through for pleasure. It is a mere list of names and offices, of places and figures, and has no other motive for compilation than to supply the statistics of the Empire. Yet it gives us the exact information that we want, and tells us the number of the soldiers stationed in Dumbarton twelve years after St. Patrick was carried off captive. We must remember that Valentia—the province between the Antonine and Hadrian Walls, including the district bounded on the south by a line stretching from the Solway Firth to Wall's End on the Tyne and on the north by the Roman Wall reaching from Dumbarton to the northern shore of the Firth of Forth—was re-conquered by the valour and skill of Theodosius in 367. It was the outlying province of the Roman Empire, and it was in immediate contact with the boldest, fiercest, and most untamed enemies of the Roman name. What wonder, then, would it be if the great bulk of the Roman army were stationed in that newly recovered province? Great bodies of troops are stationed in dangerous and exposed places, not in countries where there is nothing to fear—no enemy to oppose. The Romans were still the great masters of the military art, and surely they could not be ignorant of the elementary truth that, if the frontier were secure, the country behind was safe. Accordingly, though the seat of government was at Eboracum (York), the legions and auxiliaries were at Dumbarton and along the Antonine Wall. Mancunium (Manchester) might have a cohort of auxiliary troops, Bremetonacæ (Ribchester) its regiment of Sarmatians, and Longovicum (Lancaster) its wing of cavalry. But these were merely to preserve order and maintain communications; the great bulk of the army, under the command of the Duke of the Britains (the Dux Britanniarum), would be posted on the extreme north of the Roman dominions. So much for the probabilities of the case. Now for the actual facts. The *Notitia Imperii*—that cold, dry, impartial witness—tells us that the Duke had under him 14,000 foot and 900 horse, and that, of these, 8000 foot and 600 horse were set aside for the defence of the great Northern Wall. The date of the *Notitia* (the army list of those days) is 401—thirteen years later than the captivity of St. Patrick—but these figures would be approximately correct for the earlier date. The Roman power might rise or fall, the pressure of hostile barbarians might vary from time to time at different points, but the Campus Tabernaculorum (the Magh Tabern—the Field of Tents) was always occupied by a large and disciplined force. If, on an urgent call in another quarter, a regiment was withdrawn, it was speedily replaced, for the peace, the security, the well-being of the Britains depended on the efficiency of the Dumbarton garrison. The presence of so large a body of troops would attract a numerous body of camp-followers, and a large civil population would gather around to supply the wants of officers and men. What, then, becomes of the objection that there could not have been a large civil, and so a large Christian, community residing at Theodosia in 388?

I became acquainted with these statistics of the state of Britain in the fourth century in a curious way. I was busy writing the second chapter of this history when I was honoured with a visit from the Bishops of Liverpool and Leeds—old school-fellows and friends. Dr Cornthwaite remarked how strange it was that I was interesting myself in such a subject, and said that an old pupil of his in the English College at Rome had given himself up to the study of Roman antiquities, and had sent him two or three pamphlets on the distribution of the Roman troops in Britain. On my request to see them, he kindly sent them to me. In one of them, with the not very promising title of "The Station at Greta Bridge in Yorkshire," I found the very thing I wanted. The writer—Father Hirst—was quoting the calculations of a learned German, named Scholl, as to the numbers of the Roman army in Britain. Scholl took for the basis of his paper the statements of the *Notitia Imperii*, and thus, to my surprise and joy, I ascertained the very thing I wanted to know. Few Englishmen know Father Hirst's antiquarian knowledge; it is most minute, accurate to a marvel, and drawn from original sources—often the most obscure, and, in their form and style, most repulsive to the general reader. That visit was a notable incident in my life; that chance conversation was of priceless value to me; for the rapture of a miser hugging to his breast his money-bags is not to be compared to that which fills the bosom of a student of history who suddenly finds himself unexpectedly emerging from the mists of doubt and speculation into the full light of fact and knowledge.

There is another consideration which our opponents will

do well to weigh. The country that has been honoured by the birth of a great man is for the most part foremost in setting forth its claim. How happens it, then, if France was the birthplace of St. Patrick, that she does not claim him for her son? Has France become so careless of her reputation of being the mother of great men that she remains silent when Great Britain asserts its right to call St. Patrick a child of her soil? France is justly jealous of her right to number among her glories some of the foremost men and women who were his contemporaries. She would not willingly forego the glory of being able to count amongst her children St. Geneviève of Paris, St. Germanus of Auxerre, St. Lupus of Troyes, St. Vincent of Lerins, SS. Honoratus and Hilary of Arles; but when the most glorious of the great servants of God of the time is in question she makes no sign, and experiences no motherly throbbing at her heart. She may be proud of his training; she may boast that it was her monasteries, her schools, her cathedral that fashioned him to be the brightest and sharpest of the swords that God employed in routing the enemy of souls; but she does not look upon him as a child of her soil. His birth is not one of her glories.

Again, when the hero, whose birth is being discussed, is a saint of old, a devotion has invariably sprung up in the immediate neighbourhood. Exact localities are pointed out, natural objects are associated with his name, wells and rocks, churches and hospitals are called after him. The very atmosphere becomes charged with his memory, and the religious practices of the people are coloured by it. Benefactions and foundations are gradually forthcoming, and the name of the saint is in the very air. But our opponents cannot produce a single spot in France which in any of these ways honours the memory of St. Patrick's birthplace. There is not a single strong and abiding tradition which points out any one town or district of France as so greatly honoured. Yet it is not that the French are cold in their sentiments to the great apostle of the Irish. When they really can trace his footprints they are not slow to honour them. When in the neighbourhood of Tours they are reminded year after year by the flowers at Christmas of St. Patrick's Thorn they gather in thousands to venerate his memory and invoke his intercession. If tradition could thus perpetuate the memory of the lowly traveller who only sheltered for a night on the banks of the Loire, and in the name of their commune and the dedication of their church secured the affectionate reverence of the people, surely the same vivacious and quick-witted Frenchmen would have known had he indeed been born amongst them.

Let us now turn to the north bank of the Clyde and see how it fulfils these characteristics. Why, the whole neighbourhood is full of St. Patrick; wherever you turn, his name is in your ear. The exact spot of his birth is pointed out at Kilpatrick; the church of St. Patrick is built over St. Patrick's Hill. The hills bear his name; the old church at Dumbarton is St. Patrick's Church. The little village became a place of pilgrimage, and for more than a thousand years a perpetual stream of pilgrims from Ireland testified their unquestioning belief that there and there only was their national Patron born. I have cited already numerous statements of the Irish writers of the sixth and succeeding centuries, and Jocelyn, who must have been well acquainted with the district, for he was on the most intimate terms with the then Bishop of Glasgow, having written at his urgent request a life of St. Kentigern, expresses in precise and definite terms the belief of the twelfth century. Is not this a case of the judgment of Solomon? That wisest of men recognised the true mother of the child in the one who loved and cherished it, and bade the heartless woman who was indifferent even to its life depart a proved impostor. Scotland has shown her love for her offspring, and for ages has persistently and consistently asserted her claim to be his true mother; France has equally consistently and persistently repudiated it. When the honour is thrust upon her after the lapse of fifteen centuries she makes no sign, and surely we may, without any disrespect to that glorious country, believe that she is not entitled to it.

No doubt the blighting influence of Protestantism has dimmed the tradition at Dumbarton, but it has not obliterated it; and no traveller can visit the north bank of the Clyde without stumbling against memorials of our saint. Even the name of the village where his father lived has been preserved. About twelve miles east of Glasgow a river from the south called Avon falls into the Clyde, and this was apparently the true "River Mouth," the Bannaven of St. Patrick, and the village stood in the fork formed by the confluence of the two streams, and, wonderful to say, the range of hills skirting the Avon still bears the name of Bannauk, an evident variation of the original name.

To conclude, though the point has been many times hotly contested, it is after all a mere matter of fact to be determined by evidence. That evidence is forthcoming in abundance (for I have given only a tithe of what might have been adduced), and it is all on one side. For upwards of fifteen hundred years that evidence has been deemed conclusive, and it is not yet seventy years since Dr. Lanigan propounded his new theory that St. Patrick was born at Boulogne. But it cannot be that all this weight of evidence and authority is to vanish into thin air because an ingenious and learned writer surprises and dazzles the world with a novel and unsupported hypothesis.

APPENDIX II.

ST. PATRICK IN LANCASHIRE.

It is now some years ago since I began to interest myself in the early religious history of Lancashire. At first I was under the impression that we could go no further back than the times of St. Wilfrid, in the latter half of the seventh century. I thought that whatever Christianity might have existed in our county previous to that date, it had left no trace behind. I need not recount the steps by which I arrived at a very different conclusion—namely, that Christianity had been planted in Lancashire in Roman times, and that after a dark interval of nearly 250 years it was found still flourishing on the banks of the Ribble by the Angles, under King Egfrid. Among the most interesting facts which I slowly ascertained was that of the presence amongst us of St. Patrick, the great light of the West, and the Apostle of Ireland. Strange as it may appear, it is certain that he landed on our shores, and traversed our hills and dales; that he left on the very soil indelible marks of his presence, and that a pilgrimage was established in his honour by the devout Irish people, which endured for 1000 years, and of which we can find traces at this day.

Morecambe Bay and its winding coast are studded with sites consecrated by his presence and wondrous deeds. Even before the sailor touches the land, St. Patrick's Sker is pointed out to him. When he reaches the rocky shore and lands at Heysham, St. Patrick's Chapel attracts his attention, and as he journeys northwards he finds himself passing by St. Patrick's Well, at Slyne. St. Patrick's Sker is marked on the Ordnance map, and is about two miles from the shore, just opposite Heysham. The ruins of St. Patrick's Chapel still crown the precipitous cliff of Heysham; they have stood there braving the winds and storms of the Irish Sea since the sixth or seventh century. The architecture is of the rudest, but the form of the chapel, its size, everything about it reminds one of similar chapels scattered up and down the country districts of Ireland. From time immemorial the roof has fallen in, but the walls still stand, and the mortar made with the sea-sand has become harder than the rock itself. There is only one period to which the erection of this building can be assigned, and that is before the Angles became settled in Lancashire. It was in the sixth and seventh centuries that the Irish, newly converted to the Faith by the preaching and miracles of St. Patrick, poured themselves like a torrent on the western nations of Europe, carrying with them their Faith, and becoming missionaries of true religion and learning, as far as the Danube and beyond the Alps. But what was it that attracted them to Lancashire? In the first place, it was the actual nearness of the land. When Columbanus left Bangor, on the shores of Belfast Lough, the coast of Lancashire was the most convenient for him to land upon. But there was a far higher attraction. When, in 394, Patrick left his master's house in Antrim, in the valley of the Braid, he journeyed across Ireland to the western coast, washed by the Atlantic, and it was at Killala that he took ship. He was driven by the north-western gales into Morecambe Bay. Tradition tells us that his vessel stuck fast on the sands at the mouth of the Duddon. The rising tide might free him from this peril, but it was only for him to be wrecked on the shore near Heysham. When the crew escaped from the breakers, and climbed the cliff, they had to determine what course they should pursue. It was to their young passenger that they turned, and him they followed on their wearisome and dangerous journey to Dumbarton. When they were perishing from thirst on the sandy coast of Bare, a fresh and vigorous local tradition tells us that at his bidding a spring gushed forth from the ground, and the spot is perfectly well known to the inhabitants of Lancaster and its neighbourhood as St. Patrick's Well.

In his account of this journey St. Patrick gives no names of places, but the nomenclature of the district is a sufficient guide, and all the way to Dumbarton occur spots bearing the name of this lowly traveller of the fourth century. The romantic but desolate Patterdale is none other than St. Patrick's Dale, and the ancient church is dedicated to him. The route became sacred in the minds of the Irish of the sixth and subsequent centuries. Many a devout servant of St. Patrick looked upon himself as peculiarly blessed if his feet could tread the path which had been made holy for ever by the footsteps of his nation's Patron Saint. A continuous flow of pilgrims from Dumbarton on the north to Heysham on the south, or from Heysham to Dumbarton, was kept up during the next one thousand years, and was only interrupted by the Reformation in Henry VIII.'s time. Hospitals for the reception of the pilgrims were established at Dumbarton and, as time went on, at Lancaster. As the hospital at Lancaster is little known, I give the authority for its existence. A chatty and well-informed writer in the *Lancaster Gazette*, who styles himself Cross Fleury, tells us that Dr. Kuerden, the famous Lancashire antiquary of James I.'s reign, writes of a deed of pre-Reformation date, which conveyed a house in Lancaster for the reception of pilgrims to the Church of St. Patrick at Heysham. Here we have hospitals for pilgrims, the humble clients of St. Patrick, at the northern and southern end of the chain which connected the birthplace of St. Patrick with the spot where he reached the shore after escaping from the waves of Morecambe Bay. Here and there, at wide intervals, we can pick up isolated links, and perhaps some one better acquainted with the route may know of others with which I am not familiar; but certain it is that the memory of St. Patrick was kept alive in North Lancashire, in Westmoreland, and Cumberland, and the south-western counties of Scotland, from the fourth to the sixteenth century, by a constant stream of pilgrims. Patterdale and Preston Patrick are names which speak with no uncertain voice. In Dumfriesshire immediately after the traveller passes the English border on his northward journey he comes to Kirkpatrick, not far from Gretna Green so well known with a different kind of celebrity; and if our traveller turns aside a little to the west he finds a second Kirkpatrick, on the little stream of the Urr in Kirkcudbrightshire. These are striking instances of the way in which the memory of St. Patrick has been preserved. Of course since the times of the Reformation all this has ceased; the name of St. Patrick is no longer held in veneration in those parts, save by the recent immigrants from the sister isle, but the evidences of the old devotion remain, and in dale and church, and well, are to be found by a painstaking antiquary, by one who is a lover of the ancient histories of our land. For my present purpose it is enough to observe that this pilgrimage arose in far-off times, not later than the conquest of Lancashire and the Lake districts by Egfrid, of Northumbria. The land has gone through great changes since; it has had many masters who have spoken diverse languages. The Angle has conquered the Celt; the Angle has had to submit to the harsh yoke of the Dane and Norseman; and the mailed warriors of William the Conqueror have from their castles held in subjection generations of serfs and franklins, but the old traditions have kept their ground, and are as fresh in the mouths of the country people on the sandy shores and in rock-strewn dales as if St. Patrick and his pilgrimage were things of yesterday.

Nor are these the only witnesses to us of the nineteenth century of the piety of the Celtic inhabitants of Lancashire in the fifth and sixth centuries. In the time of Leland there was standing in Liverpool, not far from the present Exchange Railway Station, in what yet bears the name of Crosshall Street, a cross called St. Patrick's Cross. The street took its name from an ancient mansion named Cross Hall, and this in turn bore the name of a family which had resided there from the time of King John. It was about this time that family names began to be common, and the resident in the Hall took his surname from the Cross immediately adjoining. At what exact period the Cross was raised cannot now be ascertained, but it is all but certain that neither Norman, nor older Dane, nor even earlier Angle, entertained any great devotion for the Apostle of Ireland, and we can scarcely err in believing that St. Patrick's Cross was a mark of the veneration entertained for him by his Celtic fellow-countrymen, or at least by some early settlers from Ireland.

Nor is Manchester behind her great commercial rival in memorials of St. Patrick. Patrick Stone, not far from her grand collegiate church, was a well-known landmark until the end of the reign of James I.; and Patricroft is but a corruption of Patrick's Cruagh, the hillock from which the saint preached when, in 430, he accompanied St. Germanus in his apostolic journey to the West of England.

Lancashire has had a varied history, and has been the fruitful mother of many glorious sons. The first name associated with her is the honoured name of Agricola, the brave soldier, the skilful general, and the consummate statesman. The darkest hours of the sixth century were lighted up for a moment by the preaching of St. Kentigern. In the seventh century the pure and holy St. Oswald hallowed the soil of Winwick by his blood, shed in defence of his Faith and country. In the ninth century the incorrupt body of St. Cuthbert was carried through the length and breadth of the county by his faithful disciples, flying from the pursuit of the Danes; and the churches of Halsall of Lytham, and Upper Kellet, dedicated in his honour, testify to the profound impression produced by that memorable pilgrimage on the minds of the people. After the Conquest, Stephen, Earl of Boulogne, afterwards King of England, founded the great Abbey of Furness; Nigel, baron of Halton, that of Stanlawe, and Henry de Lacy that more famous still of Whalley. A Robert **Greslet**, or Greddle, baron of Manchester and governor of Lancaster Castle, was with the **barons at** Runnymede when they won the great charter of English liberties, the Magna Charta, **and, later on, he gave** to Manchester its first Charter in 1222, and Manchester **still honours his** memory by bearing on its shield **the three** bars *or* on field of gules. In the fourteenth century a Sir John de Coupland, **and in the** sixteenth a Sir Edward Stanley, distinguished themselves in the hotly contested fields of Neville's Cross and Flodden Field, bearing aloft the banner of Lancashire men. Under Elizabeth, a Lancashire man— Cardinal Allan of Rossall—by his foundation of Douay College, baulked the schemes of the crafty Burleigh and the imperious will of the Queen. **Sir Thomas** Tyldesley gave his life at Wigan, fighting for **Charles I.** Mr. **Butler, of** Kirkland, sacrificed his estates, and Mr. John Brockholes, of Claughton, **died** of his wounds, inflicted at Preston, in maintaining the cause of the **Stuarts.** In later times Lancashire **has sent to the Councils of the Queen three of the** most brilliant statesmen of the age—Sir Robert **Peel, Lord Derby, and Mr.** Gladstone. We have had men eminent in literature **like** Lingard, **in** invention like Arkwright, **in science** like Dalton **and Joule.** But, strange to say, no one name in all this galaxy **of worthies has so** stamped itself **on our soil as that of the fugitive slave from** Milcho's **homestead** under the shadow **of** Mount Slemish. Hill and dale, **well and stone, church** and **cross, after the lapse of well-nigh 1500 years, still, in** busy, hard-working Lancashire, **remind us of his presence in our county, in** Manchester, **in Liverpool, and on the shores of Morecambe** Bay.

In this brief sketch I have done little more than refer to the facts upon which the conclusion rests that St. Patrick was in Lancashire. To examine them in detail would have taken up too much space, though, perhaps, it would have given greater value to this paper. But I may conclude with the assurance that what I have stated as facts are really such, and that I have not drawn upon my imagination for any one of them. That they have been overlooked by previous writers may be true, but that is no argument against their reality. Lancashire has been rich in warriors and statesmen, in merchants and manufacturers, but till recent times it has been deficient in local annalists and historians, and it is only within the last few years that Catholic pens, like those of the Rev. T. E. Gibson and Joseph Gillow, not to mention others, have aroused an interest in the subject. Names and places familiar to us as household words have been around us; they have had tales of heroism and endurance to tell us, but they required a voice to convey their lessons, and for a time that voice was not forthcoming. But happier days are at hand, and the stories of Lancashire men and women, sequestered spots and crowded cities, and especially those of interest to Catholics, are gradually being collected and given to the world. Surely among them the story of St. Patrick in Lancashire is worthy of a place.

APPENDIX III.

TRAVELS OF ST. PATRICK.

I. 388. From Alclyde to the Coast of Louth, landing in Antrim.
II. 394. From Mount Slemish to Focklut on Killala Bay.
III. 394. From Killala Bay by Giant's Causeway into the Irish Sea; touches at the mouth of the Duddon and on St. Patrick's Sker, and lands at Heysham.
IV. 394. From Heysham passes Slyne, traverses Patterdale. A prisoner at Carlisle; reaches Alclyde.
V. 394. From Alclyde southwards, probably to Chester. Voyage to Bourdeaux, and land journey to Tours.
VI. From Marmoutier to Lerins. Date uncertain.
VII. 318. From Lerins to Auxerre.
VIII. From Auxerre to Armorica; return to Auxerre. Date uncertain.
IX. 329. By Paris to Havre. Lands in Britain, probably near Southampton. Visits St. Albans. Goes to Mold, Mancunium and Patricroft. Returns to Auxerre.
X. 332. Crosses the Little St. Bernard. Stops at Ivrea. Goes to Rome.
XI. 332. Returns to Auxerre.
XII. 332. Journeys to Britain; stays in Cornwall and Wales.
XIII. 333. Sails from St. David's Head to Bray in Wicklow.

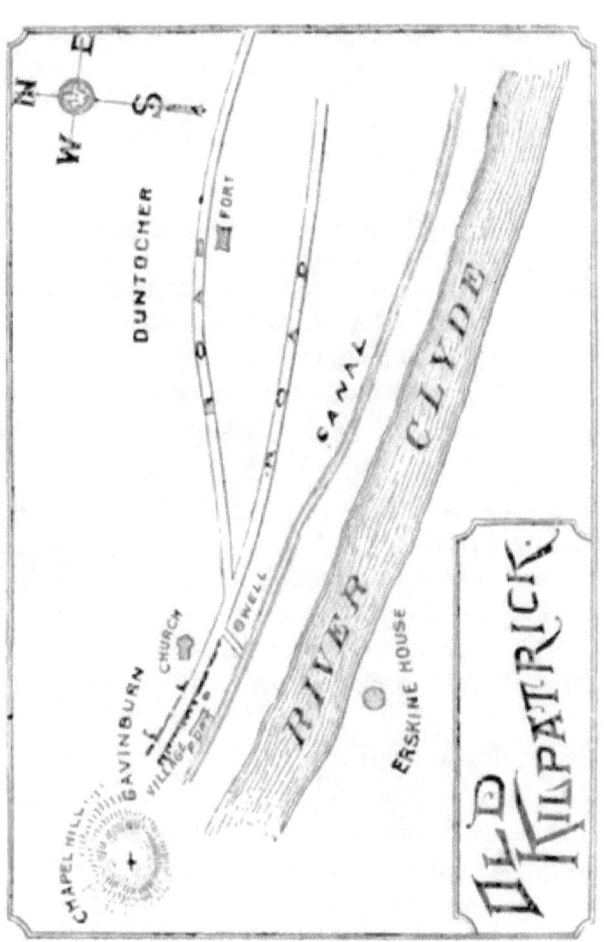

COMMUNICATED BY THE MOST REV. C. EYRE, ARCHBISHOP OF GLASGOW.

APPENDIX IV.

ST. PATRICK AND OLD KILPATRICK.

THE village of Old Kilpatrick is on the north bank of the Clyde, and situated on a fertile plain at the base of the Kilpatrick Hills. It is one and a half miles on the west from Bowling and four and three-fourths from Dumbarton, and on the east three miles from Clydebank and eleven and a half from Glasgow. The village consists mainly of one street, forming a portion of the turnpike road between Glasgow and Dumbarton.

Kilpatrick means in the Celtic language, "The church of St. Patrick". The district or parish that was known as Kilpatrick was divided in the year 1649, and formed into two parishes, *i.e.*, New or East Kilpatrick and Old or West Kilpatrick.

The ground plan will give a fair idea of the site of the old church, of the Holy Well, and of the present parish church. A print of the old church from a drawing made by Mr. Cumming, Dalmuir, from information given to him about it, can be seen in D. Macleod's *Clyde District of Dumbartonshire*, p. 82. It stood close to the site of the present church, and what remained of it was razed just before 1812. The exact site was the spot now called "Chapel brae".

The late Miss Hamilton, of Cockero, who was ninety years old when she died, told Mr. Donnelly that in her girlhood she often looked at piles of *broken, carved*, ancient stones piled near the church which was standing in her time, and was near the site of the present parish church. Some of these stones, she said, were *parts of saints and other figures*, all evidently very old.

Lord Blantyre is about to open a drain course through

that part of the ground, and some discoveries may then be found.

The ancient cross belonging to the old churchyard was dug up some three years ago in the churchyard, when making a grave for the remains of the late Andrew Buchanan of Auchintorlie. It was found buried deep in the soil. The workmanship and design are very like the Iona and Glendalough crosses, and it was very probably of about the eleventh century.

A stone font was also dug up at the same time, but was put back into the ground. The above-named carved figures, etc., were buried when the present church was built.

These notes were furnished me by Mr. Donnelly and Mr. Bruce. Mr. Donnelly, of Milton, has given me a large drawing of three portions of the shaft of the cross.

The old well of St. Patrick is quite neglected, and is nothing but a common puddle.

Some old records show that the farms in the Kilpatrick district were formerly let under a condition that the tenants were to supply pilgrims who came to St. Patrick's shrine with bed and board.

A fair used to be held here, and was known as "Patrickmas Fair".

Chapel Hill is a piece of rising ground a quarter of a mile west of Old Kilpatrick, and was the site of the western terminal fort of the great wall of Antoninus. A chapel is said to have been built near to the present group of Scotch fir trees. If excavations were made here the foundations of a chapel would probably be found, and made of the stones of the old fort or wall.

APPENDIX V.

HEYSHAM AND SLYNE.

The engravings on the backs of the volume are taken from two paintings by a young and talented artist of **Walton-le-Dale, Mr. Charles** Turner. Besides their merits as pictures, and they are of **a high** order, they possess an **interest for the** antiquary and **historian.** The **first is a view of the ruined chapel at** Heysham, known as St. Patrick's Chapel. **There has been** no attempt on the **part of the artist at drawing a striking** landscape—his aim **has been to give an exact and accurate** representation **of the ruin as it stands, and in this he has been eminently successful. In standing before the picture it appears as if every stone forming the wall, its shape and colour, had been minutely studied and faithfully** reproduced. **The architecture is extremely rude, and the** masonry **is equally so, for the building is of great** antiquity. **It has been exposed to all the inclemencies of the weather for about 1300 years, and so exhibits a time-worn and storm-tossed appearance. And well it may. Perhaps in all Lancashire there is not a building in existence which goes so** far **back into the distant past. As far as we can decide such a** matter, **this tiny chapel, for it is only twenty feet long by seven feet broad, dates from the sixth or seventh century. It was erected by the Celtic inhabitants of the coast, who had preserved some fragments of Roman civilisation, and who, above all else, retained the great treasure of the Christian religion, a precious legacy bequeathed to Britain by Rome. At the close of the fourth** century, **in the year 394, a fugitive slave from Ireland had been** driven by the wind and waves into Morecambe Bay. He landed near Heysham; and such was the veneration which, as time went on, grew up in the minds of the inhabitants of the coast for this apparently forlorn stranger that they built a chapel in his honour, and styled it by his name, the **Chapel of St. Patrick.** Misfortune had made St. Patrick, though the son of a Roman officer and a noble matron from Gaul, an exile from the land of his birth. For six years he had served as a slave on the coast of Antrim; he at length fled from his bondage and set out to return home. In all probability it was mere accident that brought him to Lancashire, and landed him on our coast. There was nothing to detain him on the spot, and so he at once started for his far-distant home on the banks of the Clyde. As we follow his steps we soon ascertain the cause of the lasting impression he produced on the minds of the simple natives of the neighbourhood. The remembrance of it is still treasured by the country folks, for they have received it from their fathers and mothers, who in their turn had heard it from the lips of those who had gone before them, and they receive it with unquestioning belief. Near Slyne he asked a woman for a drink of water; she rudely refused this slight request, when he bade her beware, for he had power from God to bid a spring rise up from the ground at the touch of his staff. He struck the ground, and the clear stream obeyed the summons, and it runs to this day. As time crept on it became a place of pilgrimage, and was known as St. Patrick's Well. It was and is still held in the highest reverence, and its waters, even amongst those who are not Catholics, are credited with marvellous virtues. To protect it from pollution a wall has been built about it. This forms the subject of the second painting. Here again the artist has not sought for effect in ingenious arrangement of tree and shrub; his object was to delineate St. Patrick's Well just as it is, without adding any ornament or hiding any defect. So we have the well pure and simple, with the coarse grass about, the stones loosened from the upper parts of the wall and thrown into the well. The ruins of neither chapel nor well are as well cared for as they ought to be. No attempt seems to be made to arrest the ravaging hand of time, nor the more ruthless mischief of the chance visitor, who in pure heedlessness disturbs a stone or chips off a piece of mortar. Yet there is nothing in the whole county which has a more wonderful tale to tell. Its whole length and breadth does not contain a monument more venerable for its antiquity, more interesting to the Christian and student. Should this neglect continue, a time may come when the paintings just described may be the only memorials left of those records in stone of St. Patrick's presence in our county.

SELECTION

FROM

BURNS & OATES'

Catalogue

OF

PUBLICATIONS.

LONDON: BURNS AND OATES, Lᴅ.
28 ORCHARD ST., W., & 63 PATERNOSTER ROW, E.C.
NEW YORK: 12 EAST 17ᴛʜ STREET.

1892.

NEW BOOKS.

Saint Ignatius Loyola and The Early Jesuits. By STEWART ROSE. With more than 100 Illustrations by H.W. and H.C. Brewer and L. Wain. The whole produced under the immediate superintendence of the Rev. W. H. Eyre, S.J. Super Royal 8vo. Handsomely bound in Cloth, extra gilt. Price 15s. net.

"This magnificent volume is one of which Catholics have justly reason to be proud. Its historical as well as its literary value is very great, and the illustrations from the pencils of Mr. Louis Wain and Messrs. H. W. and H. C. Brewer are models of what the illustrations of such a book should be. We hope that this book will be found in every Catholic drawing-room, as a proof that 'we Catholics' are in no way behind those around us in the beauty of the illustrated books that issue from our hands, or in the interest which is added to the subject by a skilful pen and finished style."—*Month.*

The Letters of the late Father George Porter, S.J., Archbishop of Bombay. Demy 8vo. Cloth, 7s. 6d.

"Brimful of good things. . . . Will instruct and amuse widely-differing classes of readers. In them the priest will find a storehouse of hints on matters spiritual; from them the layman will reap crisp and clear information on many ecclesiastical points; the critic can listen to frank opinions of literature of every shade; and the general reader can enjoy the choice bits of description and morsels of humour scattered lavishly through the book. It would be hard to find a correspondence which, in style, more closely observes the golden rule of letter-writing—'write as you speak.'"—*Tablet.*

Ireland and St. Patrick. A study of the Saint's character, and of the results of his Apostolate. By the Rev. W. B. MORRIS, of the Oratory. Crown 8vo. Cloth, 5s.

May be called a sequel to the author's "Life of St. Patrick," being a study chiefly in the 5th, 12th, 17th, and 19th centuries of those influences which have preserved the Faith in Ireland, and obtained for that country the exalted, if unintentional praise of Lord Macaulay, when he says, "Alone amongst the Northern Nations Ireland adhered to the Ancient Faith."

Immediately.

The Wisdom and Wit of Blessed Thomas More. Edited, with Introduction, by the Rev. T. E. BRIDGETT, C.SS.R., author of "Life of Blessed Thomas More," "Life of Blessed John Fisher," &c.

Aquinas Ethicus; or, the Moral Teaching of St. Thomas. A translation of the principal portions of the second part of the *Summa Theologica*, with Notes. By the Rev. JOSEPH RICKABY, S.J. Quarterly Series.

The Spirit of St. Ignatius, Founder of the Society of Jesus. Translated from the French of the Rev. Fr. XAVIER DE FRANCIOSI, of the same Society.

Succat; or, Sixty Years of the Life of St. Patrick. By the Very Rev. Mgr. ROBERT GRADWELL.

No. 1.   1892.

SELECTION

FROM

BURNS AND OATES' CATALOGUE OF PUBLICATIONS.

ALLIES, T. W. (K.C.S.G.)

    Formation of Christendom. Vols. I., II., and III., (all out of print.)

    Church and State as seen in the Formation of Christendom, 8vo, pp. 472, cloth . (out of print.)

    The Throne of the Fisherman, built by the Carpenter's Son, the Root, the Bond, and the Crown of Christendom. Demy 8vo £0 10 6

    The Holy See and the Wandering of the Nations. Demy 8vo. 0 10 6

    Peter's Rock in Mohammed's Flood. Demy 8vo. . 0 10 6

"It would be quite superfluous at this hour of the day to recommend Mr. Allies' writings to English Catholics. Those of our readers who remember the article on his writings in the *Katholik*, know that he is esteemed in Germany as one of our foremost writers."—*Dublin Review*.

ALLIES, MARY.

    Leaves from St. John Chrysostom, With introduction by T. W. Allies, K.C.S.G. Crown 8vo, cloth . 0 6 0

"Miss Allies' 'Leaves' are delightful reading; the English is remarkably pure and graceful; page after page reads as if it were original. No commentator, Catholic or Protestant, has ever surpassed St. John Chrysostom in the knowledge of Holy Scripture, and his learning was of a kind which is of service now as it was at the time when the inhabitants of a great city hung on his words."—*Tablet*.

ALLNATT, C. F. B.

    Cathedra Petri. Third and Enlarged Edition. Cloth 0 6 0

"Invaluable to the controversialist and the theologian, and most useful for educated men inquiring after truth or anxious to know the positive testimony of Christian antiquity in favour of Papal claims."—*Month*.

    Which is the True Church? Fifth Edition . . 0 1 4

    The Church and the Sects 0 1 0

    Ditto, Ditto. Second Series . . . 0 1 6

ANNUS SANCTUS:

    Hymns of the Church for the Ecclesiastical Year. Translated from the Sacred Offices by various Authors, with Modern, Original, and other Hymns, and an Appendix of Earlier Versions. Selected and Arranged by ORBY SHIPLEY, M.A.

    Plain Cloth, lettered 0 5 6

    Edition de luxe 0 10 6

ANSWERS TO ATHEISTS: OR NOTES ON

 Ingersoll. By the Rev. A. Lambert, (over 100,000 copies sold in America). Tenth edition. Paper £0 0 6
  Cloth 0 1 0

B. N.

 The Jesuits: their Foundation and History. 2 vols. crown 8vo, cloth, red edges 0 15 0

"The book is just what it professes to be—*a popular history*, drawn from well-known sources," &c.—*Month*.

BAKER, VEN. FATHER AUGUSTIN.

 Holy Wisdom; or, Directions for the Prayer of Contemplation, &c. Extracted from Treatises written by the Ven. Father F. Augustin Baker, O.S.B., and edited by Abbot Sweeney, D.D. Beautifully bound in half leather 0 6 0

"We earnestly recommend this most beautiful work to all our readers. We are sure that every community will use it as a constant manual. If any persons have friends in convents, we cannot conceive a better present they can make them, or a better claim they can have on their prayers, than by providing them with a copy."—*Weekly Register*.

BORROMEO, LIFE OF ST. CHARLES.

 From the Italian of Peter Guissano. 2 vols. . . 0 15 0

"A standard work, which has stood the test of succeeding ages; it is certainly the finest work on St. Charles in an English dress."—*Tablet*.

BOWDEN, REV. H. S. (of the Oratory) Edited by.

 Dante's Divina Commedia: Its scope and value. From the German of FRANCIS HETTINGER, D.D. With an engraving of Dante. Crown 8vo . . 0 10 6

"All that Venturi attempted to do has been now approached with far greater power and learning by Dr. Hettinger, who, as the author of the 'Apologie des Christenthums,' and as a great Catholic theologian, is eminently well qualified for the task he has undertaken."—*The Saturday Review*.

BRIDGETT, REV. T. E. (C.SS.R.).

 Discipline of Drink 0 3 6

"The historical information with which the book abounds gives evidence of deep research and patient study, and imparts a permanent interest to the volume, which will elevate it to a position of authority and importance enjoyed by few of its compeers."—*The Arrow*.

 Our Lady's Dowry; how England Won that Title. New and Enlarged Edition 0 5 0

"This book is the ablest vindication of Catholic devotion to Our Lady, drawn from tradition, that we know of in the English language."—*Tablet*.

BRIDGETT, REV. T. E. (C.SS.R.)—continued.

Ritual of the New Testament. An essay on the principles and origin of Catholic Ritual in reference to the New Testament. Third edition . . . £0 5 0

The Life of the Blessed John Fisher. With a reproduction of the famous portrait of Blessed JOHN FISHER by HOLBEIN, and other Illustrations. 2nd Ed. 0 7 6

"The Life of Blessed John Fisher could hardly fail to be interesting and instructive. Sketched by Father Bridgett's practised pen, the portrait of this holy martyr is no less vividly displayed in the printed pages of the book than in the wonderful picture of Holbein, which forms the frontispiece."—*Tablet.*

The True Story of the Catholic Hierarchy deposed by Queen Elizabeth, with fuller Memoirs of its Last Two Survivors. By the Rev. T. E. BRIDGETT, C.SS.R., and the late Rev. T. F. KNOX, D.D., of the London Oratory. Crown 8vo, cloth, 0 7 6

"We gladly acknowledge the value of this work on a subject which has been obscured by prejudice and carelessness."—*Saturday Review.*

The Life and Writings of Sir Thomas More, Lord Chancellor of England and Martyr under Henry VIII. With Portrait of the Martyr taken from the Crayon Sketch made by Holbein in 1527 . . 0 7 6

"Father Bridgett has followed up his valuable Life of Bishop Fisher with a still more valuable Life of Thomas More. It is, as the title declares, a study not only of the life, but also of the writings of Sir Thomas. Father Bridgett has considered him from every point of view, and the result is, it seems to us, a more complete and finished portrait of the man, mentally and physically, than has been hitherto presented."—*Athenæum.*

BRIDGETT, REV. T. E. (C.SS.R.), Edited by.

Souls Departed. By CARDINAL ALLEN. First published in 1565, now edited in modern spelling by the Rev. T. E. Bridgett 0 6 0

BROWNE, REV. R. D.:

Plain Sermons. Sixty-eight Plain Sermons on the Fundamental Truths of the Catholic Church. Crown 8vo 0 6 0

"These are good sermons. . . . The great merit of which is that they might be read *verbatim* to any congregation, and they would be understood and appreciated by the uneducated almost as fully as by the cultured. They have been carefully put together; their language is simple and their matter is solid."—*Catholic News.*

BUCKLER, REV. H. REGINALD (O.P.)

The Perfection of Man by Charity: a Spiritual Treatise. Crown 8vo, cloth. 0 5 0

"We have read this unpretending, but solid and edifying work, with much pleasure, and heartily commend it to our readers. . . . Its scope is sufficiently explained by the title."—*The Month.*

CASWALL, FATHER.

Catholic Latin Instructor in the Principal Church Offices and Devotions, for the Use of Choirs, Convents, and Mission Schools, and for Self-Teaching. 1 vol., complete £0 3 6

Or Part I., containing Benediction, Mass, Serving at Mass, and various Latin Prayers in ordinary use . 0 1 6

May Pageant: A Tale of Tintern. (A Poem) Second edition 0 2 0

Poems 0 5 0

Lyra Catholica, containing all the Breviary and Missal Hymns, with others from various sources. 32mo, cloth, red edges 0 2 6

CATHOLIC BELIEF: OR, A SHORT AND

Simple Exposition of Catholic Doctrine. By the Very Rev. Joseph Faà di Bruno, D.D. Tenth edition . . . . Price 6d.; post free, 0 0 8½

Cloth, lettered, ... 0 0 10

Also an edition on better paper and bound in cloth, with gilt lettering and steel frontispiece 0 2 0

CHALLONER, BISHOP.

Meditations for every day in the year. New edition. Revised and edited by the Right Rev. John Virtue, D.D., Bishop of Portsmouth. 8vo. 6th edition . 0 3 0

And in other bindings.

COLERIDGE, REV. H. J. (S.J.) *(See Quarterly Series.)*

DEVAS, C. S.

Studies of Family Life: a contribution to Social Science. Crown 8vo 0 5 0

"We recommend these pages and the remarkable evidence brought together in them to the careful attention of all who are interested in the well-being of our common humanity."—*Guardian.*

"Both thoughtful and stimulating."—*Saturday Review.*

DRANE, AUGUSTA THEODOSIA, Edited by.

The Autobiography of Archbishop Ullathorne. Demy 8vo., cloth 0 7 6

"Admirably edited and excellently produced."—*Weekly Register.*

"Told in manly, vigorous English, and filled with bits of descriptions of sea-life that are quite as good as anything Dana ever wrote, and characterized by a certain quaint humour that has frequently reminded us of the writings of Charles Waterton, the naturalist; this autobiography is certainly the most entertaining book that has been added to Catholic literature for many a long year."—*Caxton Review.*

EYRE, MOST REV. CHARLES, (Abp. of Glasgow).

The History of St. Cuthbert: or, An Account of his Life, Decease, and Miracles. Third edition. Illustrated with maps, charts, &c., and handsomely bound in cloth. Royal 8vo 0 14 0

"A handsome, well appointed volume, in every way worthy of its illustrious subject. . . . The chief impression of the whole is the picture of a great and good man drawn by a sympathetic hand."—*Spectator.*

FABER, REV. FREDERICK WILLIAM, (D.D.)

All for Jesus	£0	5 0
Bethlehem	0	7 0
Blessed Sacrament	0	7 6
Creator and Creature	0	6 0
Ethel's Book of the Angels.	0	5 0
Foot of the Cross	0	6 0
Growth in Holiness	0	6 0
Hymns	0	6 0
Notes on Doctrinal and Spiritual Subjects, 2 vols. each	0	5 0
Poems (a new edition in preparation).		
Precious Blood	0	5 0
Sir Lancelot	0	5 0
Spiritual Conferences	0	6 0
Life and Letters of Frederick William Faber, D.D., Priest of the Oratory of St. Philip Neri. By John Edward Bowden of the same Congregation	0	6 0

FOLEY, REV. HENRY, (S.J.)

Records of the English Province of the Society of Jesus. Vol. I., Series I. . . . . net	1	6 0
Vol. II., Series II., III., IV. . . . net	1	6 0
Vol. III., Series V., VI., VII., VIII. . . net	1	10 0
Vol. IV. Series IX., X., XI. . . . net	1	6 0
Vol. V., Series XII. with nine Photographs of Martyrs. . . . . net	1	10 0
Vol. VI., Diary and Pilgrim-Book of the English College, Rome. The Diary from 1579 to 1773, with Biographical and Historical Notes. The Pilgrim-Book of the Ancient English Hospice attached to the College from 1580 to 1656, with Historical Notes. . . . . net	1	6 0
Vol. VII. Part the First : General Statistics of the Province ; and Collectanea, giving Biographical Notices of its Members and of many Irish and Scotch Jesuits. With 20 Photographs . . . . net	1	6 0
Vol. VII. Part the Second: Collectanea, Completed ; With Appendices. Catalogues of Assumed and Real Names: Annual Letters ; Biographies and Miscellanea. . . . . net	1	6 0

"As a biographical dictionary of English Jesuits, it deserves a place in every well-selected library, and, as a collection of marvellous occurrences, persecutions, martyrdoms, and evidences of the results of faith, amongst the books of all who belong to the Catholic Church."—*Genealogist.*

FORMBY, REV. HENRY.

Monotheism : in the main derived from the Hebrew nation and the Law of Moses. The Primitive Religion of the City of Rome. An historical Investigation. Demy 8vo.	0	5 0

FRANCIS DE SALES, ST.: THE WORKS OF.
Translated into the English Language by the Very Rev. Canon Mackey, O.S.B., under the direction of the Right Rev. Bishop Hedley, O.S.B.

Vol. I. Letters to Persons in the World. Cloth . £0 6 0

"The letters must be read in order to comprehend the charm and sweetness of their style."—*Tablet.*

Vol. II.—The Treatise on the Love of God. Father Carr's translation of 1630 has been taken as a basis, but it has been modernized and thoroughly revised and corrected. 0 9 0

"To those who are seeking perfection by the path of contemplation this volume will be an armoury of help."—*Saturday Review.*

Vol. III. The Catholic Controversy. . . 0 6 0

"No one who has not read it can conceive how clear, how convincing, and how well adapted to our present needs are these controversial 'leaves.'"—*Tablet.*

Vol. IV. Letters to Persons in Religion, with introduction by Bishop Hedley on "St. Francis de Sales and the Religious State." 0 6 0

"The sincere piety and goodness, the grave wisdom, the knowledge of human nature, the tenderness for its weakness, and the desire for its perfection that pervade the letters, make them pregnant of instruction for all serious persons. The translation and editing have been admirably done."—*Scotsman.*

*** Other vols. in preparation.

GALLWEY, REV. PETER, (S.J.)
Precious Pearl of Hope in the Mercy of God, The. Translated from the Italian. With Preface by the Rev. Father Gallwey. Cloth. 0 4 6

Lectures on Ritualism and on the Anglican Orders. 2 vols. (Or may be had separately.) . 0 8 0

Salvage from the Wreck. A few Memories of the Dead, preserved in Funeral Discourses. With Portraits. Crown 8vo. 0 7 6

GIBSON, REV. H.
Catechism Made Easy. Being an Explanation of the Christian Doctrine. Eighth edition. 2 vols., cloth 0 7 6

"This work must be of priceless worth to any who are engaged in any form of catechetical instruction. It is the best book of the kind that we have seen in English."—*Irish Monthly.*

GILLOW, JOSEPH.
Literary and Biographical History, or, Bibliographical Dictionary of the English Catholics. From the Breach with Rome, in 1534, to the Present Time. Vols. I., II. and III. cloth, demy 8vo . . each. 0 15 0

*** Other vols. in preparation.

"The patient research of Mr. Gillow, his conscientious record of minute particulars, and especially his exhaustive bibliographical information in connection with each name, are beyond praise."—*British Quarterly Review.*

The Haydock Papers. Illustrated. Demy 8vo. . 0 7 6

"We commend this collection to the attention of every one that is interested in the records of the sufferings and struggles of our ancestors to hand down the faith to their children. It is in the perusal of such details that we bring home to ourselves the truly heroic sacrifices that our forefathers endured in those dark and dismal times."—*Tablet.*

GROWTH IN THE KNOWLEDGE OF OUR LORD.

Meditations for every Day in the Year, exclusive of those for Festivals, Days of Retreat, &c. Adapted from the original of Abbé de Brandt, by Sister Mary Fidelis. A new and Improved Edition, in 3 Vols. Sold only in sets. Price per set, . . . £1 2 6

"The praise, though high, bestowed on these excellent meditations by the Bishop of Salford is well deserved. The language, like good spectacles, spreads treasures before our vision without attracting attention to itself."—*Dublin Review.*

HEDLEY, BISHOP.

Our Divine Saviour, and other Discourses. Crown 8vo. 0 6 0

"A distinct and noteworthy feature of these sermons is, we certainly think, their freshness—freshness of thought, treatment, and style; nowhere do we meet pulpit commonplace or hackneyed phrase—everywhere, on the contrary, it is the heart of the preacher pouring out to his flock his own deep convictions, enforcing them from the 'Treasures, old and new,' of a cultivated mind."—*Dublin Review.*

HUMPHREY, REV. W. (S.J.)

Suarez on the Religious State: A Digest of the Doctrine contained in his Treatise, "De Statû Religionis." 3 vols., pp. 1200. Cloth, roy. 8vo. . . . 1 10 0

"This laborious and skilfully executed work is a distinct addition to English theological literature. Father Humphrey's style is quiet, methodical, precise, and as clear as the subject admits. Every one will be struck with the air of legal exposition which pervades the book. He takes a grip of his author, under which the text yields up every atom of its meaning and force."—*Dublin Review.*

The One Mediator; or, Sacrifice and Sacraments. Crown 8vo, cloth 0 5 0

"An exceedingly accurate theological exposition of doctrines which are the life of Christianity and which make up the soul of the Christian religion. . . . A profound work, but so far from being dark, obscure, and of metaphysical difficulty, the meaning of each paragraph shines with a crystalline clearness."—*Tablet.*

KING, FRANCIS.

The Church of my Baptism, and why I returned to it. Crown 8vo, cloth 0 2 6

"A book of the higher controversial criticism. Its literary style is good, its controversial manner excellent, and its writer's emphasis does not escape in italics and notes of exclamation, but is all reserved for lucid and cogent reasoning. Altogether a book of an excellent spirit, written with freshness and distinction."—*Weekly Register.*

LEDOUX, REV. S. M.

History of the Seven Holy Founders of the Order of the Servants of Mary. Crown 8vo, cloth . . 0 4 6

"Throws a full light upon the Seven Saints recently canonized, whom we see as they really were. All that was marvellous in their call, their works, and their death is given with the charm of a picturesque and speaking style."—*Messenger of the Sacred Heart.*

LEE, REV. F. G., D.D. (of All Saints, Lambeth.)

Edward the Sixth: Supreme Head. Second edition. Crown 8vo £0 6 0

"In vivid interest and in literary power, no less than in solid historical value, Dr. Lee's present work comes fully up to the standard of its predecessors; and to say that is to bestow high praise. The book evinces Dr. Lee's customary diligence of research in amassing facts, and his rare artistic power in welding them into a harmonious and effective whole."—*John Bull.*

LIGUORI, ST. ALPHONSUS.

New and Improved Translation of the Complete Works of St. Alphonsus, edited by the late Bishop Coffin:—

Vol. I. The Christian Virtues, and the Means for Obtaining them. Cloth 0 3 0

Or separately:—
1. The Love of our Lord Jesus Christ . . . 0 1 0
2. Treatise on Prayer. *(In the ordinary editions a great part of this work is omitted)* . . . 0 1 0
3. A Christian's rule of Life 0 1 0

Vol. II. The Mysteries of the Faith—The Incarnation; containing Meditations and Devotions on the Birth and Infancy of Jesus Christ, &c., suited for Advent and Christmas. 0 2 6

Vol. III. The Mysteries of the Faith—The Blessed Sacrament 0 2 6

Vol. IV. Eternal Truths—Preparation for Death . 0 2 6

Vol. V. The Redemption—Meditations on the Passion. 0 2 6

Vol. VI. Glories of Mary. New edition . . 0 3 6

LIVIUS, REV. T. (M.A., C.SS.R.)

St. Peter, Bishop of Rome; or, the Roman Episcopate of the Prince of the Apostles, proved from the Fathers, History and Chronology, and illustrated by arguments from other sources. Dedicated to his Eminence Cardinal Newman. Demy 8vo, cloth . 0 12 0

"A book which deserves careful attention. In respect of literary qualities, such as effective arrangement, and correct and lucid diction, this essay, by an English Catholic scholar, is not unworthy of Cardinal Newman, to whom it is dedicated."—*The Sun.*

Explanation of the Psalms and Canticles in the Divine Office. By ST. ALPHONSUS LIGUORI. Translated from the Italian by THOMAS LIVIUS, C.SS.R. With a Preface by his Eminence Cardinal MANNING. Crown 8vo, cloth 0 7 6

"To nuns and others who know little or no Latin, the book will be of immense importance."—*Dublin Review.*

"Father Livius has in our opinion even improved on the original, so far as the arrangement of the book goes. New priests will find it especially useful."—*Month.*

Mary in the Epistles; or, The Implicit Teaching of the Apostles concerning the Blessed Virgin, set forth in devout comments on their writings. Illustrated from Fathers and other Authors, and prefaced by introductory Chapters. Crown 8vo. Cloth 0 5 0

MANNING, CARDINAL.

	£	s.	d.
England and Christendom	0	10	6
Four Great Evils of the Day. 5th edition. Wrapper	0	2	6
Cloth	0	3	6
Fourfold Sovereignty of God. 3rd edition. Wrapper	0	2	6
Cloth	0	3	6
Glories of the Sacred Heart. 5th edition	0	6	0
Grounds of Faith. Cloth. 9th edition. Wrapper	0	1	0
Cloth	0	1	6
Independence of the Holy See. 2nd edition	0	5	0
Internal Mission of the Holy Ghost. 5th edition	0	8	6
Miscellanies. 3 vols. the set	0	18	0
National Education. Wrapper	0	2	0
Cloth	0	2	6
Petri Privilegium	0	10	6
Religio Viatoris. 4th edition, cloth	0	2	0
Wrapper	0	1	0
Sermons on Ecclesiastical Subjects. Vols. I., II., and III. each	0	6	0
Sin and its Consequences. 7th edition	0	6	0
Temporal Mission of the Holy Ghost. 3rd edition	0	8	6
Temporal Power of the Pope. 3rd edition	0	5	0
True Story of the Vatican Council. 2nd edition	0	5	0
The Eternal Priesthood. 9th edition	0	2	6
The Office of the Church in the Higher Catholic Education. A Pastoral Letter	0	0	6
Workings of the Holy Spirit in the Church of England. Reprint of a letter addressed to Dr. Pusey in 1864 Wrapper	0	1	0
Cloth	0	1	6
Lost Sheep Found. A Sermon	0	0	6
On Education	0	0	3
Rights and Dignity of Labour	0	0	1

The Westminster Series

In handy pocket size.

	£	s.	d.
The Blessed Sacrament, the Centre of Immutable Truth, Wrapper	0	0	6
Confidence in God. Wrapper	0	1	0
Or the two bound together. Cloth	0	2	0
Holy Gospel of Our Lord Jesus Christ according to St. John. Cloth	0	1	0
Holy Ghost the Sanctifier. Cloth	0	2	0
Love of Jesus to Penitents. Wrapper	0	1	0
Cloth	0	1	6
Office of the Holy Ghost under the Gospel. Cloth	0	1	0

MANNING, CARDINAL, Edited by.

	£	s.	d.
Life of the Curé of Ars. Popular edition	0	2	6

MEDAILLE, REV. P.

Meditations on the Gospels for Every Day in the Year. Translated into English from the new Edition, enlarged by the Besançon Missionaries, under the direction of the Rev. W. H. Eyre, S.J. Cloth £0 6 0
(This work has already been translated into Latin, Italian, Spanish, German, and Dutch.)

"We have carefully examined these Meditations, and are fain to confess that we admire them very much. They are short, succinct, pithy, always to the point, and wonderfully suggestive."—*Tablet*.

MIVART, PROF. ST. GEORGE (M.D., F.R.S.)

Nature and Thought. Second edition . . 0 4 0

"The complete command of the subject, the wide grasp, the subtlety, the readiness of illustration, the grace of style, contrive to render this one of the most admirable books of its class."—*British Quarterly Review*.

A Philosophical Catechism. Fifth edition . 0 1 0

"It should become the *vade mecum* of Catholic students."—*Tablet*.

MONTGOMERY, HON. MRS.

Approved by the Most Rev. G. Porter, Achbp. of Bombay.

The Divine Sequence: A Treatise on Creation and Redemption. Cloth 0 3 6

The Eternal Years. With an Introduction by the Most Rev. G. Porter, Achbp. of Bombay. Cloth . 0 3 6

The Divine Ideal. Cloth 0 3 6

"A work of original thought carefully developed and expressed in lucid and richly imaged style."—*Tablet*.

"The writing of a pious, thoughtful, earnest woman."—*Church Review*.

"Full of truth, and sound reason, and confidence."—*American Catholic Book News*.

MORRIS, REV. JOHN (S.J.)

Letter Books of Sir Amias Poulet, keeper of Mary Queen of Scots. Demy 8vo 0 10 6

Two Missionaries under Elizabeth . . . 0 14 0

The Catholics under Elizabeth 0 14 0

The Life of Father John Gerard, S.J. Third edition, rewritten and enlarged 0 14 0

The Life and Martyrdom of St. Thomas Becket. Second and enlarged edition. In one volume, large post 8vo, cloth, pp. xxxvi., 632, ... 0 12 6

or bound in two parts, cloth 0 13 0

MORRIS, REV. W. B. (of the Oratory.)

The Life of St. Patrick, Apostle of Ireland. Fourth edition. Crown 8vo, cloth 0 5 0

"The secret of Father Morris's success is, that he has got the proper key to the extraordinary, the mysterious life and character of St. Patrick. He has taken the Saint's own authentic writings as the foundation whereon to build."—*Irish Ecclesiastical Record*.

"Promises to become the standard biography of Ireland's Apostle. For clear statement of facts, and calm judicious discussion of controverted points, it surpasses any work we know of in the literature of the subject."—*American Catholic Quarterly*.

NEWMAN, CARDINAL.

Church of the Fathers £0 4 0
Prices of other works by Cardinal Newman on application.

PAGANI, VERY REV. JOHN BAPTIST,

The Science of the Saints in Practice. By John Baptist Pagani, Second General of the Institute of Charity. Complete in three volumes. Vol. 1, January to April. Vol. 2, May to August. Vol. 3, September to December . . . . each   0 5 0

"'The Science of the Saints' is a practical treatise on the principal Christian virtues, abundantly illustrated with interesting examples from Holy Scripture as well as from the Lives of the Saints. Written chiefly for devout souls, such as are trying to live an interior and supernatural life by following in the footsteps of our Lord and His saints, this work is eminently adapted for the use of ecclesiastics and of religious communities."—*Irish Ecclesiastical Record,*

PAYNE, JOHN ORLEBAR, (M.A.)

Records of the English Catholics of 1715. Demy 8vo. Half-bound, gilt top 0 15 0

"A book of the kind Mr. Payne has given us would have astonished Bishop Milner or Dr. Lingard. They would have treasured it, for both of them knew the value of minute fragments of historical information. The Editor has derived nearly the whole of the information which he has given, from unprinted sources, and we must congratulate him on having found a few incidents here and there which may bring the old times back before us in a most touching manner."—*Tablet.*

English Catholic Non-Jurors of 1715. Being a Summary of the Register of their Estates, with Genealogical and other Notes, and an Appendix of Unpublished Documents in the Public Record Office. In one Volume. Demy 8vo. . . 1 1 0

"Most carefully and creditably brought out ... From first to last, full of social interest and biographical details, for which we may search in vain elsewhere."—*Antiquarian Magazine.*

Old English Catholic Missions. Demy 8vo, half-bound. 0 7 6

"A book to hunt about in for curious odds and ends."—*Saturday Review.*

"These registers tell us in their too brief records, teeming with interest for all their scantiness, many a tale of patient heroism."—*Tablet.*

POOR SISTERS OF NAZARETH, THE.

A descriptive Sketch of Convent Life. By Alice Meynell. Profusely Illustrated with Drawings especially made by George Lambert. Large 4to. Boards . . 0 2 6

A limited number of copies are also issued as an *Edition de Luxe*, containing proofs of the illustrations printed on one side only of the paper, and handsomely bound. 0 10 6

"Bound in a most artistic cover, illustrated with a naturalness that could only have been born of powerful sympathy; printed clearly, neatly, and on excellent paper, and written with the point, aptness, and ripeness of style which we have learnt to associate with Mrs. Meynell's literature."—*Tablet.*

QUARTERLY SERIES Edited by the Rev. H. J. Coleridge, S.J. 77 volumes published to date.

Selection.

	£	s.	d.
The Life and Letters of St. Francis Xavier. By the Rev. H. J. Coleridge, S.J. 2 vols.	0	10	6
The History of the Sacred Passion. By Father Luis de la Palma, of the Society of Jesus. Translated from the Spanish.	0	5	0
The Life of Dona Louisa de Carvajal. By Lady Georgiana Fullerton. Small edition	0	3	6
The Life and Letters of St. Teresa. 3 vols. By Rev. H. J. Coleridge, S.J. each	0	7	6
The Life of Mary Ward. By Mary Catherine Elizabeth Chalmers, of the Institute of the Blessed Virgin. Edited by the Rev. H. J. Coleridge, S.J. 2 vols.	0	15	0
The Return of the King. Discourses on the Latter Days. By the Rev. H. J. Coleridge, S.J.	0	7	6
Pious Affections towards God and the Saints. Meditations for every Day in the Year, and for the Principal Festivals. From the Latin of the Ven. Nicolas Lancicius, S.J.	0	7	6
The Life and Teaching of Jesus Christ in Meditations for Every Day in the Year. By Fr. Nicolas Avancino, S.J. Two vols.	0	10	6
The Baptism of the King: Considerations on the Sacred Passion. By the Rev. H. J. Coleridge, S.J.	0	7	6
The Mother of the King. Mary during the Life of Our Lord.	0	7	6
The Hours of the Passion. Taken from the *Life of Christ* by Ludolph the Saxon	0	7	6
The Mother of the Church. Mary during the first Apostolic Age	0	6	0
The Life of St. Bridget of Sweden. By the late F. J. M. A. Partridge	0	6	0
The Teachings and Counsels of St. Francis Xavier. From his Letters	0	5	0
Garcia Moreno, President of Ecuador. 1821—1875. From the French of the Rev. P. A. Berthe, C.SS.R. By Lady Herbert	0	7	6
The Life of St. Alonso Rodriguez. By Francis Goldie, of the Society of Jesus	0	7	6
Letters of St. Augustine. Selected and arranged by Mary H. Allies	0	6	6
A Martyr from the Quarter-Deck—Alexis Clerc, S.J. By Lady Herbert	0	5	0
Acts of the English Martyrs, hitherto unpublished. By the Rev. John H. Pollen, S.J., with a Preface by the Rev. John Morris, S.J.	0	7	6
Life of St. Francis di Geronimo, S.J. By A. M. Clarke.	0	7	6

QUARTERLY SERIES—*(selection) continued.*
VOLUMES ON THE LIFE OF OUR LORD.
The Holy Infancy.

The Preparation of the Incarnation	£0	7	6
The Nine Months. The Life of our Lord in the Womb.	0	7	6
The Thirty Years. Our Lord's Infancy and Early Life.	0	7	6

The Public Life of Our Lord.

The Ministry of St. John Baptist	0	6	6
The Preaching of the Beatitudes	0	6	6
The Sermon on the Mount. Continued. 2 Parts, each	0	6	6
The Training of the Apostles. Parts I., II., III., IV. each	0	6	6
The Preaching of the Cross. Part I.	0	6	6
The Preaching of the Cross. Parts II., III. each	0	6	0
Passiontide. Parts I. II. and III., each	0	6	6
Chapters on the Parables of Our Lord	0	7	6

Introductory Volumes.

The Life of our Life. Harmony of the Life of Our Lord, with Introductory Chapters and Indices. Second edition. Two vols.	0	15	0
The Works and Words of our Saviour, gathered from the Four Gospels	0	7	6
The Story of the Gospels. Harmonised for Meditation	0	7	6

Full lists on application.

RAM, MRS. ABEL.
"Emmanuel." Being the Life of Our Lord Jesus Christ reproduced in the Mysteries of the Tabernacle. By Mrs. Abel Ram, author of "The most Beautiful among the Children of Men," &c. Crown 8vo, cloth — 0 5 0

"The foundation of the structure is laid with the greatest skill and the deepest knowledge of what constitutes true religion, and every chapter ends with an eloquent and soul-inspiring appeal for one or other of the virtues which the different scenes in the life of Our Saviour set prominently into view."—*Catholic Times.*

RICHARDS, REV. WALTER J. B. (D.D.)
Manual of Scripture History. Being an Analysis of the Historical Books of the Old Testament. By Rev. W. J. B. Richards, D.D., Oblate of St. Charles; Inspector of Schools in the Diocese of Westminster. Cloth. — 0 4 0

"Happy indeed will those children and young persons be who acquire in their early days the inestimably precious knowledge which these books impart."—*Tablet.*

RYDER, REV. H. I. D. (of the Oratory.)
Catholic Controversy: A Reply to Dr. Littledale's "Plain Reasons." Sixth edition — 0 2 6

"Father Ryder of the Birmingham Oratory, has now furnished in a small volume a masterly reply to this assailant from without. The lighter charms of a brilliant and graceful style are added to the solid merits of this handbook of contemporary controversy."—*Irish Monthly.*

SOULIER, REV. P.
Life of St. Philip Benizi, of the Order of the Servants of Mary. Crown 8vo — 0 8 0

"A clear and interesting account of the life and labours of this eminent Servant of Mary."—*American Catholic Quarterly.*
"Very scholar-like, devout and complete."—*Dublin Review.*

STANTON, REV. R. (of the Oratory.)
A Menology of England and Wales; or, Brief Memorials of the British and English Saints, arranged according to the Calendar. Together with the Martyrs of the 16th and 17th centuries. Compiled by order of the Cardinal Archbishop and the Bishops of the Province of Westminster. Demy 8vo, cloth £0 14 0

THOMPSON, EDWARD HEALY, (M.A.)
The Life of Jean-Jacques Olier, Founder of the Seminary of St. Sulpice. New and Enlarged Edition. Post 8vo, cloth, pp. xxxvi. 628 . . . . 0 15 0

"It provides us with just what we most need, a model to look up to and imitate; one whose circumstances and surroundings were sufficiently like our own to admit of an easy and direct application to our own personal duties and daily occupations."—*Dublin Review.*

The Life and Glories of St. Joseph, Husband of Mary, Foster-Father of Jesus, and Patron of the Universal Church. Grounded on the Dissertations of Canon Antonio Vitalis, Father José Moreno, and other writers. Second Edition. Crown 8vo, cloth . . 0 6 0

ULLATHORNE, ARCHBISHOP.
Endowments of Man, &c. Popular edition. . . 0 7 0
Groundwork of the Christian Virtues: do. . . 0 7 0
Christian Patience, . . do. do. . . 0 7 0
Ecclesiastical Discourses 0 6 0
Memoir of Bishop Willson. 0 2 6

VAUGHAN, ARCHBISHOP, (O.S.B.)
The Life and Labours of St. Thomas of Aquin. Abridged and edited by Dom Jerome Vaughan, O.S.B. Second Edition. (Vol. I., Benedictine Library.) Crown 8vo. Attractively bound . . 0 6 6

"Popularly written, in the best sense of the word, skilfully avoids all wearisome detail, whilst omitting nothing that is of importance in the incidents of the Saint's existence, or for a clear understanding of the nature and the purpose of those sublime theological works on which so many Pontiffs, and notably Leo XIII., have pronounced such remarkable and repeated commendations."—*Freeman's Journal.*

WARD, WILFRID.
The Clothes of Religion. A reply to popular Positivism. 0 3 6
"Very witty and interesting."—*Spectator.*
"Really models of what such essays should be."—*Church Quarterly Review.*

WATERWORTH, REV. J.
The Canons and Decrees of the Sacred and Œcumenical Council of Trent, celebrated under the Sovereign Pontiffs, Paul III., Julius III., and Pius IV., translated by the Rev. J. WATERWORTH. To which are prefixed Essays on the External and Internal History of the Council. A new edition. Demy 8vo, cloth 0 10 6

WISEMAN, CARDINAL.
Fabiola. A Tale of the Catacombs. . . 3s. 6d. and 0 4 0
Also a new and splendid edition printed on large quarto paper, embellished with thirty-one full-page illustrations, and a coloured portrait of St. Agnes. Handsomely bound. 1 1 0

www.ingramcontent.com/pod-product-compliance
Lightning Source LLC
Chambersburg PA
CBHW030320240426
43673CB00040B/1225